China's
Modernization
and
Transnational
Corporations

China's Modernization and Transnational Corporations

N.T. Wang
Columbia University

LexingtonBooks
D.C. Heath and Company
Lexington, Massachusetts
Toronto

84-7938
Library of Congress Cataloging in Publication Data

Wang, N.T. (Nian-Tzu), 1917-
    China's modernization and transnational corporations.

    Includes index.
    1. China—Economic policy—1949-   . 2. China—Foreign economic
relations. 3. International business enterprises—Government policy—
China. I. Title.
HC427.9.W33   1984   338.951   82-48530
ISBN 0-669-06266-9

Copyright © 1984 by D.C. Heath and Company

Published simultaneously in Canada

Printed in the United States of America

International Standard Book Number: 0-669-06266-9

Library of Congress Catalog Card Number: 82-48530

To my father,
whose entrepreneurship
I wish could be passed on
to future generations
and
whose grants to Chinese scholars
I wish could be renewed

To my mother,
whose love and self-sacrifice for the family
is forever remembered

Contents

Tables

Preface

My interest in China's modernization started with my own great leap from the security of a classical Chinese education into the adventure of Western learning. While under the influence of tutors in a private academy in Shanghai, I was thoroughly absorbed by the pragmatic humanism and statecraft of Confucius, the boundless and sophisticated speculation of the "hundred schools of thought," the artistry of the prose of the Han and Six dynasties, and the ecstasy of the poems of Tang and Song. I felt completely self-sufficient. Any learning external to that world appeared unimportant if not trivial. My acquiescence to learning from the West did not, therefore, evolve from an innate realization of inadequacy but was forced upon me by necessity. True to the basic values of the classical Chinese scholar, I was not prepared to suffer the consequences of being excluded from the mainstream of the educational system and to jeopardize my chance of playing a role in this world.

As the influences of modern learning accumulated in me, the views and values I had previously held were increasingly called into question. At the same time, the metamorphosis in my thought reinforced an old wish to apply myself to the future of China. This future would inevitably involve a fundamental transformation of virtually everything from beliefs to social structure, and thus, in a sense, would also involve modernization.

On the other hand, I had never believed in the cloning of Western civilization in China. This attitude was probably influenced by my respect for, not to mention attachment to, the historical and cultural roots of China. But the main reason for my attitude was practical. Indeed, my first choice was to make a contribution not in the realm of ideas but in the realm of action. As a result of the great upheavals in China, however, my personal involvement in its affairs was cut short. My work was for many years concerned mainly with issues relating to all the developing countries and subsequently with transnational corporations.

The announcement of the Four Modernizations program after the passing of Mao rekindled my interest in the China connection. The only question was, and still is, what exactly I should do. The answer is again pragmatic. Since I have been living abroad for a long time, my role in China must be limited to an advisory one at most. Because of my experience in the East and the West, however, I may be able to serve as a bridge for both sides. At the technical level, I can take China as a case study of development issues and concentrate on the role of transnational corporations in its development.

Despite the relevance of years of work to this study, the task of linking China's modernization and transnational corporations remained formidable. It was necessary for me to mobilize the knowledge accumulated by all the actors concerned. This was attempted through the establishment of the China-International Business Project at the Graduate School of Business and the School of International and Public Affairs in the East Asian Institute, at Columbia University. The Project included research into emerging relations between China and international business; the organization of conferences in which government officials, business executives, and academicians took part; the setting up of monthly seminars in which informal views could be exchanged among the actors; and the offering of courses and lectures on the subject in the United States, China, and Hong Kong, as well as other, less formal exchanges and discussions.

Despite the mobilization of these resources into this study, it became obvious that a more definitive work on the subject must await the future. For one thing, information remains grossly inadequate, although more openness on the part of the Chinese is evident. For another, numerous theoretical underpinnings remain to be worked out, despite the explosion of literature on economic development as well as on transnational corporations. Most models bear little resemblance to reality, especially in socialist economies.

Yet, given the speed at which things are evolving, the wish to be definitive is outweighed by the desire to influence the process. If this study succeeds in affecting the future course of events in a small way—whether for a better understanding by the Chinese, the transnational corporations, or the governments concerned—it will not have been undertaken in vain.

In preparing the study I am indebted to many individuals. They are too numerous to list, but a few require special mention. I always remember the priority my parents placed on my education and on excellence. I also feel obliged to my teachers, especially Joseph Schumpeter—who constantly urged me to put my ideas into book form—and Wassily Leontief, whose distaste for risk aversion has been my constant source of encouragement in overcoming an Oriental reluctance to print anything which is not worthy of posterity. My immediate debt is to my wife, who has endured a lifestyle far more onerous and less elegant than she would have liked, just to suit my preferences.

Many of the ideas and facts in this study can be traced to the writings and informal communications of those I have been in contact with. Only a few of the identifiable ones are explicitly acknowledged. As in most of my previous writings, Marianna Oliver has improved the readability and presentation of this work. Much of the manuscript was typed by my daughter, Geraldine, who felt it was not beneath the dignity of a professional and was one way of getting to know me. I have promised to let her repeat the feat when I become old enough to write my memoirs.

Introduction

Viewed from a broad historical perspective, the Chinese have been outstanding both as innovators and as adapters. Not only are such epoch-making discoveries and inventions as paper, printing, gunpowder, and the compass traceable to the Chinese, but many philosophies and sociopolitical institutions can be attributed to the same origin. One need only glance over the long list in Needham's careful and scholarly documentation of the history of science and technology in China to gain an idea of the depth and breadth of the Chinese contribution to the common human heritage. Any casual observer at or before Marco Polo's time, journeying along the historic silk route, would certainly have characterized China as more modern than its contemporary empires or principalities. The level of economic development, the lifestyle of the people, and the complexity of sociopolitical organization had no match elsewhere in the world.

The adaptability of the Chinese to changing circumstances is less evident. The very heights achieved by the Chinese in the economic, cultural, and military realms, especially in comparison to neighboring areas, had instilled in them a sense of exaggerated self-confidence and ethnocentrism. The Chinese saw themselves as the center of the world and as standard setters. The need for thoroughgoing adaptation hardly arose, consciously at least. Even during periods of foreign rule, notably in the Yuan and Qing dynasties, it was the conquerors who, by and large, had to adapt to Chinese ways. Most of these "foreigners," as well as many other ethnic groups, have now been assimilated and become part of the greater family. Indeed, if one goes back further into history, one will find that the people currently inhabiting the most populous and prosperous areas on the southeast coast were once regarded as foreign. China has gone through a subtle process of change by constantly embodying and digesting foreign elements without admitting that it has given up anything or made any adaptation itself.

A more direct evidence of Chinese adaptability is the relative ease of overseas Chinese in comingling with local populations. This is in contrast to, for example, the greater degree of insularity of overseas Japanese. Although in some communities the adaptability of the Chinese has been inhibited by Chinese snobbery and conservatism, or local discrimination, the trait appears to reassert itself when the need arises. For example, in Southeast Asia, when local law requires the use of the local language, the Chinese have no hesitation in mastering it.

The repeated failure of modernization attempts by the Chinese since the Opium War is surprising in the light of this early historical record, and is examined in chapter 1. While the reasons are complex and subject to varied interpretations and emphases, the historical concurrence and processes rather than the innate character of the Chinese stand out.

First, the modern history of China can be characterized as a hundred years of war. Ever since the humiliating defeat of the 1840s, China had been in constant turmoil from either external invasion or internal strife. While this may be expected during the transitional period in dynastic cycles, the intensity and duration was unprecedented at a time when modernization was taking place in earnest in all the advanced countries. It is true that wars are not necessarily an obstacle to modernization. The very requirements of military operations provide a strong argument for modernization. The contrast between Western firepower and the Chinese invocation of mystical and magical forces, as in the case of the Boxer Rebellion, was too apparent for even the most recalcitrant minds to ignore. Defense was thus the first motive for modernization. Yet, the constant destruction wrought by repeated warfare sapped the power of the center to mobilize resources and made any sustained effort at modernization impossible. Repeated though enfeebled attempts in this direction were nipped in the bud before the fruits could be reaped. In an atmosphere of extreme uncertainty, the dilemma was that private entrepreneurs placed a high premium on risk aversion while the public sector was too weak to perform the true entrepreneurial function.

Second, modernization's defense orientation was too narrow a base on which to conceptualize. There was very little understanding of the forces, processes, and interrelated components of the advanced countries, save a sense of their awesome military power. Small wonder the initial Chinese aim was to obtain the superior weapons of the "barbarians." This soon proved an aim too limited, of course, since importing Western weapons was useless unless there were trained and disciplined soldiers to handle them! Foreign mercenaries had even to be utilized, despite the obvious dangers, especially when the threat of foreign invasion and occupation was ever present. It was also gradually realized that in order to ensure a constant supply of weapons, an indigenous defense industry would have to be established, which in turn must rely on steel and coal, as well as on railways, and so on. But even all these were hardly an adequate concept of modernization.

Third, although China was never a colony, a semicolonial status is sometimes worse than being a colony as such from the point of view of economic development, which is central to modernization. China was a semicolony to be milked or even plundered rather than a territory receiving metropolitan protection. The indemnities paid to the victorious Powers were time and again as much as the traffic could bear. They were comparable to the gold systematically requisitioned from American Indians by their Spanish conquerors. They were far more burdensome and sustained than the German reparations after World War I, whose far-reaching impact on the course of postwar events was so well analyzed by Keynes. Moreover, the activities of foreign enterprises in China were too limited to bring about a fundamental transformation of the economy, and were highly detrimental to the development of national enterprise. In foreign trade, for example, Chinese exports were limited mainly to a few traditional native products in exchange for consumer goods. Although foreign enterprises performed the useful function of assembling, cleaning, sorting, grading, packaging, and marketing the produce, precious little was either received or learned by the Chinese. Even the key Chinese business aides who acted as important intermediaries in sourcing and credit guarantees played an auxiliary role, as their designation as *compradores* implied. As far as imports were concerned, importers had a field day since Chinese tariff autonomy was not restored until after World War II. In industry, the privileges enjoyed by foreign firms were blatant. Not only were the firms sheltered by extraterritoriality but they were also exempt from burdensome local levies (*lijin* or interregional tariffs). Competition between foreign and national enterprises was hardly of equal footing.

Fourth, the role of the government in whatever indigenous economic activities there were was more deleterious than simple neglect or incompetence; it imposed innumerable obstacles. The private sector was looked upon mainly as a source of revenue. Moreover, because of the exhaustion of possible sources and the government's uncertainty of effective control over them, the prudent rule of not killing the goose that lays the golden egg was frequently violated. This tendency was accentuated as the goose was sought after by different layers of authority, public and private. The latter ranged from hit-and-run bandits to entrenched local mafias.

It is true that for selected industries, such as iron and coal, the government had long recognized the need for public support, including finance, and the ability to deal with bureaucrats. Yet, the very model chosen, called "official supervision and private management," implied that official involvement was a necessary condition of such activities. The supply of entrepreneurial talent in such cases was necessarily of mixed origin. The public sector had the last word and exerted severe constraints on sustained development. The ineptness of the bureaucracy to engage in industrial activities is dramatically illustrated by the story of a Chinese official who requested a British firm to supply a steel furnace without indicating the kind of steel or capacity desired. When asked to give specifications, the official reacted with indignant refusal since otherwise he would have had to reveal his original error.

It was therefore not the lack of appreciation for modernization nor the total absence of effort that characterized a century of Chinese history after the Opium War, but rather the narrowness of conception and the feebleness of the effort that condemned the Chinese to lag behind. There were, of course, numerous promising early starts. For example, the first modern shipyard was established as early as 1865. In 1918, it was able to construct four 10,000-ton class ships for export. Yet the industry was not developed, at least until recently.

The establishment of the People's Republic was a major historic event which ought to have heralded the period of modernization that had been aborted so many times previously. For one thing, 1949 marked the final liquidation of the semicolonial heritage. There was no more doubt that China was independent. No foreign power maintained any military presence in China. The only exception to national unification was Taiwan, which fortunately is an island and is geographically insulated from the mainland. By the early 1950s, even the remnants of foreign economic establishments had been either nationalized or dispersed.

On the domestic front, the liquidation of all opposition forces was also complete save for the continued separation of Taiwan. This is in sharp contrast to the Republican era, post-1911, when rebellious forces of many persuasions were always active and military flare-ups arose intermittently across the land. The authority of the government was no longer to be questioned, nor were there any underground or guerilla activities that usurped the functions of the nominal authorities. Indeed, the extension of the government's power was unprecedented both in breadth and in depth. Not only were all regions and localities under its control, but also every neighborhood and even household. The types of activity involved were equally far reaching. They extended literally from the womb to the tomb: The virtual removal of all family tombs from farmland in order to increase agricultural production was symbolic of the revolution's attitudes and social values. China had come a long way from the days when the construction of railways had to be suspended and existing tracks torn up for fear of unfavorable effects on the environment (*feng-shui*) of ancestral tombs, and thus the fortunes and destiny of the next generation.

The general direction in the economic sphere was also unmistakable. Industrialization was top priority. The dual emphasis on small as well as large industries—the strategy of "walking on two legs"—was not a halfhearted drive at industrialization but a strategic move to make full use of the existing resources. It is therefore different from the Gandhian cottage industries pitted against the modern sector, or even the Soviet model of "big is beautiful."

The actual movement toward modernization between 1949 and 1976 was impressive, as judged by the usual indicators or total output in agriculture, industry, technology, and defense. Indeed, many observers, dissatisfied or even frustrated with the stagnation and underdevelopment of the Third World, hailed the Chinese model of development as worthy of emulation, apart from or in spite of the priority placed on social goals such as egalitarian distribution, full employment, and the prevention of excessive urban growth. During this period—or rather, after 1952, when reconstruction or recovery had been accomplished—China achieved an overall rate of growth that was surpassed by few other developing countries. Thanks to the increase in irrigation, improvement in seed varieties, greater use of fertilizers and, above all, sheer hard work, the growth of agricultural production surpassed the rate of population increase, this despite periods of bad harvests. The advance in industry was even more spectacular. The output of steel, the key link, increased from 1.35 million tons in 1952 to over 23 million tons in 1976. The capacity to build machines that made machines was unequaled save in a few advanced countries.

The announcement of the Chinese Four Modernizations program in 1978 was at first greeted by most observers as an intensification and continuation of past programs. Indeed, the cavalier manner in which targets were set strongly suggested such an interpretation. The subsequent revelation, step-by-step, that China's modernization was to take a sharply different route came as a shock to most observers. It was particularly painful to the many China watchers whose views were politicized. On the one hand, there were those fundamentally opposed to everything that emanated from a socialist state. Any variation on the major theme would not, in their view, make much difference. This is not unlike the popular view in the socialist states of development in capitalist countries, whether under Republicans or Democrats, Conservatives or Liberals. On the other hand, there were those who were the self-proclaimed friends of New China, having extolled the virtues of everything since the establishment of the People's Republic, including the Great Leap Forward of the late 1950s or even the Cultural Revolution. The change in direction presented a dilemma. If they now admitted that the policy change was in the right direction, they would have to retract much of what they had previously published or defended. Many were too stubborn or too timid to do so. If they continued to hold their past views, they would have to regard the current change as revisionist, renegade, or even a betrayal. Consequently, they would also appear less friendly towards the new, post-Mao China.

Despite initial uncertainties in appraising the real reasons for the policy break, the unfolding of events after 1976 has left little doubt that the Chinese economy inherited from Mao was in fundamental difficulty. This is not to deny or belittle the significant achievements of the regime as indicated earlier; but these very achievements were often at the expense of the future, and could not possibly be sustained for very long. The most dramatic illustration is the reported high rate of increase in the production of steel. This was accompanied first by a lack of proper maintenance of plant and equipment. Moreover, as is now common knowledge, many products were substandard or incapable of being absorbed into the productive system. As a result, they simply piled up in the warehouses. In the case of coal, although output-quality considerations were less important, the pursuit of high production targets at the expense of proper maintenance was still more devastating, as many mines became dilapidated, flooded, and unsafe. This was all the more detrimental to sustained production since there was a growing proportion of underground workers who had grown old but whose tenure was protected by the system of the "iron rice bowl." Wages were frozen and virtually unrelated to workers' contributions.

If the high rate of industrial growth masked the fundamental difficulties in that sector, the heroic efforts of the Dazhai agricultural model made an even more emotional appeal to ignore all its defects. Few could fail to be moved by the sheer determination to transform a barren mountain into a farmland. Slopes could be leveled by hand with the help of only the simplest tools; topsoil could be transported from neighboring land and water guided or siphoned from remote places through tunnels and mountains to where it was needed. Nothing was too difficult if the will was there!

Yet, quite apart from the cost in terms of human labor or falsification of data, the opportunity cost of all the other inputs was either forgotten or deliberately ignored. It was forgotten because to even raise the question of cost appeared contrary to the spirit of the times. Hence it was deliberately ignored, and any evidence which might raise questions about the accepted model was considered disrespectful if not counterrevolutionary.

The guiding principle of "take grain to be the key" also appeared at first to be extremely reasonable. This was certainly so when the chief preoccupation of the people was whether or not there was enough to eat. Hunger had been a frequent occurrence in China throughout history. Good and bad times alternated, partly as a result of natural climatic and topographical conditions whereby periodic drought in the north and flooding in the south was endemic, and partly because of the collapse of disaster-prevention systems during dynastic declines. Even in recent years, the poor harvest at the beginning of the 1960s led to famine in some localities. Yet a rigid application of the principle, combined with the narrow interpretation of self-reliance, introduced great distortions in the rational allocation of resources; these distortions have surfaced only gradually. The constant shortage and continued rationing of such daily necessities as edible oil and cotton goods were reflections of the highly monolithic structure of production. The virtual disappearance of a rich variety of vegetables and aquatic products— used not only in the traditional cuisine of the wealthy but also in the common household—was less apparent to the outside observer. It was only belatedly that the vast destruction of orchards and fish resources was revealed. Similarly, the folly of converting steppes suitable for animal husbandry and tropical lands suitable for the cultivation of coffee and cocoa into low-yielding rice or wheat farms was exposed only when economic calculations were reinstated.

No sector was more neglected or suppressed than the service sector. This neglect was partly influenced by the emphasis on material products, (a view symbolized by the very concept and measurement of the aggregate national output, which is limited to material product). Presumably most services were considered to be unproductive in the Marxian tradition. There was also a confusion of "service" and "servitude." Despite the ubiquitous motto "serve the people," there was in fact great reluctance to provide services. Public servants acted like officials or rulers. In an economy of general scarcity, the provision of services such as selling and personal care was tantamount to granting a favor. At the same time, the services usually provided by individuals or small enterprises virtually disappeared, as they were regarded as the "tails of capitalism." As a result, it was virtually impossible to have anything mended, for example, except through a personal relationship.

It became increasingly clear that the future of Chinese development was in great jeopardy. The way out was certainly not more of the same; instead, it would require a fundamental change in ways of doing things tantamount to a new revolution. This is explained in chapter 2.

The most immediate task was the abandonment of the unrealistically high growth targets inherited from the Maoist big-push strategy and implied in the grandiose projects announced in connection with the Four Modernizations. The inevitability of this change was clearly demonstrated in subsequent developments. While there was no dispute about the importance of developing petroleum resources as rapidly as possible, the plan to build ten Daqings, for example, was not based on any serious investigation of what it would take to fulfill the target. Offshore reserves may one day enable China to become a major oil-producing and -exporting country, but when the ten Daiqings were announced, even the tentative results of the seismic surveys (subsequently conducted with the help of foreign oil companies and with an expenditure of over $200 million, at no cost to the Chinese) were unavailable. Even after these surveys, the precise nature and economic worth of the reserves could not be known until the actual drilling was carried out.

In the case of coal, it was not uncertainty of reserves but the availability of inputs and infrastructure that constituted the bottleneck. The improvement of the latter especially is both expensive and time-consuming. Transport and port facilities had already been strained once interregional and international exchanges were activated.

The virtually flat output of both oil and coal during much of the early 1980s should alone have dictated a more moderate rate of expansion for the rest of the economy, since aggregate growth is to be fed by greater use of energy. At the same time, the energy bottleneck had a sobering effect on existing waste and inefficiency in its use, much like the shock administered to the Western economies by the oil crises.

A related change in policy was a shift of emphasis from an unusually high rate of capital accumulation. Although the recorded accumulation ratio, at times as high as thirty to forty percent, may be somewhat exaggerated due to statistical biases, the fanatical pursuit of high growth, high accumulation was a textbook illustration of the limits of a policy based on a simple positive relationship between growth and accumulation. This was aggravated by the command system of planning, under which capital was accumulated virtually for its own sake. On the other hand, there was a high degree of underutilization of capital. Machine tools, for example, were left idle in the warehouses and underutilized in the factories. Under the system as it was then, many factories were completely equipped with maintenance and repair shops to minimize the risk of bottlenecks. Yet shortages of capital were prevalent even in the priority sectors, since growth targets were unrealistically high.

The complement to a more moderate rate of capital accumulation is the greater availability of consumer goods. It is true that many developing countries suffer from excessively high levels of consumption that they cannot afford. The imbalance created by a level of production of the Middle Ages and a twentieth-century pattern of consumption is at the root of many fundamental fiscal, monetary, and social difficulties. The great emphasis the Chinese placed on frugality and a simple lifestyle was both necessary and wise. Yet the prolonged suppression of any significant rise in the level of consumption had an unfavorable effect on incentives and discipline. There was little material reward for work, neither was there much to lose for slacking, for disciplining and depriving anyone of the bare necessities of life would seem morally repugnant. At the same time, the low level of living departed from the promise that a socialist victory would bring a good life and prosperity to everyone. People began to wonder why living conditions were so poor, especially as compared with other presumably inferior social systems.

The de-emphasis on high growth and accumulation also implied a shift of priority from heavy to light industry, at least in the transitional period. The reforms were, however, much more than short-run adjustments to restore balances, as attempted by anticyclical policies. These were more fundamental and of a structural nature. They involved systemic changes in the workings of the economic system as a whole, in incentives and disincentives, and in the decision-making and organizational setups.

In carrying out such structural reforms, there are two alternative approaches. One is comprehensive, whereby the processes and the final model are totally worked out so that the various measures and parts will fit together and reinforce each other. This is, in theory, ideal. It is sometimes credited to the Hungarian model of reform, although in reality this is also far less systematic, comprehensive, or predictable than imagined. The other approach is step-by-step, which is the way chosen by China. Obviously, the second approach is intellectually unsatisfactory, simply because the parts will often not fit together. However, the conditions for the first approach were not present in China, at least in the first stages of reform. For one thing, precise knowledge about the state of the economy was largely non-existent, as many economists, statisticians, and other planners were condemned to the "ox pens" and have been only recently rehabilitated. ("Ox pens" were places where the accused were confined for thought reform, usually less formal than a prison or labor camp.) Many of them had lost their professional connections and had been out of touch with current economic developments. In any case, even the most fundamental economic data such as production, trade, and finance were classified as state secrets and unavailable to ordinary scholars. This is in sharp contrast to the role of economists and statisticians in Hungary or the United States, for example. Moreover, the decision makers in China had to be concerned with the art of persuasion in order to achieve a political consensus. A comprehensive model would not only be difficult to generate in theory and in practice but would also be hard to sell to the people concerned, who had not been greatly exposed to the intricacies of economic reasoning. Indeed, some of the reforms appeared to be diametrically opposed to everything that the Chinese had been led to believe. The step-by-step approach was thus not so much a deliberate choice as a practical and political necessity.

As has already been suggested, the workings of the planning system were at the root of China's fundamental difficulties. Those who made the rules and issued commands were out of touch with reality. One had only to look at the condition of the steel mills to have known the folly of setting production targets so high. The managers of the steel mills knew, of course, that the targets were too high, but they would hardly protest since to do so might be taken as a reflection of their lack of ability or enthusiasm.

Two essential ingredients are embodied in the reform of the planning system. One is a greater degree of decentralization, or, more correctly, a re-definition of the powers of the center and the lesser economic units. The other is a greater use of the market mechanism. The first is not simply a choice between centralization and decentralization. In almost all societies, there is always a debate as to whether there should be more or less centralization. Indeed, a cyclical pattern is frequently discernible since excessive centralization tends to create rigidity and bring about decentralization, which in turn breeds chaos and recentralization. At the beginning of the establishment of the People's Republic, the primary concern was to restore order and a unified purpose, as had been the concern of new regimes throughout Chinese history. As early as the 1950s, it was found necessary to redress the balance between the center and the periphery. However, the focus was almost exclusively geographical or administrative. The distin-

guishing feature of the current redressing of the balance is the greater authority conferred upon enterprises. While there are altogether some 400,000
enterprises, the major ones are under direct control of the center. Indeed,
many local enterprises are not very efficient. Some of them have been
fostered by regional protectionism. For example, in tobacco-producing
regions, a number of local governments have restricted the export of tobacco
to other regions in order to protect their own cigarette manufacturers. The
central authority may, in extreme cases, force the closing of these facilities
when they are found to be below certain minimum standards. In some
cases, they have been merged with facilities in other regions.

The key to greater decision-making power on the part of enterprises is
closely related to the second major ingredient in planning reform, greater
use of the market mechanism. Instead of relying exclusively on central command of what is to be produced, how much, and using what inputs, and to
whom the output is to be allocated, enterprises are now being given greater
autonomy in these decisions. The complete supplanting of command planning
by market forces has, however, been rejected. The ideological reasons for
this position are clear since a socialist economy is generally equated with a
planned economy. The main reason is pragmatic. The supply of the means
of production and major items of daily necessity is considered too important to be subject to the invisible hand. Planning by command remains an
important tool. It is, however, to be complemented by indicative and parametric planning as well as market adjustment. The chief feature of parametric planning is the deliberate use of levers—such as prices, taxes and
subsidies, and credit—to influence the decisionmaking of enterprises. In addition, many less fundamental decisions—such as the variety, style, and color
of consumer goods—may be left to the choice of consumers through the
market mechanism. Even here, the official visible hand may continue to
play an important role. To illustrate, in a locality where five vendors who
specialized in mending pots and pans changed their profession in anticipation of greater reward or security elsewhere, local officials invited the vendors to return to their profession with a contract of services and a guaran-
teed minimum income.

On the whole, structural reforms plus readjustment policies have already brought about revolutionary changes in the economic scene. The
security of the "iron rice bowl" has become more and more questionable, if
it has not been demolished. The idea that poverty is virtue has been replaced
by the tenet "to be rich is glorious." Enterprises are beginning to be profit-
and market-conscious. This is especially evident in the agricultural sector,
where literally hundreds of millions of farmers, like their counterparts in
most countries, are again being given much leeway to play the role of entrepreneurs. The central feature in a variety of contract work is that they will
be rewarded by results rather than by arbitrary rule.

Despite the broad popular support for these reforms, the mixed and step-by-step approach has given rise to new problems. The source of these problems lies mainly in the price system. With the rediscovery of the market, prices are supposed to give signals for the allocation of resources, but they may give the wrong ones when they do not reflect relative economic scarcities.

Under the system of command planning, practiced for decades, the role of prices was unimportant for allocation purposes. Since enterprise surpluses would be mopped up and deficits made up by the government, the price of inputs or outputs did not significantly concern the enterprises. At the same time, price stability was an important goal in itself in view of the nightmarish experience of the 1940s. (The Chinese dread of inflation is comparable to that of the Germans, who also have experienced hyper-inflation in which confidence in money was totally destroyed.) As a result, prices have been maintained as far as possible where they are government-administered. Even where prices have had to be raised, for such purposes as stimulating production of grains or other important goods, the prices to consumers have been kept at fairly stable levels.

Given the existing price system, the profit of enterprises may reflect the relative prices of their inputs and outputs rather than their operational efficiency. For example, coal production may lose money simply because coal prices are kept artificially low. The adjustment of coal prices might, it was feared, run into the serious danger of triggering an inflationary spiral. There was, therefore, a dilemma in regard to price policy.

The long-term solution rests in an adjustment of the price system. A shorter-term solution is to use accounting prices, together with differential taxes, to calculate the profits of enterprises. This implies a detailed system of central intervention.

In practice, a mix of the solutions is indicated, and this further reinforces the need for a step-by-step approach. At the same time, to the extent that complementary steps have not as yet been taken, the danger of guidance by the wrong signals continues to exist. This applies especially to those enterprises selected for experimental reform. The apparent results may not be attributed to the success or future of the reform measures adopted. The uncertainty thus created is likely to reinforce the pattern of continued experimentation and great variation in actual practice, as ad hoc measures are introduced to deal with obvious irrationalities and inequities. In the same vein, numerous complementary reforms are likely to unfold as years go by. Already, reforms in the tax system, the banking system, the labor market, and the wage structure are emerging.

The return to economic calculus has had inevitable implications for the Chinese attitude towards transnational corporations, as shown in chapter 3. Realizing the goals of modernization, in economic terms, depends upon the efficient utilization of existing resources. The question is whether China should also make use of the resources in the hands of transnational corporations. The answer is affirmative, if the net effect befits the purpose of modernization.

The actual development of relations with transnationals has, however, been dominated by the uncertainties of inexperience and constant experimentation. The initial pronouncement of an open-door policy generated euphoria on the part of the Chinese as well as the transnationals. Still influenced by the desire to attain high production targets, the Chinese perceived modernization to be attainable through the import of machinery and equipment to increase productive capacity. This was greeted with equal enthusiasm by foreign enterprises. It looked as though the billion-customers market could finally be reached.

The consequences of this episode of the "great foreign leap forward" between 1977 and 1979 are now familiar. The burden on Chinese foreign-exchange reserves created by a rush to order imported goods proved too heavy when all the commitments were added up. The imported equipment was frequently wasted. Much of it actually laid on the docks and the warehouses. Even the equipment already installed fell victim to bottlenecks caused by shortages of electricity or other inputs. At the same time, the exaggerated expectations of many foreign enterprises were unfulfilled.

The move toward readjustment and the subsequent cancellation of contracts, involving some major projects such as the Baoshan iron and steel mill, set shock waves everywhere. The potential and the credibility of the Chinese were seriously questioned.

In terms of policy direction there was, of course, no retreat to insularity. The characterization of the new policy as an open door was in a sense an exaggeration, since foreign participation in economic activities in China continues to be severely limited. It is an open door only in contrast to the previous closed-door policy, under which the doctrine of self-reliance was very narrowly defined. The new policy does not reject self-reliance but reinterprets it. Foreign trade is no longer regarded with suspicion but is to be encouraged. The emancipation of thought extends to the acceptance of all forms of cooperation with foreign enterprises, ranging from licensing, compensation trade, and joint ventures to direct foreign investment.

A direct consequence of this reinterpretation is the new role assigned to transnational corporations. For a long time, the Chinese were influenced by Marxian and neo-Marxian literature about transnational corporations. These mammoth companies, it was thought, were monopolistic exploiters, and their impact on host countries was generally adverse. Without fundamentally redefining transnational corporations, however, the new policy admits that it is possible for dealings with them to result in mutual benefit. A Chinese delegate to the United Nations Commission on Transnational

Corporations agreed that the Chinese might also have some transnational corporations insofar as Chinese corporations engage in transnational activities. This position is in contrast to the posture taken by the Soviet Union and some developing countries. To them, transnational corporations are intrinsically bad and by definition they do not exist in their countries. The new Chinese view is that the positive effects of transnationals may outweigh their negative effects. From this viewpoint, even direct investment in China by transnational corporations may be beneficial because the finance, technology, know-how, and market access resulting from it may outweigh the exploitation of workers by transnational capitalists. The issue, then is not whether transnational corporations are always good or always bad for host-country development, but whether they can be made to make a positive contribution if appropriate policies are adopted.

The employment of a great variety of forms of cooperation with transnational corporations is an indication of Chinese willingness to explore alternatives to suit particular purposes and circumstances. The theoretical and practical considerations involved in matching substance and form and weighing costs and benefits are the theme of chapter 4. It is significant that despite the fact that a patent law does not as yet exist in China, licensing from transnational corporations is practiced. This is especially suitable where the Chinese capacity to absorb the new technology is high. In some cases, notably where advanced technology is involved, the Chinese absorptive capacity may be low. In any case, transnational corporations are often unwilling to licence the technology because it is more profitable to make use of it themselves and it is necessary to guard against its dissipation. It must be either purchased in an embodied form, as is the case with computers, or shared jointly in a mutually agreeable shape, as in joint ventures or direct investment where the transnational corporations retain a degree of control. Often, the precise arrangement contains numerous ingredients in special packages. For example, licensing may be combined with the export of the final product in order to facilitate Chinese payment. Similarly, new materials, intermediate products, or designs may be supplied by transnational corporations in connection with Chinese exports. In these cases the Chinese may receive a processing fee or they may undertake to export all or part of their production to the transnational corporations to pay for the materials, equipment, or investment. In such arrangements, divestment is built in.

Some arrangements may take the form of joint ventures. These ventures do not necessarily involve foreign equity capital; they may, for example, be coproduction arrangements in which the production takes place in an existing Chinese plant and no new entity is created. Even if foreign capital is involved, the contractual party may merely arrange for financing by a third party.

The flexibility and variety of forms indicate that the Chinese are less influenced now by doctrinaire considerations. No form is considered taboo in itself. Many forms, such as depackaged finance, technology, know-how, and market access, advocated by many developing host countries and their advisors, are not always insisted upon. There is still, of course, a Chinese preference for importing technology rather than final products, where possible. The main reason may be illustrated by a simple example: If the Chinese import fish, they must continue to do so all the time; if they import a fishing device, they can get the fish themselves; and if they learn how to make the fishing device, they do not even have to import the final product. But the same illustration leaves out many questions about the general applicability of simplistic rules. What is the use of the fishing device, if the waters are not endowed with fish that the device can catch? What about the fishermen? How expensive is the fishing device, and how much fish and what kind can it yield? Similarly, what is needed to make the fishing device? How long would it take to learn to do it? What happens when the device becomes obsolete?

There is also a Chinese preference for engaging in compensation trade. The main reason for this preference is to promote exports and save foreign exchange. A further reason is that is is relatively easy to administer, especially when trade decisions are somewhat decentralized. In such circumstances, a rule of thumb for administering import permits is that as long as no official foreign exchange is required, local authorities or enterprises may make their own decisions. However, reliance on foreign enterprises to push exports may be a useful expedient in the short run, since Chinese access to foreign markets has been severely restricted by years of isolation. In the longer run, a greater penetration of foreign markets may require direct export experience and contact with end-users. Some of the exports in compensation trade are moreover limited by supply or by quantitative restrictions imposed by the importing countries. Many raw materials have a ready world market, and items that may potentially be limited by quantitative restrictions are tending to increase. Furthermore, compensation arrangements tend to favor firms which are equipped to engage in such activities, notably Japanese general trading companies, European firms experienced in similar arrangements with Eastern European countries, and a few relatively large U.S. firms with their own trading organizations.

In natural resources, considerations of national sovereignty are an important factor. In the case of petroleum exploitation, for example, the Chinese have so far insisted on joint ventures. A greater degree of flexibility in dealings with transnationals is permitted in the Special Economic Zones. (To the extent that these zones may serve as showpieces for possible administrative arrangements for Hong Kong and Taiwan and demonstrate that a predominantly private enterprise system can be maintained within the Chinese system, relationships with foreign enterprises there may take many forms more familiar to the West.) Other areas (such as Shanghai), though not the same as Special Economic Zones, have also been designated to specialize in attracting foreign firms. These areas will tend to multiply as more and more ports are opened up for direct dealings in foreign commerce.

It is clear that both the role of transnational corporations in China's modernization and the appropriate forms of cooperation are affected by the policies pursued by China as well as by the home countries, and by the international environment, as stressed in chapter 5. What is not always evident is that the very decision to permit transnational corporations to play a positive role in China's modernization has prompted a series of new policy measures. The question is whether these measures have actually served or are likely to serve the intended purpose.

The traditional Chinese attitude of relying on personal trust rather than law is inadequate from the point of view of transnational corporations. This is especially true since whatever legal institutions existed were dismantled during the Cultural Revolution. Moreover, there is of course no more extra-territoriality. The movement toward a greater degree of rule of law, fortunately, is also in line with the general objective of modernization. Law is needed to protect the rights of citizens from arbitrary action as well as to govern the relationship between parties in economic contracts.

Since 1978, China has promulgated a series of laws every year. A number of them have been addressed mainly to relations with foreign enterprises. Some laws, such as the Company Law and Patent Law, are still in the drafting stage. A nagging question often raised by foreign enterprises is whether these laws are sufficiently detailed. In comparison with laws and regulations in the West, most of the new laws appear to be very brief and to raise more questions than provide answers. This has been in part remedied by the subsequent issuance of somewhat more detailed regulations. A further problem is that official interpretation of the laws and regulations may deviate from what is apparent in the written text. Such an interpretation is rarely made public before an actual case arises. Generally, inasmuch as most of the laws have not been tested in the courts, their precise application remains unknown. This is particularly disturbing to transnational corporations used to case law, such as those of the United States. The degree of uncertainty thus remains high for many transnationals.

In practice, it is hardly feasible for the Chinese to anticipate all contingencies by enacting new laws, since their experience is as yet limited. Moreover, the new laws are not the whole story. Other laws, some of which were enacted when the political climate was quite different, are still on the books and continue to be applicable. Ideally, all the relevant laws should be reconsidered and revised, but practical steps must be first taken in the priority areas.

Another way to provide a greater degree of certainty is to specify the various contingencies in the contract with transnationals. This is at the cost of increasing difficulties in negotiations, however, as pointed out below.

With respect to home-country policies, home governments are in general supportive of the activities of transnational corporations in China. The desire to promote trade and investment is stressed at the highest levels. The methods used differ from country to country. In the United States, for example, the government plays no more than a facilitating role. The officially stated policy with respect to foreign investment is indeed neutrality, although the impact of actual policies is usually far from this. For instance, accelerated depreciation does not apply to investment in China, while export credit contains a degree of subsidy. In other countries, government support for trade and investment is usually stronger. In Japan, especially, the activities of transnational corporations are often coordinated closely with government measures. A notable example is the provision of easy credit, which may be financed partly by aid agencies and aimed at assisting Japanese projects.

As far as imports from China are concerned, virtually all the developed countries have extended most-favored-nation treatment to China. Most of them have also accorded preferential tariffs. Although the effect remains limited because of numerous safeguards and the erosion of the preferential margin following several rounds of tariff reductions, this preference has enabled the Chinese to compete more effectively with other developing countries. The United States has not as yet applied the preferential system to China. While China is regarded as a developing country in accordance with the bilateral trade treaty, a further condition is membership in the General Agreement on Tariffs and Trade (GATT). At the moment, the Chinese have observer status in GATT.

Despite the relatively small amount of China's trade with the developed countries, a number of restrictions have been imposed on imports from China. Textiles trading stands out, and there is a tendency toward stricter curtailments. In the United States, the limitations were originally confined (in the first bilateral agreement) to a few major categories, but there have been U.S. attempts to include more and more items. Moreover, when the Chinese did not agree to the restrictions proposed by the United States, unilateral quotas were imposed. The situation is complicated by restrictions imposed on China elsewhere, often more stringent than those of the United States. In Japan, for example, even though no explicit quota limitations are imposed on textile imports from China, access to that market may be limited by lack of retail outlets. An increasing number of imports from China have been subject to antidumping proceedings in the developed countries. This arises partly from the intrinsic difficulty of determining the internal cost or price of Chinese products, and partly from the fact that most Chinese exports are labor-intensive products which affect declining sectors and employment in the importing countries. An aggravating factor is Chinese inexperience with conditions in the developed countries. The high degree of concentration of a few items into a few markets and great volatility reflect the absence of a long-term export strategy. Moreover, threats of antidumping action against the Chinese in the developed countries may serve the purpose of creating disruption and uncertainty even if there is no merit in the case.

An important restriction placed on exports to China by developed countries relates to dual technology, which may be used for military as well as civilian purposes. This restriction is controlled at the national level as well as the international level. In the United States the level of restriction has been progressively liberalized by separating China from the Soviet bloc. In actual implementation, however, two problems remain: first, the interpretation of what is permissible by the various departments concerned, especially Commerce and Defense, has varied, with the result that the stricter one has in practice exercised virtual veto power. Some of the cases have therefore been discussed at the highest level between the governments. Second, transnational corporations have encountered different treatments for similar products, reflecting the degrees of success in lobbying or obtaining information. This differential treatment increases the uncertainty on the part of the Chinese, not only with respect to the categories of technology in question but also the specific firms involved.

At the international level, coordination is attempted through the Coordinating Committee for Communist Trade (COCOM). It is generally known, however, that other countries tend to be more liberal than the United States. Doubts are raised therefore as to whether there truly is a coordination of policy and practice. To the extent that bargaining takes place between the exporting countries within COCOM, the outcome may be influenced more by horse trading than by objective criteria.

The above suggests that the expanding relationship between China and the transnationals requires a more serious realignment of the relations between the host and home countries involved than has evolved so far. For the developed countries, an old-fashioned mercantilist policy is obviously self-defeating. The market of a billion customers can never be a reality if the potential customers are not allowed to earn their foreign exchange. On China's part, simply attacking protectionism is inadequate because one cannot ignore the political realities in democratic societies where sectional interests play an important role. There are also intrinsic problems in a free-market solution in relations between predominantly capitalist and predominantly socialist economies. There is no substitute for detailed negotiations in order to arrive at mutually satisfactory arrangements.

A prerequisite for such negotiations is an articulation of policies on both sides. The bilateral trade agreements, and, more recently, the investment and tax agreements being negotiated, are a step in this direction.

A further step must necessarily involve multilateral relations and restrictions. In trade, it involves the future role of China in GATT, as well as the future rules of that organization. As far as the international monetary regime is concerned, China is already a preeminent member of the International Monetary Fund (IMF) and the World Bank. Its role in matters such as the creation of international liquidity, flexible or fixed exchange rates, and the decision-making processes in these institutions will inevitably affect the general environment within which China's relations with transnationals are to be structured. More directly, the codes of conduct relating to transnational corporations currently being negotiated in the international agencies should provide a guideline for the behavior of transnationals as well as appropriate policies for home and host countries.

As China progresses in modernization, its relationships with other developing countries as well as with Eastern European countries will also become more complicated both as a partner and as a competitor in the international economic arena. The warming toward the West should not imply alienation from the other blocs. There are already signs that relations between China and the Third World and socialist countries are rapidly developing.

While room for negotiations expands on all fronts, there are reasons why the relationship between China and transnationals is governed particularly by negotiations, as elaborated in chapter 6. In general, the need for negotiations reflects the absence or scant use of overall policies that structure their relations. If the transnationals were all welcome or were all limited to specific activities under prescribed conditions, little negotiation would be necessary. This does not mean that the general framework within which negotiations are taking place has not been improved. Relevant laws and regulations have gradually been enacted. Visa applications have been more speedily processed. Channels of communication have been widened. The negotiations are no longer confined mainly to the Canton Fairs, as in the early days. On the transnational-corporation side, the cultural distance has been shortened by the employment of Chinese-speaking personnel, often of Chinese origin, in negotiations. Lawyers, political scientists, and business consultants who are familiar with China have also been increasingly engaged. Yet, important gaps remain. A main difficulty for transnational corporations continues to be a lack of knowledge about whom to negotiate with. While the establishment of the new Ministry of Foreign Economic Relations and Trade has streamlined China's administrative structure, the institutions and personalities that count remain numerous. The drastic reorganization of government units and changes of personnel have introduced an element of uncertainty into relations built upon trust and friendship between persons. The decentralization of decision making in China accentuates this uncertainty. For giant firms, this difficulty is overcome by access to the very top, but implementation remains in the hands of people at the working level.

Another difficulty lies in misleading signals. Since many transnational corporations have very little experience in China, they have been anxious to break into the new market through heavy outlays in development expenditures. Not only have they been willing to provide all sorts of unusual free services—such as flying their counterparts to the home country for visits, technical assistance and training, wining and dining—but they have also been willing to pare down their profits to a minimum, sometimes to negative levels. Consequently, the initial assumption by the Chinese that the transnational corporations are extremely rich and derive exorbitant profits from China has been reinforced. In the meantime, many transnational corporations are having second thoughts about the China connection, since in the longer run it is the bottom line that counts.

On the other hand, the possibility that the Chinese may be defrauded is real. This arises largely from lack of information on their part. Although the Chinese have been able to compensate for the usually low bargaining power of developing countries by attempting to build a united front and dividing the other side, the apparent victories won in the contractual provisions may be illusory. The low prices negotiated may be offset, or more than offset, by less desirable quality, delivery dates, maintenance or replacement services. The tying of export credit to purchases from a given source may entail disadvantages that outweigh the gains from concessionary terms. As the Chinese gain more experience in these matters, the hidden costs will become apparent and new contradictions and strains in the relationship with transnationals will emerge. Some of the negotiations may have to be reopened, as in a number of other developing countries.

The evolving relationship between China and transnational corporations should not, therefore, be expected to be entirely smooth. There are too many actors, institutions, and issues involved. At the same time, the prophets of doom show a singular lack of vision even as compared with the naiveté of the euphoric optimists. China is not another backward country. Apart from its territorial span, which envelops a wealth of climate, topography, and natural resources as well as a quarter of humankind, there is a sense of self-respect and historical mission shared by most Chinese. The mission to modernize is not simply in order to get rich and strong but to make a contribution to the entire human civilization. Their orientation is again bound to be global once abject poverty and national survival are no longer the burning issues. This is also the orientation of the transnational corporations. It is unavoidable that their paths will meet and their relations expand.

All this may sound somewhat abstract and sweeping. Some practical details will be found in the subsequent pages, in particular the case studies in chapter 7, which examine experiences at the industry and enterprise levels. These case studies supplement the general discussions and illustrative examples given throughout the volume.

1

The Striving for Modernization

In a world of rapid change and intense competition, modernization is virtually a universal goal. Certainly it is not limited to developing countries. Developed countries also feel the constant pressure of either going ahead or falling behind. Europe has been made painfully aware of the technological gap which still exists between the Old World and the New. The United States is increasingly worried about the latecomers who are catching up or surpassing them in a number of areas, such as the conquest of space by the Soviet Union and the rise of the engineering and electronics industry in Japan and Western Europe. In the developing countries, the drive for modernization is hardly controversial, as the gap between the haves and have-nots is so glaring and the very survival of peoples and nations is at stake.

What is unusual about the current Chinese drive to modernization is not that it is taking place but that it is still taking place at this late date. An irrepressible question is whether or not the Chinese ever thought of or attempted modernization earlier, and if so, whether something went so drastically wrong that they are forced to start all over again. Otherwise, a smooth transition into the modern era without much fanfare would have been adequate. As it now stands the implication is that basic changes in the strategies as well as the structure and the system must take place. These changes are still taking shape and may head in some uncertain directions. A further implication is that, for the first time since the establishment of the People's Republic, what is happening in China matters directly to the outside world, including transnational corporations. The transnationals are now perceived by the Chinese not as adversaries but as potential partners or instruments for Chinese purposes. Immense opportunities thus lie ahead, not only for potential business with China, but also for subtle influence on the course of events in China and in the rest of the world. What happens in the future may very well depend on the success or failure of the current Chinese experimentation. Understandably, many await the outcome in China with breathless anticipation. Those who believe that transnational corporations are the root of the underdevelopment of developing countries greet every instance of friction and frustration between China and the transnationals with a sense of triumph. Those who have always considered China a model of self-reliant development are seized with a mixed feeling of disbelief and amazement. Most people, however, will be persuaded more by results than by theory.

1

The present chapter attempts to lay the foundations for an analysis of the implications of the Chinese experience by explaining why China's early attempts were abortive and why China experienced such fundamental difficulties as late as 1976.

The Burden of the Past

The reasons for the failure of attempts at modernization since the Opium War are subject to varying interpretations. Some would emphasize the external factors, while others would stress internal problems.[1] Some would point a finger at political and institutional inadequacies, while others would delve deep into cultural and personality weaknesses.[2] These various forces have obviously interacted and reinforced each other. The following pages single out three basic difficulties from which the forces at work may be elucidated.

The Conceptual Problem

The Chinese concept of modernization has been greatly affected by recurrent crises throughout modern history. A main consequence of the pervasive atmosphere of crisis is that the proponents of modernization have been more interested in the art of persuasion than in the dispassionate development of the concept. During the Imperial period, when the Emperor, or in actual practice his regent or counsellor, had absolute power, any new idea could be dangerous and cost the heads of its originators and the lives of their entire families. While Chinese history is marked by very brave men who felt compelled to act in accordance with the highest principles despite the enormous risk or even futility of doing so,[3] their ideas were channeled mainly toward influencing those in power.

The posture of these loyal persuaders was one of acceptance of the existing institutional framework as well as the unenlightened state of mind of the audience. They were careful not to raise serious fundamental issues and were content to confine themselves to the practical possibilities of persuasion. The system of requiring formal written memorials for Imperial scrutiny and decision aggravated the risk and restrained the content. A memorial which appeared to be insane or unlawful would not only incur enormous risks but also had little chance of reaching its destination because it would be suppressed in the course of preliminary screenings.

In the circumstances, the writings of the memorialists dealt generally with what was practicable. The periodical emphasis on defense responded to the needs of the times. Thoughts of modernization for military strength were obviously triggered by China's slow realization of the superiority of Western arms, first brought about by the Opium War of 1840 and repeatedly demonstrated thereafter by a series of defeats and humiliations. Notable among these were the sack of the Summer Palace, in 1860; the Invasion of Taiwan, in 1874; the Sino-French War, of 1884-85; the Treaty of Shimonoseki, in 1895; and the scramble for concessions by Russia and Germany, in 1897-98. Even after the overthrow of the Manchu Empire, the Chinese were still frequently reminded of foreign military superiority by the twenty-one demands of Japan in 1914 and the award of Germany's Shangdong holding to Japan despite the fact that China had been on the side of the victorious Allies. More recently, the Japanese invasion of the northeastern provinces in 1931, the total war from 1937 until 1945, the Korean War of 1951, the Vietnamese War of the 1960s, the border incidents with the Soviet Union, India, and Vietnam, as well as the unfinished business of reunification with Taiwan, have left little doubt about the continued need for Chinese military strength.

Two important twists in history frustrated the attainment of this objective despite the recurrent emphasis on defense modernization. The first was manifested at the turn of the century by the Boxer Movement, which relied on indigenous methods bordering on mysticism and magic.[4] What was strange was not that such popular beliefs and movements should exist but that they should be officially sanctioned and that wanton attack should be launched on all things foreign. It was a manifestation of madness and stupidity unparalleled in the annals of civilized nations. The second major twist is of more recent vintage. The brilliant successes of the Red Army achieved on the basis of inferior matériel but high revolutionary spirit, convinced some leftists of their invincibility. They believed that sheer heroism and the deployment of vast waves of manpower were all that was needed to defeat adversaries possessing modern technology. The flaws of this generalization could not be exposed as long as any questioning of the dominant opinion was considered tantamount to counterrevolutionary even though the nature of potential enemies and possible future weapons, electronic systems, nuclear warheads, spacecraft, and still more unthinkable means of destruction rendered past experience hardly relevant.

Of course, seen in historical perspective, these twists were mere temporary aberrations in a major trend toward modernization. The emphasis on defense soon led to the import of modern technology. Yet the concepts of technology and modernization remained extremely narrow as long as they were largely limited to the immediate requirements of the military. There was insufficient understanding of the way in which technology needed to be absorbed and generated so that it would take root in Chinese soil. There was a lack of balance between the hard and the soft sciences. This imbalance remained until recently, as may be seen from the concentration of Chinese visiting scholars and students abroad in the hard sciences.

The logical link between defense and industry also became apparent fairly early. Arsenals and navy yards obviously required supporting industries such as iron and steel, coke and coal, as well as infrastructures like electricity, telegraphs, telephones, roads, railways, and ports. Nevertheless, a national program of industrialization or infrastructure development was conspicuously absent until recently. The programs drafted by such leaders as Sun Yat-sen were largely on paper only.[5] This does not mean that all the Chinese avoided the larger question of thoroughgoing modernization. Most of those who did emphasize institutional and structural reform were, unfortunately, short-lived. The fate of the reformists at the hands of the reactionary Empress Dowager served as a warning to many visionaries. The advocates of complete Westernization also exposed themselves to the charge of naiveté or lack of understanding of China's special conditions, so that few followers were attracted. The dominant intellectual conception of modernization centered upon "Chinese learning for fundamental principles and Western learning for application to mundane affairs." How the two strains were to be synthesized or to manifest themselves was generally left unclear.

While the conception of modernization held by China's intellectuals or practitioners was highly constrained by their preoccupation with the need for persuasion and immediate practicality, that of the revolutionaries was colored by conditions of combat. But since persuasion was equally important to them also, appeals to emotion rather than reason became imperative. Moreover, in order to win popular support, the issues had to be greatly simplified and reduced to bare essentials. Everything to be found in the existing order must be negated since otherwise their followers could not be motivated to dedicate their very lives to the purpose of revolution.

The ideas of modernization associated with the Taiping revolutionaries in the 1850s illustrate the above characteristics. The veneration of the new was paralleled by distaste for the old. What was to be abolished included not only such customs as long finger nails and foot binding but also native religion, the wearing of ornaments, and the raising of birds. Even the Republican revolutionaries indulged in the smashing of temples and monasteries and the banning of traditional medical practices such as acupuncture. During the New Life Movement of the late 1930s, zealous students would be asked to see to it that all pedestrians including manual workers were properly dressed by buttoning every button. The most recent episode was, of course, the smashing of virtually all the works of art in sight as well as the banishing of old books by the Red Guards during the Cultural Revolution.

These naivetés and excesses might not have caused irreparable damage if they had been merely a temporary transitional phenomenon in which an old order was giving way to the new. The failure to articulate the concept of modernization might not have made much practical difference if new ideas had gradually evolved together with material progress. The tragedy of the last 130 years or so in China is that no sooner did one transitional period pass than another one set in. Rarely was there enough time for a sustained period of orderly development. The period of restoration in the latter part of the nineteenth century after the collapse of the Taiping Rebellion was a golden opportunity that was missed. The Republican era after the fall of the Manchu Empire, in 1911, saw a succession of military campaigns among factions, interspersed with repeated Japanese invasions. The establishment of the People's Republic, in 1949, gave the first hope for more than a century that China would finally embark on the Long March towards modernization. Yet the ideas and methods that had proved invincible in winning the revolution and the postwar reconstruction grew more and more ossified and less and less adaptable to the new requirements. It is now common knowledge that the Great Leap Forward was a disaster symbolized by the total physical and emotional exhaustion of a whole nation. The subsequent return to rationality showed signs of great promise for a resurgence, only to be cut short by the Cultural Revolution, which proved an even greater disaster than the Great Leap. The revolutionaries had failed to learn the eternal truth that the attributes required to govern are different from those needed for revolution. Certainly the simplistic revolutionary slogans were no substitute for practical policies and programs.

The Leadership Crisis

In a society where decision making was extremely centralized, the personal equation of the leaders played a crucial role in shaping actual policies and programs. The abortive modernization attempts during the latter part of the nineteenth century were obviously connected with the long reign of the Empress Dowager. The filtering through to the throne of the external influences and new ideas was extremely limited, sheltered as it was by an enormous entourage and endowed with absolute power. The very top was even slower than the memorialists to admit the need to learn from the West, since modernization threatened to erode the power and prestige of the throne. Certainly the ideas of the revolutionaries had to be rejected outright. Even when reforms were staged by the Emperor himself, he had to be imprisoned and his aides executed in order to preserve the power of the Dowager.

Whatever secondhand new knowledge filtered through to the very top was either diluted or distorted. First, there was a real problem of communication when foreign ideas were expressed in the traditional Chinese language and style. A face-to-face discussion between men of ideas and the throne was a rarity, given the hierarchical distance. One recorded event illustrates the enormous distance between the ruler and the ruled. An appointment with the Emperor at 8 A.M. had to start before midnight. The total lack of understanding of the requirements of the state, even in the area of defense, is illustrated by the transfer of funds earmarked for the navy to the beautification of the Summer Palace for the personal pleasure of the Empress Dowager. The ignorance of the capabilities of the Western powers as well as of international standards of conduct is exemplified by the use of the Boxers to declare war on all foreigners.

During the Republican era, the crisis of leadership arose from the vacuum created after the easy overthrow of the corrupt and the inept rulers. Suddenly, everyone with some ambition and a few guns aspired to lead the country. The centers of power were preoccupied incessantly with struggles and intrigues for self-preservation and aggrandizement. There was little time or opportunity to modernize the nation as a whole. If some degree of modernization did occur during this period it was despite the leadership rather than because of it.

A strong hand was certainly called for when the leadership question was finally solved with the establishment of the People's Republic. At last China had escaped from the multitude of regional warlords who tyrannized over and exploited their subjects to satisfy their individual greed or whims. Once again, there was the semblance of one nation and one purpose. Despite the origins of the mass line of the new regime, however, the dynamics of factional strife and skillful manipulation of public opinion produced a personality cult unparalleled in Chinese history. Mao was accepted as the single source of truth and wisdom. He was revered like an emperor and a god. The entire nation was virtually under a hypnotic spell. There was no room for the exercise of independent thought. Absolutism and orthodoxy were on a scale unmatched by the bygone dynasties.

The Obstacle to Implementation

The oversimplified conceptual framework and the endemic leadership crises meant that there was no consistent direction and strategy for a workable modernization program. The purpose of modernization was rarely articulated. Sometimes it was identified with nationalism. At others it was linked with the promotion of socialism. Only occasionally was lip service paid to the betterment of the people's livelihood. The strategy for modernization was correspondingly unclear. It was fashionable to Westernize but at the same time the Chinese substance had to prevail. The difficulty was to know which traditional values must be given up and which modern values were to be embraced. Only surface phenomena appeared to be unmistakable. For example, the modernization of the economy could mean no more than industrialization. Even the modernization of agriculture might not go beyond mechanization, irrigation, the use of chemical fertilizers and pesticides, and electrification.

Progress was further stifled by the difficulties of implementing actual programs. It was clear from the outset that the major modernization programs had to be carried out mainly by the public sector. The defense orientation accentuated this tendency.[6] The private sector was too weak to undertake such tasks as large-scale coal mining, iron and steel works, railways, and the like. Where private interests did exist in such sectors, they were largely limited to small-scale operations. In any case, the blessing of the government, which was always sufficiently powerful to impose obstacles or even to break any private enterprise, was a practical necessity.

It is true that official supervision was often combined with the private management of enterprises. However, the dividing line between supervision and management was thin. Top managers often had important official connections. When they lacked such linkages they were at the mercy of the officials operating within the system of perquisites, or "squeeze," which was openly practiced from the Emperor to the clerks. The enterprises served mainly as vehicles for personal enrichment.

Even in the absence of corruption in the strictest sense, the bureaucratic behavior of public officials constituted an obstacle to modernization. Although the inefficiency of bureaucracy is not limited to the public sector, nor is it a universal phenomenon of that sector (as some public enterprises, for example, those in France, are well run), the old-style Chinese bureaucracy was hardly equipped to assume the new responsibility of modernization. The dominant motive of the bureaucracy was self-preservation and risk avoidance. The rules of the game provided very little link between efficiency and reward. Indeed, modernization posed a threat to the entrenched positions and security of the bureaucracy, especially those who were not qualified or too old to learn new tricks.

The redeeming feature within the system was that individual variations were possible. This was partly due to the need to give more power to local officials during periods when the center was in decline in order to deal with immediate crises. In the Republican era, the decentralization of power took place not by design but by necessity. At times, even private enterprises had sufficient power to engage in numerous activities, which gave the appearance of rapid economic development.[7] Even during the People's Republic, when the hands of the managers of enterprises were tied, at least until recently, great unevenness was evident in the performance of different enterprises.

On the Eve of the Modernization Drive

The current belated drive for modernization stems from the lack of success of China's past attempts to attain this goal. A closer examination of the fundamental difficulties that existed on the eve of the present drive will explain its inevitability. It is true that events might have turned out differently if the present leadership had failed to dislodge its opponents. It is the thesis of the author that the same state of affairs could not have dragged on for very long without a collapse that could hardly be entirely ignored by any functioning government. A historical parallel may indeed be found in the changes introduced belatedly by Mao after the disasters of the Great Leap Forward. The main difference is that the situation in the mid 1970s was far more serious than in the late 1950s. The seriousness of this situation escaped most students of China until recently. Even today, many observers cannot at once see how a bleak picture can be reconciled with China's apparently brilliant performance in the economic growth league of the past three decades.

The Cocooning of the Mind

Nothing is more serious than the effect on a people's mental state when all knowledge and ideas regarded as dangerous are banned. The burning of books during the Cultural Revolution was certainly more thorough than similar acts by Shihuang Ti and later despots. Virtually all libraries withdrew everything from public view except what was considered absolutely safe. Even historical tracts and novels were not exempted from the purge, since they might suggest parallels in the contemporary scene. This again was far more severe than during the height of the Confucian orthodoxy when the teachings of a hundred schools of thought or contending philosophies were available for study despite the clear definition of orthodoxy.

A few privileged people were granted access to the forbidden materials, but they were used mainly for polemics rather than serious analysis. Anyone suspected of harboring unorthodox ideas could be labelled an antirevolutionary or capitalist roader.[8] This applied especially to the cadres who were the pioneers of the revolution, since the bourgeois thinkers had long been silenced. A consequence of this close mindedness was the vulgarization of the Marxist-Leninist-Maoist line of thought. Again, this was far worse than the vulgarization among the Qing literati of the Confucian thought in the so-called eight-legged essays. For there were many Qing scholars who despised the vulgarized form and refused to indulge in it. Even though they risked their official careers, they were not singled out for punishment nor ostracized by their contemporaries. Their writings could even be published. The orthodox classics included, moreover, various interpretations of Confucian learning, such as The Annals. In contrast, only one interpretation of Marxist-Leninist-Maoist orthodoxy was permitted. It was frequently lifted out of context. In some cases, even these leaders' own writings proved unsafe and therefore had to be expurgated. Mao's essay on the Ten Great Relations, for example, was not available before 1976. On the eve of 1976, the intellectual atmosphere was such that virtually all the disciplines—economics, management, political science, sociology, and anthropology—had been abandoned. The few remaining intellectuals of the pre-1949 or pre-antirightist movement variety were either put in the ox pens or were assigned to posts that were completely unrelated to their training.

This self-imposed cocooning of the mind had far-reaching implications for the way of doing things. It was unsafe to think for oneself, not only in the case of major philosophical or national issues but also in everyday life. Consequently, the mental paralysis tended to extend to all realms of activity. Those that concerned man or society were most seriously affected. Even those concerned with other matters did not entirely escape the shackles imposed by orthodoxy.

The Loss of Incentives and Discipline

What motivated a revolutionary to dedicate his life to the cause was certainly not the same as what made the common man tick. The continued pursuit of the revolutionary goal with revolutionary motivations during the period of reconstruction and beyond contributed to the achievements of the People's Republic in its formative days. Genuine heroism and idealism set standards for emulation. Yet, the lofty ideal of changing the nature of man so that people would toil incessantly for the good of society without regard for self proved more and more elusive with time. First, virtual success in conquering starvation, with the exception of the early 1960s and certain isolated cases, tended to weaken zeal.[9] Social consciousness in a situation where life or death was the overriding question differed significantly from a state where the question was far less basic. One's enthusiasm to toil to allow one's fellow man to purchase fine grains and meat instead of merely coarse grains was understandably limited. When it eventually amounted to converting a black and white television into a color set, willingness could be even less. Moreover, the gap between the expected outcome and the actual results of zealousness became more apparent. It was not zeal alone that could produce steel of usable quality from backyard furnaces. Mass mobilization for such projects as irrigation and reclamation may have been successful in many localities; but even here ecological damage has resulted where serious investigations were not made. Furthermore, the egalitarian goal, at first a moral force, began to seem more and more unfair as laziness and carelessness went unpunished and diligence and meticulousness went unrewarded. This was accentuated as revolutionary zeal eroded, and the process became cumulative as economic performance was affected. Lastly, the erosion tended to accelerate as the old revolutionaries aged and a younger generation arose that expected a good life in a socialistic society. It was asked why life had to continue to be so hard and drab. In many localities, for example, despite significant achievements on the national front, people still had to rely mainly on the coarse grains used for animals in richer countries. They could not afford to have more than one egg or half a kilo of pork a week. The question also arose as to whether life in a socialistic society was indeed superior to that in other forms of society, as people had been led to believe.

The loss of incentive was compounded by erosion of discipline. The weakening of nonmaterial and material incentives also weakened self-discipline. At the same time, apart from political considerations, disciplinary measures were seldom used by managers. Workers could not be fired regardless. Even fines for misconduct were hardly levied since slowdowns were common and any disciplinary action would appear harsh or unegalitarian. Salaries could not be reduced from the already very low level of living of the offenders. Even in the communes, where rewards were supposed to be linked with work via a point system, in practice the nature of work was often ignored and rewards had no reference to effort or result. Indeed, poverty was equated with virtue, especially during the Cultural Revolution. Housewives who worked diligently to raise a few chickens or pigs would be running counter to the official line.

The Growing Economic Irrationality

The economic implications of this mental paralysis, loss of incentive, and laxness in discipline deepened with time. At first, things did not appear to need a complete overhaul. In part, thinking people were willing to give the benefit of the doubt to an alternative to all other known models with their well-known defects. In part, there was a gap between policy and actual implementation. This was especially true in certain areas, such as Shanghai, which had been favorably treated as a showplace. It was also true of sectors that were somewhat insulated from central policy, such as the armed forces and certain ministries. As time went on, however, the cumulative effect became more and more evident. The official line conflicted so much with human experience that no amount of propaganda or theology was any longer convincing to the innate common sense of the ordinary people. There was a crisis of confidence. The only thing which retained a semblance of credibility was the reverence for Mao. Paradoxically, this was also the reason why the forces of the Gang of Four collapsed so quickly, and with so little resistance, upon Mao's death.

Economic decision making by slogans, as has been pointed out, had its reasons initially. The communization of agriculture was linked to the desire to break the power base of the peasants, who were traditionally individualistic and even capitalistic because they behaved like small entrepreneurs. From the technological point of view, communization was a means of promoting the consolidation of fragmented fields and of pushing irrigation and mechanization schemes as well as scale economies. It was likewise a device for spreading the risk intrinsic to agricultural pursuits, which continued to be affected by the vagaries of nature. Yet, the failure of agricultural production per capita in the mid 1970s to surpass the level of the mid 1950s posed a serious threat to the ability of the nation to continue to feed itself.[10] Prospects for expanding the amount of land under cultivation were extremely poor. The reported arable land area had declined in the 1970s as compared with the 1950s owing to competing uses such as industries, housing, hydropower, and roads.[11] The use of fertilizers was also approaching the point of diminishing returns. Even better irrigation had meant a rapid drop of underground water levels in many areas. The conversion of forest and hilly land into crop land caused serious soil erosion and threats of flooding. The sorrows of the Yellow River and the Yangtze threatened to recur, as the river bed rose and protective vegetation gradually disappeared.

However, the growing irrationality of the guiding principles of agricultural development was realized only slowly. The Dazhai Model appeared both noble and practical—because heroic efforts would conquer all obstacles and harsh conditions and because people would then be able to take care of themselves without state or external aid. It was not revealed until much later that in economic calculations the cost and benefit relations of such a scheme were not altogether favorable. The subsidies by the state were often hidden, and the reported increases in production were found to be exaggerated.[12]

Likewise, the motto "take grain as the key" appeared at first to be extremely reasonable. In a land-hungry, developing country like China, grains remained the most essential life-sustaining substance. In terms of yield per land area, they compared favorably with legumes; and hogs, cattle, and poultry were by and large less efficient convertors of caloric value. In so large a country, the possibility that domestic grains might be supplemented by imports was severely limited, apart from security considerations. A ten-percent shortage of grains in China would require more than thirty million tons of imports, which could strain the supply of all the grain-surplus countries. The foreign-exchange cost would be of such magnitude that it would impose a heavy burden on the country's balance of payments, especially if the increased demand affected the world supply price of grains.

The rigid application of the grains strategy, moreover, brought about widespread diseconomies. First, it ignored the distribution of land and water resources within China. Inasmuch as about nine-tenths of the area was unsuitable for grain production under existing conditions, the lopsided emphasis meant the misuse as well as the underutilization of scarce resources.

Thus, arid and hilly land produced a low yield of grains. In some instances, valuable orchards and other economic crops were destroyed to make room for grains. Soil erosion was aggravated. Lake areas, which served as a buffer in periods of heavy rain, shrank progressively. Many aquatic products and legumes that were common in the Chinese cuisine became rare luxuries.

Achievements in industry appeared at first sight to be even more impressive than in agriculture. They were indeed dramatic, if comparison is made between 1949 and the 1970s. The level of gross industrial output in 1975 was almost 3,000 percent of the 1949 figure. In terms of the share of industry in the structure of output, China could already be classified as industrialized. A comparison with 1952, though somewhat less dramatic owing to the recovery from the depressed levels, does not alter the main picture.

Nevertheless, the reported fulfillment or overfulfillment of expanding industrial output had become less and less real. First, under the motto for industrial development, "take steel as the key," a considerable amount of output had no outlet and was simply stockpiled. The bulk of this arose not because of a temporary slack in demand, as in inventory accumulation during cyclical downswings in industrial countries, but because of unsuitable qualities or specifications. The story that the diameter of some stockpiled nails was over a foot, as factories tried to meet their output targets in tons, might be an exaggeration. Yet the total unconcern of producers about the marketability of their products was built into the system: it was not their responsibility to make sales as the whole of their production was taken over by the state. This attitude was reinforced by the general breakdown of discipline and the behavior of the bureaucracy. There was laxness in quality control. Neither the distributor nor the end-user exercised much indirect control by checking against quality specifications. Frequently, the end-user's only choice was take it or leave it.

The emphasis placed on the development of heavy industry rather than light industry also appeared reasonable at first. The reversal of the traditional stages of industrial development was consistent with deliberate industrialization. This had been the strategy of the Soviet Union, and the initial foundations of industrial development in China were laid mainly with the Soviet aid for 156 major projects before Sino-Soviet relations turned sour. The strategy had the advantage of generating its own demand, since heavy industry required supplies from other heavy industries. It could also build up pressure for the development of other sectors, such as railways, construction, and light industries. The importance attached to heavy industry was especially designed to redress the initial imbalance in the industrial structure. Furthermore, international conditions at the time were such that China had little choice but to rely on its own basic industries.

The pivotal role assigned to machine tools reflected this strategy. The number of machine tools China accumulated was indeed impressive. The same figure showed, however, their redundant and inefficient use. The ratio of the value of industrial output per machine tool in China was a small fraction of that in Japan. This was because in China many machine tools were simply hoarded by enterprises that attempted to be self-sufficient. Virtually every plant kept its own tooling and repair shops, though they were used only occasionally. The inefficient use of machine tools also reflected the concentration on the production of simple tools, since there was little incentive on the part of enterprises to innovate and improve the variety.

The development of transport and communications reflected the overall strategy as well as the stage of development. The relative emphasis placed on the development of heavy industry meant a corresponding demand for bulk cargo. The need to introduce new modes of transport and communications—whether on land, in the air, or over the seas and rivers—mandated a higher rate of growth of that sector than for the economy as a whole. On the other hand, self-reliance (or, more correctly, the inward-looking orientation, both regionally and internationally) and the relatively low stage of development minimized the demand for traffic. On balance, the pattern of Chinese development can be characterized as transport-saving or communications-saving in comparison with countries at similar levels of development. The main difficulty with this sector was that it imposed a severe constraint on a shift from the inward-looking orientation. With the introduction of an outward-looking policy, bottlenecks naturally arose, as is discussed in the next chapter. Suffice it to mention here that a severe strain would be placed not only on the total demand but also on its structure. For example, the development of foreign trade placed a special burden on port facilities. The increased demand for short hauls in goods and passengers particularly strained road transport.

It was the service sector that was woefully neglected. This seemed to fly in the face of the ubiquitous slogan "serve the people," to be seen on virtually every government building during the Maoist era. At the same time, this neglect was deeply rooted in Chinese society. First, Mao himself sensed the danger that the once-revolutionary cadres who owed their brilliant victories to mass support might relapse into the posture of the traditional elite officialdom. The system of government controls in numerous areas of activity, whether food rationing, clothing, lodging or travel, tended to induce a ruling-class attitude rather than the one of public service.

Second, even among the populace in general, there was a strange aversion to providing services. The memory of class relationships was still fresh, whether between the feudal lord and the serf, between the master and the servant, or between the imperialist and the colonial subject. Service was thus easily confused with servitude. This confusion was evident to virtually all visitors to China in the early days in their encounters with service personnel. One had almost to beg for any service, which was then rendered reluctantly. This attitude was reinforced by the general shortage of goods and services, and it in turn accentuated the shortage. For instance, it was almost impossible to find anybody to repair household objects.

The third reason for the weakness in the service sector was the narrow interpretation of what was productive and what was not. The material-product concept inherited from the Soviets excluded many of the service items. The innocent categorization in statistical terms was confused with what was useful or less useful to socialist construction. Consciously or unconsciously, the service sector was down-played.

All the fundamental difficulties did not disappear with the passing of Mao and the downfall of the Gang of Four. Even in the Four Modernizations program, officially introduced in 1978 by Premier Hua Guofeng, the offhand nature of the lofty targets clearly showed a lack of any fundamental understanding of the real problems of the day. The idea of four modernizations was not to be faulted. The need for China to accomplish the comprehensive modernization of agriculture, industry, science and technology, and national defense was, indeed, stressed by Premier Zhou Enlai in his report in 1975. It was useful to reaffirm the fundamental goal. Yet the meaning of modernization was hardly spelled out. Little was said about how the Four Modernizations were to be achieved. One can certainly add a host of other basic conditions, such as democratization and human rights as the fifth and sixth modernizations. It was basically in the economic realm that the irrationality persisted. The list of targets came virtually out of the blue. Between 1978 and 1985, agriculture was to be 85 percent mechanized. Grain output was to achieve a 4.3 percent annual average growth rate, which was more than twice that for the twenty-year period 1957-77. No less than 120 major projects were to be constructed. These included 10 iron and steel complexes, 9 nonferrous metal complexes, and 8 coal mines, with an output of 1 billion tons per year by 1987 as compared with 550 million tons in 1977. There would be 10 Daqings, 30 power stations, and 6 new trunk railways. Even for an outside contemporary observer, such as one economist with the Japan Economic Research Center, it was not difficult to make a few rough calculations showing that the goals were too ambitious.[13] One wonders what had happened to the Chinese planners.

The sudden opening of the door to a flood of foreign business was also carried out in an offhand manner. Little thought was given to the overall foreign-exchange implications. The total obligations of various contracts were apparently not added up until much later. Moreover, machines were ordered without regard to the supply of other inputs. For example, advanced equipment for steel-rolling mills could not be fully utilized owing to shortages of electricity and intermediate products. Refining equipment was forced to lie idle as the promised crude was not forthcoming.

It was only in 1979 that China truly embarked on serious efforts at modernization.[14] These efforts were reconfirmed and consolidated at the twelfth Congress of the Party, in 1982. A major characteristic of the current program of modernization is structural reform as well as the readjustment of the economy. The nature of these reforms and their implications are discussed in the following chapter.

2 The Nature of the Reforms

The peaceful transition of political power from the blind worshippers of Mao to those who saw fundamental flaws in the existing system did not take place overnight. The power structure built upon the personality cult of Mao was too strong and deep-rooted to be challenged in one stroke. Whether in theory or in practice, the unquestioning disciples were well entrenched and unyielding. It was not until the Third Plenum of the eleventh Central Committee of the Chinese Communist Party, in December, 1979, more than three years after the passing of Mao, that a turning point was reached. With the progressive consolidation of power by the new leaders in the Party and the government in successive years, the reform movement has also gathered momentum, although the course has not been entirely clear or smooth.

The Eight-Character Policy

The Two Eight-Character Policies

The broad outline of the new direction was succinctly summarized in eight Chinese characters, or four concepts (two characters for each concept): readjustment, restructuring, "consolidating" (see below for a reinterpretation of this concept), and improving. These are reminiscent of the Eight-Character Policy of 1961, which had followed the disasters of the Great Leap Forward. The similarities between the two policies are striking. Apart from the superficial identity of the labels, both policies signalled significant changes in direction following great disruptions in the economy. Both can be traced to the central role played by Chen Yun.[1]

The differences between the policies in the two periods are even more important than their similarities. First, despite the powerful support for Chen Yun's ideas and program from Liu Shaoqi, Zhou Enlai, and Deng Xiaoping in the early 1960s, Mao's dominance persisted. Chen Yun was able to exert his influence only to the extent that Mao permitted him to do so. There were fundamental divergences in their approaches, and the answer to the question of whose line would prevail in the case of a showdown was obvious. In contrast, the post-1979 leadership has become increasingly unified under Chen's or Deng's allies. Secondly, the eight characters in the two periods differ in one important aspect. While readjustment

17

and improving are common to both, the early period included consolidating (*gonggu*), and solidifying or strengthening (*zhongshe*), while the latter period puts forward the second concept of restructuring, which strikes at the root of the entire system.

Failure to appreciate the important differences between the two periods has led to the mechanical application of the cyclical theory, which is based on the historical observation that occurrences in China tend to reverse themselves, implying future instability. This failure has also led to a misinterpretation of the nature of the current reforms. In particular, their revolutionary import and complexities have been underestimated.

The Concepts Reinterpreted

Of the four current concepts in the policy, the first two, readjustment and restructuring, are central. The last two, *zhendun* and improving, are less specific and are complementary to the first two. *Zhendun* is incorrectly translated as consolidating, which conveys the erroneous notion of preserving the existing order. It actually implies that there is something wrong, such as laxness in discipline, which should be righted or rectified. At any rate, the emphasis is not simply on putting things together and solidifying but on putting the house in order. This should include a change in the organization of the Party leadership, and the reimposition of discipline for cadres and workers. With respect to more mundane matters, it could also include orderly procedures and the keeping of good records in productive activities. *Zhendun* is therefore reformist in orientation and closely related to restructuring.

The concept of improving is extremely broad. It can very well be the outcome of the first three. The purpose is probably to emphasize a basic objective which was strongly negated by ultraleftists. The raising of levels of living and the improvement of one's lot is now accepted. No longer is poverty a virtue in an atmosphere of perpetual class struggle. Concomitantly, improvement in the quality of goods and services and in all aspects of endeavor such as arts and sciences is now consistent with socialist goals.

In terms of development strategy, improving productivity implies a move from extensive to intensive development. The former relies on more of the same inputs for the expansion of output, while the latter seeks to economize inputs through new technologies and greater efficiency.[2]

Readjustment

The focus of readjustment is mainly short run. In view of the existing imbalances, their correction has a special urgency and is expected to show results within a relatively short period of time. Events have shown, however, that the time required for redress is much longer than the original estimate of three years. This is because the imbalances were numerous under the Maoist strategy of unbalanced growth. Readjustment has to be made between consumption and capital accumulation, between agriculture and industry, between light industry and heavy industry, between subsectors within each industry, and in interindustry relations.

There are also new problems of fiscal and foreign-exchange imbalances. The imbalance between consumption and capital accumulation resulted from the single-minded pursuit of a very high rate of accumulation before 1979. Obviously, what is accumulated is not available for consumption. Levels of living are therefore depressed. To be sure, in a developing society, tightening the belt to attain a rate of accumulation of at least ten to fifteen percent of income is needed in order to achieve a rate of aggregate-output growth at least as high as the population increase. A high rate of accumulation is imperative to achieve an initial thrust and momentum as well as future rises in the level of living. The Chinese rate of accumulation, however, had been pushed to unprecedented levels, exceeding one-third in 1978.[3] This surpassed the records of almost all other countries, developed and developing. In view of the neglect of capital efficiency, such a rate did not result in a commensurate rate of growth of aggregate output, because the incremental capital output ratio had declined. Moreover, over the years, even reported growth had been exaggerated since nonusable goods were included in the figures. Furthermore, the prolonged suppression of consumption had an unfavorable effect on incentives and therefore also on production.[4] This is perhaps clearest in the case of agriculture. Peasants have little incentive to produce surplus goods for sale if they are not able to obtain needed consumer goods in exchange.

The realignment of the priorities between agriculture and industry and between light and heavy industry is related to the realignment between consumption and accumulation. The position of agriculture had, of course, never been officially downgraded. During the revolutionary days much support was derived from the agricultural sector. Indeed, to many contemporary observers, the entire communist movement was one of agrarian reform. In reality, the emphasis placed on industrialization, especially the development of heavy industry, as well as on capital accumulation, placed a heavy burden on agriculture to provide the needed resources. This is reminiscent of the strategy of the leftists in the Soviet Union, where agriculture was to be exploited for development, although the Chinese never openly endorsed such a strategy.

One instrument for improving the agricultural situation was the readjustment of agricultural terms of trade, or the relative price of its inputs and outputs. The procurement prices of a number of agricultural products were raised on the average by twenty-two percent in 1979; they were again increased by seven percent in 1980. Also, above-quota purchases were made at higher prices.[5] The rest of the surplus could be sold at fair-market prices, which were generally even higher.

The relative position assigned to light and heavy industries has been reversed in favor of the former. This is partly necessitated by the new importance attached to consumption. It is also related to a new concern for quick returns as well as comparative advantage. The main reason for the new emphasis, however, is that, following the Stalinist model of development, heavy industry was developed for its own sake with little regard for its interrelationship with the rest of the economy. Indeed, interindustry relations were surprisingly neglected, with the result that bottlenecks abounded. This was reflected, for example, in the idling of new plants because of a lack of raw materials and power.

In agriculture, increased attention is being paid to products other than grains and to such important produce as cotton. Forestry, fishery, husbandry, fruits and vegetables all have a place, especially in view of the varying natural conditions in the many parts of China. In heavy industry, stress is placed on serving the requirements of other industries—whether light industry, industries of strategic importance, or those in critical scarcity. Even in light industry, significant changes in the proportions of numerous products are called for as adjustments are made to changing demand patterns and the movement from a seller's to a buyer's market. These changes are greatly assisted by structural readjustment.

Restructuring

Restructuring is necessarily more difficult and time-consuming than readjustment. Strictly speaking, it should not cover the same time horizon. Certainly it cannot be accomplished within three to five years. Inasmuch as restructuring means a fundamental reform of the entire system, it has far-reaching implications. There is no accepted theory of how a socialist economy should be structured nor much practical experience to rely on. The classic Communist literature is not of much help, since Marx was more concerned with the shortcomings of capitalist society than the workings of a socialist one. Moreover, having been disillusioned by the Soviet model in the past, the Chinese are now rightly wary of transplanting the new Soviet and Eastern European models to their country. This is not to deny that the experiences of the Soviet Union and of the Eastern European countries, especially after the recent reforms, are instructive. They were, however, regarded as revisionist and were mainly ignored by the Chinese until recently. Even today, the aversion to things Soviet has a fall-out effect on the rest of the Warsaw Pact nations. Few Chinese are now interested in learning Russian and the Eastern European languages. Many specialists acquainted with the region are changing their field and learning English.

Restructuring is therefore being approached extremely cautiously. The divergence from the Maoist model and the lack of a detailed conceptual alternative necessitates a step-by-step approach. Even more important is the need to avoid too much controversy at a time when political power has yet to be consolidated and consensus has to be achieved by factual demonstration of the correctness of the reform measures. It should also be remembered that the readjustment is in itself not uncontroversial, especially as it affects unfavorably the turf of many powerful ministries and new problems are created by it. The pursuit of the Eight-Character Policy, especially readjustment and restructuring, is in many ways bold and revolutionary. It is thus only prudent not to proceed hastily. Further, the difficulties of implementation are staggering, as is shown below. These considerations will become clearer when the nature of restructuring, or systemic reforms, is discussed in the following section.

Toward Systemic Reforms

The Emancipation of the Mind

A prerequisite for restructuring of the Chinese economic system is the emancipation of the Chinese mind from slavish adherence to Maoist doctrines. It is not an exaggeration to maintain that Mao himself certainly did not indulge in such adherence. A distinction can therefore be made between those who believed that Mao was the source of all knowledge and wisdom and those who continue to consider him a great man. The implication of the latter is that to err is human and that no mortal can possibly foresee the distant future and prescribe in detail for posterity, since conditions change constantly. This emancipation of thought could not have taken place without drastic changes at the political level. Otherwise the risks of heresy would have been too great.

A direct consequence of this emancipation is the reexamination or reinterpretation of Maoist doctrines. Thus, socialism continues to be the desired social structure, but class struggle can be de-emphasized as the class enemies have already mostly vanished. In economic application, socialist agriculture does not preclude private plots or even individual contract labor. Self-reliance has not been discarded, but this does not mean that China has to reinvent the wheel, to close its doors, or to achieve self-sufficiency for the nation or for each region and commune. Competing systems of thought are still looked upon gingerly for fear of disintegration and disorder, but that does not preclude learning from these systems. In particular, many branches of learning have their universal as well as their particular aspects. The former are not necessarily relevant only to a particular social system, even if they are a product of that system.

Such a reexamination and reinterpretation of the new orthodoxy affects all aspects of life. The relaxation of confrontational tension among people and among social groups is conducive to social cohesion. Civility is no longer suspected of hypocrisy, and service confused with servitude. Such a change in attitude has been officially sanctioned, among other things, in the "four emphases and five beauties (gudelines for behavior, especially in interpersonal conduct, ranging from civility to concern for public welfare and morality)." The extent to which they have already been put into practice is apparent even to casual observers. For example, the service personnel of hotels and restaurants are beginning to acquire better manners and behave less as if they were doing the customer a favor. What is strange is that such a change is not entirely without controversy. There have even been theoretical attacks on such behavior in the newspapers, an illustration of the difficulty of changing people's habits of thought.

Toward New Leadership

Though the emancipation of mind had a broad base of support, given the existing excesses that bordered on the tragicomic, it would have been impossible without initiative from the top. The penalty associated with the counterrevolution is severe, as many found out. The new demnads placed on leaders who institute fundamental reforms is also severe. In contrast to traditional dynastic changes, in which the lieutenants who had brought about the revolutionary conquests were usually fairly quickly and systematically replaced by a new set of officials (as epitomized by the saying "When the rabbit is dead the hunting dog perishes"), virtually all the important positions in postrevolutionary China continued to be occupied by the Old Guard. Most of them apparently made significant contributions during the revolution, but their ability to run the country, especially its economic activities, was untested to say the least. The Cultural Revolution did succeed in ridding the ranks of many of the Old Guard, but the new recruits were chosen almost exclusively on the basis of ideological purity and loyalty in the internal struggle. Their ability to run the country was even more questionable. Indeed, the leaders of the Cultural Revolution explicitly down-played expertise, contrasting it unfavorably with Redness.

The new emphasis on expertise imposed a heavy burden on the leadership. One of the first steps in the new policy was to rehabilitate those with expert knowledge. This move was in any case required to right the wrong. At the same time, the knowledge of these experts was mostly of the pre-1950s vintage. Many of them had long been denied the opportunity to either follow or practice their profession. Another step was to retire the septuagenarians and older cadres. Despite the very generous pensions given to retirees, the loss of power and of numerous fringe benefits, such as aides, cars, and entertainment, was a serious consideration; thus the change had to be brought about gradually, and the privileges of retirees progressively restored or extended.

The main answer was in retraining. Many senior officials were sent abroad for short visits in order to broaden their horizons. In the United States alone, many institutions received frequent visits from the Chinese. At first the recipient institutions were enthusiastic, if only out of curiosity and because of the novelty. Gradually, serious contacts became difficult when the institutions found that the flow was mostly one-way traffic and that the information sought by the Chinese was fairly elementary and largely obtainable from readily accessible publications.

The establishment of domestic training programs on a rotation basis, whereby government officials take turns to be trained, is a novel feature of the new order. The main difficulty lies in the development of appropriate programs. The separation of educational institutions from operational activities is deep-rooted. Most educators have little practical experience in their fields. Economists in China, for example, normally have little access to national or enterprise data, most of which is stamped "secret" or "top" secret." Even basic aggregative statistics, such as those now printed in the *Financial Statistics* of the International Monetary Fund, were a revelation to scholars after China joined the world monetary institution.

The employment of foreign instructors supplements scarce domestic resources but also poses additional problems. Primary among them is the fact that most trainees do not possess the language proficiency needed to deal with foreign experts. The degree of success in communication depends more on the skill of the interpreter than on that of the instructor. This is especially true when terms and concepts that appear elementary to the instructor are new to the Chinese. Even when they are properly translated, the meaning is not clear and is frequently misunderstood.

The case of management training courses held in Dalien and organized by the U.S. Department of Commerce in cooperation with the Chinese Commission of Technology and Science is illustrative. While the trainees have generally benefited from a stimulating environment that included the exchange of experience and the use of case methods, the applicability of the cases to the Chinese environment, as well as the other instructional materials, is sometimes questionable. The development of appropriate materials, instructors, and methods can only be done gradually.

This instance further demonstrates that even when the leaders have all the political will to reform, the articulation of the concept, its translation into concrete measures, and its actual implementation must take time.

The Rediscovery of the Market

Although the new stress on expertise is necessary to correct its previous neglect or even deliberate suppression, the process whereby real experts are generated and recognized remains to be specified. In most countries, in addition to formal training, peer review, or the satisfactory completion of certain professional tests, the most important process takes place through the market mechanism. This is especially so with economic activities. Indeed, the most able entrepreneurs may not have much formal business management training, but have proved themselves instead in the real world or the marketplace. It is true that they may be lucky, or may engage in predatory activities that are ethically wrong and socially offensive, but their continued business success conveys an important message. The lack of formal training may be more than compensated for by practical experience, which can of course be supplemented by self-directed study as well as by the advice of trained experts and consultants.

Moreover, whatever the social system, the defects of the market mechanism are to a greater or lesser extent, remedied by social policy. Contrary to popular notins and regardless of transient political swings, the richer the society, the greater the possible scope for social action. Thus, the share of national income that is distributed through deliberate social action, such as social-security and welfare expenditures, rather than through the market mechanism, tends to be high in the rich, developed economies. Most of the capitalist countries are represented in this group. In contrast, the share tends to be low in many developing countries, even though they espouse socialism in their constitutions or political platforms.[6] Many worthy endeavors, such as the arts and the sciences, whose contribution to society is inadequately reflected in the marketplace, are frequently subsidized in capitalist societies. At the same time, lucrative activities such as drug sales, prostitution, and monopolistic exploitation are prohibited or controlled. Even the resale of tickets for sports or artistic events at a profit is sometimes punishable by law. Many other activities are encouraged or discouraged by positive or negative taxes. At the same time, the use of the market mechanism is not inconsistent with socialism, nor is it contradictory to planning.

Aversion to the marketplace, however, is deep-rooted in China. The merchant class has long been placed at the bottom of the social scale despite, or perhaps because of, its accumulation of power. Under the People's

Republic, a socialist economy is equated with a planned economy. This has in turn often been narrowly interpreted to mean the banishment of market forces in favor of administrative or command decision making.

The result of such a leaning is that the burden placed on the planners was extremely heavy. They were supposed to know everything and provide all the solutions. They were expected to be familiar with numerous production possibilities in various sectors and localities. They were also to control all resources and make the appropriate allocations. This included inputs as well as final products. In addition, prices were supposed to be stable and not play the role of arbitrating divergences between demand and supply.

To accomplish such a task would require superhuman effort even if it were performed by top experts with the aid of sophisticated computer models and complete information. This obviously did not happen. Even the rudimentary types of check for internal consistency, such as input and output balances, were absent. A great deal of waste and misallocation of resources consequently ensued.

With the emancipation of minds from doctrinaire hatred of the market, the new guiding principle has become a planned economy supplemented by market forces. There is, however, serious debate over exactly how a mixed system is to work, and how much and in what respect it is to be determined by planning or by the market. There is no ready answer. Indeed, any private enterprise economy is faced with the same difficult question.

Although in theory the use of market forces can reduce the burden on planning, in practice central planning needs to be significantly strengthened. This is because of the virtual cessation of planning in favor of arbitrary command during the Cultural Revolution. Even the Five-Year Plans were discontinued, and the meager planning staff mostly disbanded.

Planning is obviously needed in order to carry out the readjustment policies required to correct the imbalances enumerated earlier. The nature of the planning, however, has changed. It is not necessary to make administrative decisions on the precise type and variety of most consumer goods. With the exception of a few essentials, such as grains and edible oil, market forces can be the guide. Even for essentials and producers' goods, a mixed system may be used. With grains, for example, only minimum targets need to be set, and for edible oils price incentives may be enough to induce the desired expansion of output. Even producers' goods may be cleared in the market, if there are surpluses or when quotas have been fulfilled. At the same time, public intervention may be called for in order to allow the market forces to work.

Thus, a variety of systems or mixes has been introduced. The central point is that a more direct link is now being established in China between the producer and the end-user. This redistributes power to the end-user from the allocator and adds a new dimension to the function of the producer. When the end-user was given specific products under the system of command planning, his bargaining power was extremely low. If the products were unsuitable, there was no alternative. Anything seemed better than nothing. This was the case with the allocation of workers. If unsuitable or redundant workers were rejected, no others would be made available; and in any case, whether or not the workers performed they were on the producer's payroll.

Under the system of command planning, the task of the manager of a producing unit was ridiculously simple. He was unconcerned with sourcing or with the disposition of the product. The entire output would be disposed of by another organ. Producers were therefore generally in the dark as to who the users were and what their reaction was. With the re-establishment of the link with the market, the knowledge required of producers has correspondingly been greatly expanded. Risk has also increased, since there may be no market. The rediscovery of the market does not therefore simplify the work of the planner or the operational personnel entirely. Their tasks, though redefined, remain vast and complicated.

The Responsibility System

The rediscovery of the market implies the assumption of a host of new responsibilities at the enterprise level. What happens when products are unsaleable? As long as the government continues to allocate all the inputs and make up the deficit, the enterprise can function as usual. A key element of control must therefore be through the profit and loss of the enterprise.

On the cost side, some inputs have to be obtained from the market. This applies especially to finance. Instead of obtaining money from the Ministry of Finance without any repayment obligation or interest charges, at least a portion must come from the banking system, which demands interest and repayment. The bank may, of course, refuse to lend, either because of national priority considerations or purely because the soundness of business in terms of profit and loss is questionable. The survival and possible expansion of the enterprise is in this way linked to the bottom line.

A further link between profit (or loss) and the fate of the enterprise is provided by the retention of a portion of the profit by the enterprise. This can be used to augment funds for the development of the enterprise, for the collective welfare of the workers, and for bonus payments. There is therefore also a link between the interests of the workers and that of the enterprise.

A more thorough device for reform of the system is to make the enterprise completely responsible for its own profit or loss. This is contingent on the fulfillment of profit quotas, which must be turned over to the state. This enterprise autonomy is accompanied by a system of taxes as well as subsidies. The problem (as shown below), is that profit and loss are a function of many factors besides operational efficiency. Among the most important are prices, including the possibility of price-setting through the exercise of monopoly power.

In a broader context, the introduction of a responsibility system also requires the abolition of the "iron rice bowl," which meant that everyone could dig into the bowl regardless of his contribution toward filling it. The principle of distribution is now to each according to his work, rather than according to his need, which the communist ideal desires.

A further implication of the responsibility system is the shift in the locus of decisionmaking. To the extent that enterprises rather than political organs are given more room for making decisions, there is a degree of enterprise autonomy. Enterprises are therefore set up outside the administrative divisions of the state. This does not necessarily imply that central control is weakened. It could very well be strengthened, inasmuch as the central authority exercises effective planning, not chiefly through command but through parametric measures such as taxes and prices. Moreover, the major enterprises, such as shipbuilding and automobiles, are consolidated at the central and local levels so that they are under the direct purview of the central authority.

Problems of Reform

The attempt to correct existing defects tends to create new problems, even if it is more-or-less effective. Even efforts to correct old imbalances have created new ones in China. Fiscal imbalance results from sizeable increases in agricultural-procurement prices as well as in pay adjustments. Monetary imbalances stem from fiscal deficits, as well as from the expansion of credit and the surge in consumer demand. Balance-of-payments imbalances derive from a sudden rush for imports. The following discussion focuses on a few key problems created by structural reforms. Although the distinction between readjustment and restructuring is not always clear—and they frequently interact—they compete for the attention of decision makers. While readjustment is needed to provide a reasonably stable and orderly condition for long-term fundamental changes, restructuring gets at the heart of the malaise, which cannot be removed merely by readjustment.[7]

The Boundary of the Untouchable

To an outside observer, the unchangeable tenets specified in the new constitution appear constraining. In pure intellectual inquiry, nothing is beyond question. Likewise, according to the democratic ideal, the social system should be determined by the wishes of the people exercising their free choice.

In China's case, at the present historical juncture, fundamental dissent is still discouraged. The degree of actual constraint depends, however, less on the statement of principles than on their practical application. This is also true of other societies, for no functioning system exists in its pure form. It must be reinterpreted and accommodated to existing realities if it is to avoid the fate of the dinosaurs. Capitalist societies certainly do not rely exclusively on the market mechanism. Even in Hong Kong, which has been cited by its advocates as the archetype of a free market, more than half the population would be homeless if they had had to compete in the market for living space in a place where land is priced in square inches rather than square feet. Luckily they live in heavily subsidized government apartments. In the United States, income tax was unconstitutional in the early days. Today it is the chief source of government revenue. The regulation of economic activities tends to be cyclical. When the public interest is woefully ignored in the pursuit of private gain, social outcry demands regulation. When the regulation no longer serves its intended purpose, it is discarded. The relative advantages and disadvantages of particular social systems have therefore been grossly exaggerated by their respective diehard supporters.

Moreover, a social system dose not have a zero base; rather, it is the result of historical circumstances. In contrast to the goal of international communism, the Chinese have realized that revolution is not for export. Even in China itself, the essence of socialism has been reduced to public ownership of the means of production and to each according to his work. Within this framework, not only is collective (in contrast to state) ownership of land and other productive assets by individuals permitted, but private plots and service activities, such as restaurants, repair shops, and the like are increasing since they have been found to be more efficiently run privately.

Major exceptions are also made for greater private initiative in particular regions, such as the Special Economic Zones. In Macao, although Chinese sovereignty has been re-established and officially confirmed in the Portuguese constitution, the economic system remains basically capitalist. In policy statements from China on the unification of Hong Kong and Taiwan with the mainland, assurances have also been given that their economic systems will not be disturbed. As far as dissent goes, some broad social consensus about the main character of the system probably exists in most societies, if a degree of social cohesion is to be maintained and polarization avoided. Democratic societies of the Western variety are able to achieve the consensus without authoritarianism. In an overwhelming number of developing countries, the choices are often more limited. In recent Chinese history, the imperial dynasty had already been overthrown by revolution and the Republican regime, at least on the mainland, had also been displaced by revolution. More recently, Mao has been undeified. There is genuine concern that the fundamental political and ideological debate may again take the form of revolution and chaos. Nevertheless, further evolution along present lines could very well go much further than renewed convulsions and class struggles.

The question, then, is not whether there are still untouchables but in which direction the system is to move so that the country will not again be at the mercy of a few at the top against the true interests of the masses.

The Second Best Approach, Step-by-Step

There are two somewhat contradictory elements in what is required of the system in China. On the one hand, fundamental reforms are needed to cope with the cumulative distortions created by dogma. On the other hand, a new direction must be established after the old theology has been disavowed. There is a real danger lest the reforms be interpreted as a negation of everything that China has stood for and a crisis of credibility develops as a new doctrine fails to evolve in order to fill the vacuum.

The theoretical solution is for a comprehensive alternative new system to be worked out and implemented. This would ensure that the many parts of the system were coordinated and the various implications of changes in the system worked out. In economic terms, this approach is often considered to be found to be the method followed in Hungary, where reforms have been introduced in a fairly comprehensive way and worked out on the drawing board before their introduction. A close examination of the Hungarian case reveals that such a characterization is an exaggeration. At any rate, the objective conditions in present-day China do not permit this approach. There would be literally hundreds of possible models that could be considered. The top decision makers in China would have great difficulty in discriminating among them in terms of their intrinsic theoretical merits. Popular opinion about the models can hardly serve as a reliable guide before people have been confronted with actual results of experimentation.

Even after a consensus has been reached on the need for drastic reforms, their precise nature is difficult to agree upon, both at the top and at the grass-roots level. The step-by-step approach, though admittedly second best, is the price that must be paid to win political consensus. At the top, the ultimate choice of the system is postponed since the approach is experimental. New arrangements coexist with the old. If the former do not work out in practice, they can be scrapped or changed. At the grass-roots level, the art of persuasion has to be even less theoretical. In agriculture, for example, many cadres harbored initial doubts about the desirability of contracting work to teams, households, or individuals. The new arrangements were too close to the policies of Liu Shaoqi, which had been so thoroughly attacked for so long.[8] Many peasants too were truly skeptical. They were persuaded only by the superior output and personal gains enjoyed by participants in the new arrangements.

At the technical level, there is no need to solve a great number of equations, reliable data for which are not available in any case. Numerous partial solutions may be attempted with a lesser degree of sophistication and a greater degree of intuitive appeal.

At the same time, these step-by-step and partial approaches possess their own intrinsic difficulties.[9] First, the true nature of the new arrangements evidently depends on the presence or absence of complementary measures. For example, the high productivity of private plots may be partly at the expense of collective effort. If discipline is relaxed in collective work and reward is not linked with effort, there is an incentive to channel energies to the private sector. When enterprises enjoy virtual monopoly power, the introduction of profit retention may induce them to exercise that power to maximize profits. The devices employed are not limited to the restriction of output or the raising of prices. They may include the discontinuation of relatively unprofitable items such as mass-consumption goods in favor of fancy ware, or they may involve swap arrangements to hide price increases.

To the extent that the existing price system does not reflect relative scarcity values, profit rates may reflect the artificially high price of the output or the low price of inputs rather than better effort or management. The high profit from the manufacture of manmade fiber textiles and the low profit from cotton textiles provide a classic example of the effect of artificial prices. The effect of the former's relatively high price, and consequently high profits, was accentuated by the readjustment policies that permitted light industries greater latitude to expand. As a result, large unsold inventories of manmade fiber textiles accumulated while cotton textiles continued to be in short supply.

A further far-reaching effect of price irrationality is the incentive given to local or regional authorities to promote industries in their localities simply because they yield revenues. There is a tendency, for example, for tobacco-producing regions to restrict the export of tobacco leaves to other regions in order to protect local industry. All these generate new distortions and require new reforms.

Distortions in the Price System

Of all the new reforms that have to be introduced, but that have hardly begun, one of the first is removal of distortions in the pricing system. As has been indicated, when the market is rediscovered and the responsiblity system is introduced, prices play a crucial role in sending signals for economic decision making. However, these signals are not themselves determined by economic forces but by past administrative fiat. As time passes, relative prices deviate more and more from economic considerations. Witness the rising cost of price subsidies.

Yet a reform of the entire price system cannot be introduced without serious risks of inflation and distributive injustice. These risks are especially frightening in a country where the memory of hyperinflation is still fresh and the safety margin is very low for many people at subsistence levels. As in other economic systems, widespread price adjustments tend to have an upward bias. It is easier to increase prices than to cut them. The adjustment of prices of agricultural products has taken this route. At the same time, the upward pressures on prices is suppressed by pegging corresponding agricultural prices for consumers. Similarly, the prices of many essential goods are extremely low. For example, at the existing level of house rents, the cost of houses cannot be amortized in less than a century or so. The price of energy is also low, which contributes to much inefficiency in its use. At the same time, an across-the-board reduction in the absolute levels of prices of items that are relatively overvalued is administratively difficult. Even if it can be done, it will in turn seriously affect state revenues, since the high prices yield correspondingly high profits and taxes. Unless the entire tax system is also revamped, large-scale price adjustments will precipitate a fiscal crisis.

The upshot of these considerations is that great caution has been exercised in adjusting the price system. Indeed, with the predictable inflationary impact of the initial price and wage adjustment, the degree of caution has increased at least temporarily. Certainly the almost panicky administrative freeze of most prices announced in December 1982 represents a step backward. As long as quality and style cannot be adequately controlled, the freeze cannot in practice be effective in the long run. The resort to administrative command suggests, however, a tactical retreat from greater reliance on market forces. While the need for such crisis measures of administrative control may decrease with more stringent fiscal and monetary policies and the positive effect of the reform measures on output, a comprehensive readjustment of the price system remains a distant goal. In the meantime, the signals emitted by existing prices may be the wrong ones.

The distortion resulting from incorrect prices can to some extent be offset by a series of measures. For the purpose of calculating profits for retention by enterprises, the level of prices may differ from the transaction prices but may be computed at theoretical levels; in other words, at shadow prices in accordance with economic rationale. This has in fact been done in some conspicuous cases when enterprise profit or loss evidently resulted from lopsided price levels. This tends to result in haggling and bargaining about the shadow prices employed. To the extent that the levels of efficiency of enterprises in different localities or even in the same locality varies greatly, a uniform shadow price for the same product would result in great disparities between enterprises. This aggravates the tendency to bargain and imposes a great burden on administration.

Similarly, price distortions may be offset by differential taxes and subsidies. The consequent implications for bargaining and administrative burden also ensue.

The Burden of the Bureaucracy

Although the main thrust of economic reform, by invoking greater use of economic forces, reduces the burden on administrative decision and therefore on the bureaucracy, the complications arising from numerous stop-gap measures and hybrid arrangements tend to have an opposite effect. Difficulties are raised at three levels.

First, the types of problems encountered by the new bureaucrats are, as illustrated earlier, very different from those prior to the reform measures. Price adjustments, the functional role of taxes, and productivity and market considerations are all novel features. The experiences of the old bureaucrats are of questionable relevance. Indeed, their continued assertion of authority and their instinctive efforts to hide their ignorance are obstacles in the way of a smooth transition. In general, the old bureaucracy cannot be expected to be enthusiastic about the reforms, and they are likely to exert passive resistance or even engage in active sabotage against the new programs. This is the reason for drastic changes in the bureaucracy, as well as for severe disciplinary measures against wrongdoing.

Second, quite apart from the question of vested interest and competence, there is a natural tendency for a large bureaucracy to avoid making decisions. This is apparent, for example, in the Soviet Union. A wrong decision can bring punishment, but if the buck is passed upstairs, blame can be avoided. This tendency is aggravated by the need for coordination among units within an organization, and among organs with functional and geographical responsibilities. A document frequently has to collect innumerable signatures. Even at the level of vice-ministers, consensus might require as many as twenty signatures; prior to the reorganization of most ministries in 1982 (when the number of vice-ministers was considerably reduced to as few as two in some cases). A recent account of the procedure followed by the application for the establishment of a new commercial outlet in a city involved 32 units, including planning, construction, urban affairs, security, finance, commodity control, water, electricity, and environment, and 169 channels, before approval was granted. An application would normally take half a year before a permit was issued. The responsibility system is singularly difficult to apply a bureaucracy.

Third, although the traditional system of official "squeeze" has largely been eliminated, more subtle forms of corruption are more resilient. The example of the application for a permit is illustrative. The applicant will have to send a car to pick up bureaucrats in power to make their inspections, and they will have to be wined and dined.[10] Scare commodities are allocated only to those with special relations, or *guanxi*.

As long as egalitarianism rules and the allocation of scarce commodities is by rank or perceived need—such as housing by family size and concert tickets to musicians—monetary gain is of limited use. The opening of the lid to higher standards of living and the elimination of the social stigma from signs of opulence has quietly stimulated the acquisitive instinct. The motto "to be rich is glorious" may be a useful antidote to the opposite and mistaken conception "to be poor is glorious," but people may not pay enough attention to proper means of getting rich. The avenues for corruption have widened with the increasing role of market forces. In the market place, extortion is seldom necessary but offer of bribery in various degrees of sophistication will be plentiful.

In comparison with Western justice, the punishment in China for those who are corrupt is severe. This should exercise a restraining effect, provided the enforcement is not mere window-dressing. For as far as formal statutes are concerned, few countries give legal sanction to corruption. Nevertheless, these statutes are not always enforced. In some countries, even where ancient torture is still used as a punishment (as in a recent case of the blinding of an offender as a warning to would-be criminals), the selective application of justice nullifies the deterrent effect.

Further Reforms

The foregoing indicates that the experimental and step-by-step approach to structural reforms necessitates a host of further reforms. Inasmuch as these further reforms are also introduced experimentally and gradually, some of the problems associated with the reforms already introduced will continue to surface. On the other hand, numerous further reforms are introduced for the explicit purpose of correcting the problems arising from earlier measures. Some are designed to complement the earlier reforms so that serious problems may be avoided. The cumulative effect of all these reforms cannot but be revolutionary in character. This far-reaching effect is demonstrated by enumerating the key areas for further reforms.

Planning

A central element in the structural reform is the new role assigned to planning. In the first place, planning needs to be more closely coordinated with short-term readjustment so that it does not repeat the same difficulties of indefinite postponement of plans when crises of one sort or another render the plan figures academic. Such coordination is extremely difficult, as it is in most other countries, since the time horizon of the planner is by nature longer than that of the manager of day-to-day affairs, in, for example, the finance ministry or the central bank. Moreover, planners do not usually possess sufficient political power to mediate among the conflicting claims of strong ministries. It is the task of the prime minister to do the coordination, but he is usually occupied with too much work to be able to devote much effort to serious planning.

An equally urgent task is the generation of adequate information so that plans are feasible and not merely wishful thinking. Currently, relevant information is not only scarce but is also concentrated in a very few hands. Insufficient information means that true feasibility cannot be determined. The recent population census shows how expensive it is to build up even a rudimentary data base. At the same time, it also demonstrates the need for all sorts of surveys of, for example, industries and households. The new data base has also opened up new possibilities for the greater use of sampling methods, which again require new techniques and organization.

An inevitable result of the scarcity of relevant information is that rational decision making is extremely difficult. An independent assessment is even more difficult, since outsiders are even less well informed. Efforts have therefore been made to carry out investigative research by well-placed organs of the Party, the Cabinet, or the Academy of Social Sciences. An organ similar to the United States General Accounting Office, which regularly evaluates the performance of government offices has been established.

The most basic reform will have to be directed to the prime sources of information. Little attention has hitherto been paid to the collection, processing, and analysis of the basic data of administrative units and enterprises. For example, there are still no detailed foreign trade or balance of payments statistics, which are essential for formulating foreign economic policies. At the enterprise level, accounts are still very rudimentary. A new set of statistical and accounting standards will therefore have to be established. These standards must also evolve with experience.[11]

Bureaucracy

Reforms at the top political levels to streamline the decision-making process will have to be followed by similar reforms at the middle and lower levels. These further reforms will include the retirement of aged cadres, the training and retraining of those retained, and the thinning of the ranks of the bureaucracy. This will affect more than twenty million people.

To the extent that key posts at these levels are also occupied by Party members, the weeding out of those who are unqualified because of ideology, character, or ability is a complement to the bureaucratic reforms and basic to long-run political viability. This is especially true as democratic processes within the Party are to be permitted. It should be remembered that about one-half of the Party members were recruited during the Cultural Revolution, when standards of screening were altogether different from those used at present.

Labor

In a broader context, the rigid system of allocation of labor will also have to be changed. Thus far, the "iron rice bowl" has in practice largely been maintained, even though in theory a case has been made against its preservation. Obviously, if all enterprises are free to fire redundant workers, tens of millions will be thrown into the ranks of the unemployed. Some enterprises claim that a third or more of the workers assigned to them are redundant. Mass firing will raise serious questions of human and social cost. At the same time, the gradual introduction of the responsibility system will empower more and more enterprises, patterned after the model of the Capital Iron and Steel Corporation, to hire and fire workers.

Reforms are also being introduced to permit greater mobility of labor. People are currently still tied to their locality as well as their place of work. Interregional movement has been restricted, particularly in order to prevent the flooding of the rural population into urban centers such as Beijing and Shanghai. The place of work has been fixed, even to the extent that a post is passed on to an heir upon a worker's retirement or death. Indeed, the workplace is also the most direct administrative organ for managing and looking after all the aspects of the life of the worker, including marriage, birth control, and welfare. From the point of view of the employer, if a good worker is let go, replacement is generally difficult. As a result, it is virtually impossible to change jobs, even if job and job holder are mismatched. A drastic change would, however, involve great disruptions. Labor mobility is therefore being introduced only slowly, by such measures as secondment[12] and swaps between places of work.

Prices

There is a conflict between containing inflation and adjusting the price structure. Reforms are being carried out chiefly to reduce the inflationary pressure. In particular, capital expenditures have tended to be much higher than targeted by the Central Government because enterprises and regional governments have their own sources of finance fed by the new responsiblity system. The Central Government is therefore attempting to mop up these resources by earmarking a portion of them for investment into the bottle-necked areas.[13] In addition, a greater degree of control by the center has been reintroduced to restrain local investment. This gives the impression that the government is retreating somewhat from the responsibility system even though the general direction continues to be unchanged.

A broad adjustment of prices in line with scarcity levels has hardly started, since inflation remains the chief concern. Theoretical price levels corresponding to real costs have been compiled, however, in preparation for rationalizing the price structure. Minor adjustments have been made to the pricing of selected items. In these cases, the raising of some prices has been accompanied by the lowering of others. The upward adjustment of prices of cotton textiles were offset, for example, by downward price revision in manmade fiber textiles as well as several other consumer goods.[14] The achievement of better balance in the economy and the damping of in-flationary pressures should enable the Chinese to introduce further structural price adjustments.

Wages

Despite the raising of wage levels and bonuses, the wage structure has remained virtually intact. Such a structure does not adequately reflect the scarcity values of various labor groups. Preparations are being made for change, and job descriptions are being redefined. The structural change is the more necessary because past adjustments were influenced by egalitarian considerations, which meant that they were generally across the board rather than selective in reward for effort or efficiency. The issue is clearly controversial, especially as room for the market adjustment of supply and demand of labor will continue to be limited in the near future.

Taxes

There are three primary areas in which further tax reforms are being introduced or considered. First, corporate taxes will more and more replace profit to be turned over to the state. This has the advantage of solidifying the enterprise-responsibility system, since the enterprise will be in a better position to know what is to be paid to the state and what it will return. It also offers the possibility of differential rates for different types of enterprises or industries, to allow for high and low profits as a result of external factors such as distorted prices.

The second area of reform currently being considered is the shortening of the capital-depreciation period in order to promote capital renewal and technical improvement. This has gained respectability in recent times. A chief proponent of the reform, Sun Yefang, has been honored by the Party. Another, Ma Hong, has assumed important positions of responsibility.[15] Evidently, depreciation rates are closely related to corporate-income-tax rates.

The third area of reform is tax sharing with local authorities. This has already been introduced to a limited extent. A further extension is linked to the reform of the entire tax system. Such reform is essential for reducing the incentive for regional autonomy. Indeed, an essential strategy of Chinese development must be the creation of a "common market" within China, which still does not exist in practice.

Banking System

Although the enterprise responsibility system assigns new and enlarged functions to the banking system, the task of reorganizing and reorienting it to discharge these functions is gigantic. First, there are relatively few specialized banks. The People's Bank, for example, engages in deposit taking in addition to central banking functions. Since the allocation of funds for capital expenditures was the responsibility of the Finance Ministry, the banks are not equipped to extend long-term loans. Preparations have been made to introduce greater specialization within the banking system, including the establishment of industrial and commmercial banks. Concurrently, longer-term loans will be added to the financing of capital expenditures. These will also call for more monitoring of the activities of enterprises. A new generation of bankers will have to be trained to carry out the new responsibilities.

Implications for International Business Relations

The new reforms have important implications for international business relations. At first sight, the effect of the open-door policy is simple. China's one billion customers are at last becoming a reality to foreign business and are not merely wishful thinking. The true implications are far more complicated, however. Many outside observers have in fact moved from euphoria into depression and disillusionment.

The Retrenchment

The immediate effect of the Eight-Character policy on foreign business relations was retrenchment. Numerous large contracts were reported to be cancelled or suspended, a severe shock not only to those directly involved but to all China-watchers. It looked as though China had become an unreliable business partner. Indeed, the whole open-door policy was in doubt.

Despite the shock waves generated, the retrenchment did not in fact mean breaches of contract. Many memoranda of understanding were not, and were never intended to be, firm contracts. The suspension of further negotiations toward contractual agreements did not therefore violate the sanctity of contracts. As far as true contracts were concerned, nonfulfill-ment normally involved severe penalties. The Chinese elected to pay these penalties only in cases where they were unable to renegotiate. For most cases, new agreements were reached by both parties.

The retrenchment had a delayed effect on the volume of foreign trade. Total imports declined in 1982, which gave yet another superficial signal of policy reversal. On the other hand, the improved balance-of-payments situation has enabled Premier Zhao Ziyang to plan an annual rate of in-crease of 8.7 percent for total foreign trade and 9.2 percent for imports, for the Sixth Five-Year Plan period, 1980-85. This compares with the annual rate of increase of four to five percent for gross industrial and agricultural output during the same period.[16]

Political Stability

The drastic reforms were not without controversy within the top leader-ship. There have been fears that some day the political pendulum will swing again in the opposite direction. While no political analysis can ac-curately predict the future, the reforms have consolidated the power of those who support the present line. This is true of the top echelon in the Party organization as well as the government. The impending cleansing of the Party will further solidify the grip. Even in the military, where Maoist sentiment continues to be expressed, the creation of the Military Commis-sion under the new constitution, the inability of a military commander to singlehandedly issue orders to the military except in time of war, the retire-ment of overage officers, and the promotion of younger ones will minimize any possibility of a coup.

All these moves for the consolidation of power, unlike the antirightist movement of the late 1950s or the witch-hunting during the Cultural Revo-lution, have been carried out in a mild fashion. There are no class struggles and no exiles, but fadeaways with generous pensions and reduced responsi-bilities, so that effective opposition may be muted.

The main stabilizing force is of course the masses, who have had enough of movements, struggles, turmoils, and uncertainties. Their prime concern now is peace and prosperity in stable conditions. Their chief ambition is to better themselves in this environment.

The Primacy of Economic Considerations

Translated into concrete terms, the change of emphasis from political movement to economic betterment has broad implications for the Chinese attitude toward things foreign. The rediscovery of economic rationality in the management of development means that foreign resources can serve Chinese purposes. Foreign markets are also needed to obtain foreign resources. The question then is not one of principle—whether foreign business or economic relations should be developed or cultivated—but a practical one of exactly where and how foreign resources are to be utilized. This is the subject of the following chapter.

3

The Role of Transnational Corporations

The Great Debate

The Theoretical Background

The role of transnational corporations in the modernization or development of developing countries is controversial. (See endnote 1, chapter 3, for a discussion of terms.) A view often stated by Western economists is that as far as the economic effects are concerned the role of transnationals is positive; the perceived negative role is political. Such a view is a gross oversimplification that many people, especially developed-country economists, still believe. The explosion of literature in this area in the last decade has significantly complicated the picture.[1]

There are many ways in which transnational corporations may play a role in a developing country. Politically, the most blatant is that a transnational may attempt to overthrow a host government because it does not like that government's political complexion or its specific policies. In the olden days of gunboat diplomacy, corporate imperialism was inseparable from home-country imperialism. Corporations might serve as government agencies, and when the interests of corporations were unfavorably affected in the host country, home governments did not hesitate to provide their citizens abroad full military support. A more common occurrence these days is corporate alignment with local groups that advocate policies the transnationals regard as favorable. In this way, transnationals enter into direct political conflict with local groups that are opposed to such policies. Home governments become involved when they are persuaded by transnational corporations to exert various degrees of pressure on host governments, through the extending or withholding of credit or aid, for example.

The key issue is not so much the exact political role that transnationals may play as the degree and the frequency of their actions. It is significant that in the international forum no country will defend the political subversion of host countries by transnational corporations. Nor is it in the corporation's own long-term interest to engage in subversive activities. Today's success may be tomorrow's failure, as governments come and go. The prudent political activities of transnationals in host countries are often minimal and low key. Attempts by transnational corporations to influence home-country policy are an integral part of the political process of the country in question. Most home countries permit intense lobbying by various con-stituencies and sectional interests. Recent revelations indicate that the in-terests of the transnationals do not always coincide with those of the home country.[2] They may be, for instance, in alignment with certain host develop-ing countries. It is noteworthy that in spite of ideological differences, transnationals were generally in favor of normalizing relations with the People's Republic because they saw the possibility of the opening up of new markets, even though a few opposed it because of their Taiwan connections.

The political concerns of host developing countries have parallels in the sociocultural area. Consciously or unconsciously, transnational corpora-tions propagate the sociocultural values of the societies in which they orig-inate, which may clash with those of the host countries. They are commonly blamed, for example, for contaminating local cultures with egotism, ac-quisitiveness, aggressiveness, and economic corruption. The corporate culture especially is often characterized as ruthless and dehumanized. Local patterns of consumption may be unduly influenced by alien ways and styles that raise moral questions and offend aesthetic sensitivities. Concern is also expressed about the unsuitability of adopting twentieth-century living stan-dards in conditions of productive capability that belong to the Middle Ages. These political and sociocultural arguments often reinforce each other and produce a mosaic of emotions combining nationalism, anti-industrialism, and a sense of powerlessness and insecurity in the face of external influ-ences. Such a reaction is not limited to developing countries. Even in Western Europe and Japan, a mix of anti-Americanism, subnational loyalties, and nostalgia is frequently evident.

From the point of view of modernization, the sociocultural fallout may have its redeeming aspects. In developing countries especially, a change from lethargy and fatalism to a progressive and achievement-oriented at-titude may be credited to the global reach of transnational corporations. The role of transnational corporations is, however, perhaps less pervasive than that of other agents of change such as trade, and the spread of infor-mation through education, news, entertainment, and travel following the revolution in transport and communications. The demonstration effect of the consumption patterns of developed countries probably precedes the ac-tivities of transnational corporations, although clever advertising certainly speeds up the process.

It is the economic impact on host countries that has generated the greatest controversy. On the positive side, the reasoning is straightforward: modernization requires finance, technology, managerial skill and marketing. Transnational corporations will greatly facilitate the process of moderniza-tion by supplementing domestic resources and skills. The strategic impor-tance of these supplements may be more important than the quantity in-volved would seem to indicate, for the supplements may be essential to overcome domestic strategic scarcity and bottlenecks.[3]

This optimistic view has of course been challenged. The financial contribution of transnational corporations to host countries has been questioned on three counts. First, it is contended that transnational corporations often take out more money than they bring in. As a result, their balance-of-payments effect is negative. This contention is supported especially by data from many Latin American countries.[4] One reason is said to be local financing. Transnational corporations are able to secure better financial terms than local firms, and they crowd local firms out of the financial market. Moreover, they often enjoy monopolistic power and siphon out exorbitant profits. Second, the influx of foreign capital may depress the level of domestic savings. Lastly, it is contended that portfolio financing is preferable to financing through direct corporate investment, since it enables the host country to retain control.[5] This is the principal avenue employed by the Japanese utilizing external finance.

On the other hand, in assessing net inflow or outflow, the capital and current accounts are sometimes not distinguished. It is a mathematical necessity that the total outflow should exceed the total inflow over the life of the financing if capital is to reap a positive return. That is, the sum of dividend or interest plus repayments always exceeds the original investment. That does not mean that the balance-of-payments effect of all capital inflow must necessarily be negative for the host country. Moreover, for any given period, dividend or interest payments reflect the servicing of past investments and have little connection with current flows of capital. In Latin America, for example, when past investment is heavy and current inflow modest, there is a net outflow on the combined capital and current accounts. These figures do not reveal the net balance of payments contribution or otherwise of transnational-corporation activities, since they do not report the indirect effects such as foreign exchange earned through increased exports or reduced imports. The total effects are, moreover, not limited to the products of the transnationals. They involve, among other things, the foreign-exchange content of the machinery, energy, raw materials, and intermediate goods used, as well as broader macro effects such as a higher overall rate of growth as a result of the removal of bottlenecks. The precise total balance of payments effect, direct as well as indirect, depends on the interaction of transnational corporation activities with the host-country environment and policies. For example, the monopoly profit and lack of export possibilities may be closely related to import-substitution policies supported by highly protectionist measures. The negative value-added nature of certain foreign investment projects (such as aluminum) may reflect inappropriate prices of output and inputs (for example, artificially high prices of aluminum and low prices of imported fuel and materials). When all the indirect and policy effects are taken into account, the outcome is more complicated than the results of many simplified models suggest.[6] (The implications of the choice between direct foreign investment and portfolio investment will be discussed in chapter 4.)

The technological contribution of transnational corporations to host developing countries has also been questioned. Briefly, doubt has been expressed as to whether technology is really transferred. As long as the indigenous workers are confined to lowly positions, much of the technology is kept within the transnational corporation and in the hands of expatriates. Even in instances where technology is transferred, its appropriateness may be questioned. Since much of the technology is generated in the developed countries to suit conditions there, it may be ill-suited to developing countries. For instance, the technology may be too sophisticated and unable to function without a host of complementarities, such as high-quality materials and meticulous servicing. It may be too capital-intensive, since the relative price of capital to labor in developing countries may be much higher than in developed countries because of differences in relative scarcity. In addition, the cost of the technology may be too high because the transnational corporation reaps a high rent. Finally, the host country may become technically dependent on the transnational corporation, especially if restrictions are placed on certain uses of a technology, such as the export of goods using the technology in competition with other subsidiaries of the transnational.[7]

These arguments must be carefully considered. With respect to the extent of transfer of technology, conditions vary greatly among host countries. The most important determining factor in the transfer is the absorptive capacity of the host country. Another factor is that some transnationals prefer to keep their technology in their own hands because it is more profitable and less risky to do so. Yet for most types of technology of interest to developing countries, there are plenty of competitors. In industries like textiles, cement, and so on, technology may easily be acquired from consulting firms for a fee, and these firms are not usually interested in direct investment. Even if the technology remains in the hands of the direct investors, there is always some trickle-down through local skilled labor and contact with local suppliers and customers. There is a tendency as well for transnationals to employ more locals, partly because they are less expensive than the expatriates and partly because they have a comparative advantage in dealing with the local milieu.

The inappropriateness of foreign technology in many host developing countries is well documented. However in some cases, the transnationals are not the worst offenders when compared with local firms, one reason for which is that transnationals may possess better information about alternative technology. At the same time, the factors explaining complacency in the choice may be common to both transnationals and locals. When these firms are highly protected, for instance, their primary concern is timely exploitation of the market rather than cost considerations.

Inappropriateness because of capital intensity is only part of the story. Although the level of wages is relatively low in many developing countries, there is often a serious shortage of skilled labor and supervisory personnel. The shortage of such personnel may be a worse bottleneck than the shortage of capital.

With respect to the cost of technology, a distinction must be made between competitive and monopolistic market conditions. Fortunately, most of the technology that developing countries acquire has already been in existence for some time and is therefore quite competitive. The main concern here is that the developing country administration may not be aware of it, and may be cheated. This is not a transnational problem so much as it is a host-country problem. To the extent that the transnationals enjoy monopolistic power over the technology, a monopolistic price may be charged. In general, it is frequently impossible for the host country to know the exact nature and worth of the technology before it has actually acquired it. There is therefore great uncertainty as to what the exact price should be. The cost to developing countries may be relatively high because of either the high cost of transfer in relation to the volume of business, or because of ignorance of the existence of close substitute technology in the host country.[8] In some cases, the cost may be lower because transnationals may charge discriminatory prices in accordance with what the market can bear.

These debates are also relevant to managerial skill and market access. Managerial skill may be regarded as part of know-how or technology. Export-market access enters into the discussion of balance-of-payments effect. The list of possible positive and negative roles can be expanded into areas such as employment, labor relations,[9] income distribution,[10] industrial pattern and market structure,[11] which are areas not discussed in this study.

The Chinese Perception

The Chinese perception of transnationals was influenced less by the fervent debate elsewhere than by their own particular circumstances. When the People's Republic was first established, the attitude toward foreign business in China was influenced by three major considerations. First, foreign business was viewed as an extension of imperialism. Secondly, the impact of foreign business was seen as predominantly negative, as a result of exploitation and unfair competition with national enterprises. Thirdly, virtually all foreign business was regarded as unfriendly or unsympathetic to the regime. All these considerations stemmed from China's historical experiences as well as Marxist-Leninist-Maoist ideology. The policy pursued was simple: practically all foreign business was liquidated, confiscated, or let go.

The massive Soviet aid for 156 large core projects, especially in industries, during the first Five-Year Plan, is a different story. Since the Soviet Union was regarded as a comrade in the same socialist camp, the question of imperialism or exploitation did not arise. The aid package was interpreted as friendly and benevolent, particularly in view of the seige mentality that existed in China at a time when most other countries were unfriendly. These projects accounted for forty-four percent of the total industrial-investment outlay for the plan period.[12] The output from these projects accounted for a substantial portion of industrial capacity in the subsequent years, especially for producer goods.

As is now well-known, China's experience with Soviet aid turned sour. In spite of the generally positive contribution of this aid to the construction of the new China, the conditions that the Soviets attempted to impose would have meant a serious infringement of Chinese sovereignty and independence. This alone was a sufficient condition for the termination of the donor-recipient relationship. In addition, friction between the Soviet experts and their Chinese counterparts had accumulated. Soviet advice was generally not heeded either because it was not fully appreciated or because it was considered unworkable under Chinese conditions. The abrupt withdrawal of all Soviet experts as well as the blueprints of unfinished projects turned friendly feelings into deep resentment. The strained relationship was aggravated by the large-scale exodus of vital commodities from China to the Soviet Union for servicing and repaying "aid" during a period of extreme economic hardship in China.

The narrow interpretation of the doctrine of self-reliance was thus rooted in China's unhappy cumulative historical experience with foreign economic relations, private and public. Had this experience been less bitter, the virtual isolation of China in the 1950s and 1960s might have been less likely. As it was, the doctrine elicited such absolutist fervor that the isolation became more and more self-imposed.

To be sure, even in extreme self-isolation, the role of foreign business was not totally negated. To the extent that there were imports and exports, foreign partners were necessarily involved. Although their activities in China were severely limited by the monopoly of the Chinese foreign trade corporations, their role abroad was actually heightened because of Chinese unfamiliarity with, or deliberate departure from, international practices. Thus the marketing of Chinese produce abroad was almost entirely concentrated in the hands of foreign business. Financing was also the preserve of foreign institutions since the Chinese neither extended nor accepted credit.

The particular emphasis placed on imports of complete plants gave an unusually large role to a few well-established engineering consulting firms. Reminiscent of the Soviet aid packages were the fertilizer plants set up by Kellogg. They had the advantage of requiring minimum involvement on the part of the Chinese. Virtually everything was left to the foreign business partner, which set up the plant and demonstrated that it was in operative condition. It departed completely when the Chinese took over, so that difficulties of interference either of the pre-People's Republic variety of Western enterprises or of the Soviet-aid type did not arise.

Concomitant with the announcement of the Four Modernizations program was the assignment of a new role to the external sector. The nebulous concept of modernization was matched by the exaggerated importance attributed to the external factor. Suddenly, a period of "foreign great leap" was ushered in when a rush of import orders gripped the entire economy. Under the then existing system, the easiest way to meet the expanding production targets for the modernization program was to increase capital expenditures and capacity, and since imports were permitted or even encouraged, the consequence was clear.

The attitude toward transnational corporations was more difficult to change. Their image, as reflected in a few authoritative Chinese sources, remained largely negative: they were by definition monopolistic exploiters. The passage of the Law of the People's Republic of China on Joint Ventures Using Chinese and Foreign Investment in July 1979 represented a breakthrough.[13] Permission for foreign direct investment was not only novel in Chinese thinking but rarely practiced in other socialist countries. The theoretical obstacle was severe. Since according to orthodox communist theory capitalists exploit the workers through the use of the means of production, foreign investment would inevitably involve foreign exploitation of Chinese workers. The theoretical trap was circumvented by the Chinese admitting that, despite such exploitation, the disadvantages would be more than offset by the advantages of the inflow of capital, technology, and so on.[14]

With such a liberal interpretation of foreign direct investment, the legitimacy of numerous other forms of foreign involvement—such as compensation trade, coproduction, and other contractual arrangements to be discussed in the following chapter—has been easily established. Even the generally negative evaluation of the activities of transnational corporations has undergone a subtle change. At the United Nations, the Chinese delegate echoed the theme of the moderate Third World countries and the Secretariat that the positive effects of transnational corporations on developing countries should be enhanced and the negative effects minimized. This contrasts with the Soviet position that it was impossible for transnational corporations to have any positive effect, although in fact not all transnational corporations were excluded from the Soviet Union. Further, while the Soviets denied that their enterprises were transnational corporations, the Chinese not only maintained that there might be Soviet transnationals but that other socialist countries, including themselves, might also be the homes of transnational corporations in a technical sense. The implication is that not all transnational corporations are necessarily good or bad. Certainly there might be transnational corporations from social imperialists, but Third World transnational corporations might behave differently. In contrast with many Third World countries the Chinese have refrained from any prejudgment of transnational corporations.

The New Role

The foregoing has set out the conceptual foundations of the new role to be played by transnational corporations in China. This new role can best be appreciated by a closer look at the key sectors of China's economy. These sectors do not correspond exactly to the official Four Modernizations in agriculture, industry, science and technology, and defense.[15] This discrepancy is deliberate, for three reasons. First, in line with this study's broad conception of modernization, the four areas officially identified should be interpreted flexibly. Certainly many areas not specifically listed can be added. They may include political, institutional, and cultural (or what the Chinese call spiritual) aspects, none of which is dealt with in any detail here.[16] They are less important when the focus is on how transnationals may play a role in modernization rather than on the impact of transnational corporations on modernization. The latter is premature until some volume of activity has been attained. Similarly, social goals such as education and health, which must form part of the modernization effort, are only indirectly examined in connection with other issues.

Second, while agriculture and industry are necessarily included in the economic sectors, infrastructures and services should also be explicitly included. Third, defense[17] and technology[18] are not examined in themselves. To the extent that the modernization of economic sectors such as transport, communications, steel, and the automotive and electronic industries is essential for the military, defense enters the picture. Similarly, technology in the broad sense, whether hard or soft, patented or not, engineering or managerial, also enters into the picture in every sector.

Energy

No sector provides a better illustration of the positive role that transnational corporations can play than energy. To give a proper perspective, the crucial importance of this sector should be made clear. From 1980 to 2000, total output is targeted to quadruple while the supply of energy is only to double. It is obvious that the burden placed on energy saving is very heavy. The nonfulfillment of energy production would seriously affect the entire modernization program. It would also have far-reaching long-term effects on, for example, the ecology of the country, since energy shortage would accentuate the existing trend towards widespread deforestation because wood is extensively used for household heating and cooking.

Although oil was known to have been used in China centuries ago, geologists in the early twentieth century judged that reserves were unlikely to be large. More recent World Bank estimates have put the oil and gas reserves at 1.8 billion tons. It was not until the withdrawal of Soviet aid and the threat of a cut-off of the supply of petroleum products from China that large-scale discoveries of indigenous reserves were made. The initial development was accomplished almost exclusively by domestic effort. The Daqing model earned the great honor of serving as an example of self-reliant development for all industries in China.

The realization that the initial target of ten Daqings announced by Hua in 1978 was a pipedream, and the indication that there were possible rich offshore resources put the role of transnational corporations in a different light. For seismic surveys alone, the participating international oil companies[19] put up some $200 million at their own expense. By April, 1983, four international oil companies—Japan National Oil Company, Elf Aquitaine, Total Chine and Atlantic Richfield (ARCO)—were engaged in offshore drilling, accounting for twenty-one out of twenty-five total offshore wells and eight out of nine discoveries. In May, 1983, the first offshore exploration contract was awarded to a group of oil transnationals headed by British Petroleum (the other partners are Petro-Canada Exploration, Inc.; Ranger Oil, Ltd.; The Broken Hill Proprietary Company (Australia); and Petrobras International of Brazil. Subsequently, contracts were also signed with Occidental Petroleum, EXXON and Shell Oil. Other awards are expected. The cost of test drilling and exploration was expected to be several billion dollars more and the amount involved in the future development of production and processing a further multiplication.[20]

It is primarily the technical expertise that must be obtained from the international oil companies, however, as development offshore is far more involved than development on land. Deep-sea drilling platforms or ships are sophisticated. Numerous auxiliary services, such as helicopter shuttles between drilling sites and supply bases and technical personnel to deal with possible oil spills and blowouts, are required. Even if such technology were to be acquired through learning-by-doing, it would take a far longer time without close cooperation with the transnational corporations. The widely publicized collapse of a drilling platform illustrates the risk involved when the details of operating procedures are not mastered by the Chinese. China may therefore be expected to continue to seek the cooperation of a large spectrum of international oil companies in the future.

With respect to coal, Chinese reserves, estimated at 600 billion tons, rank first in the world. The share of coal in China's total energy supply remains predominant—about seventy-five percent—despite the development of alternative sources. Massive investment is required for the development of large fields, such as those in Shanxi and Shandong. Moreover, additional investments must be made in complementary activities, such as transport and port facilities. Feasibility studies are already being made by such transnational corporations as Occidental Petroleum in Shanxi and Shell Coal in Shangdong. These studies may well lead to joint venture arrangements.

China's exploitable hydropower potential is estimated at 1.9 trillion kilowatt hours per year. The main advantage of this source is that it is renewable and clean. It is often an integral part of multipurpose projects, especially those related to the control of flooding, which has been the sorrow of China for centuries and an endemic threat that has not been altogether eliminated. Where hydro sources are plentiful, they can provide base load power. Even in regions richly endowed with competing sources of energy, hydro can provide peak load power.[21] The main disadvantage is the capital intensive nature and long lead time of hydro projects. This disadvantage is sometimes mitigated by foreign involvement.

So far, the Chinese have relied primarily on their own efforts for hydropower development, a reflection of their considerable experience in this field. Even monumental projects such as Gezhouba have been both designed and implemented indigenously. Recently, the Chinese have expressed interest in foreign-government involvement in such development, and are exploring bank financing as well. Involvement with transnationals includes a cooperative agreement with Allis-Chalmers for the manufacture of hydropower equipment, the licensing of Alsthon Atlantique and ASEA transmission equipment, and pre-investment and feasibility studies conducted by Snowy Mountain, International Engineering Company, Le Group SNC, Shawinigan, and Acres International.[22]

Although nuclear power has generated much controversy elsewhere, especially in relation to safety, the Chinese are not averse to its development. A main consideration is that the energy-using regions in the coastal areas are relatively poor in other energy resources. Moreover, the peaceful use of nuclear power appears to be a logical sequel to the successes in the military application.

The main project with transnational involvement is a planned 1,800-megawatt plant in Guangdong. Such involvement is complicated by home country export control measures, as discussed in chapter 5.

Other Minerals and Metals

China's tungsten, antimony, zinc, rare-earth metals, and lithium resources are the largest in the world. Other metallic minerals—copper, tin, lead, iron ore, molybdenum, mercury, manganese, and nickel—rank among the top three.[23]

Many minerals are important in world exports, and numerous transnationals are engaged in their trade. With some, such as tungsten, Chinese reserves account for more than one-half of the world total. There is advantage in organizing joint ventures such as the New York-based Chi Mei Metals (between China National Minerals and Metals Import and Export Corporation and Li Tungsten).

China is a net importer of copper and aluminum. Copper reserves are estimated to rank third in the world. Transnationals approached for work on copper mines include Fluor for Dexing Mines. Bauxite reserves are also believed to be rich although they are probably of low quality. ALCOA, ALCAN, Pechiney, Sumitomo Aluminum, and Showa Denko have been approached for an aluminum project in Guizhou. Negotiations with other transnationals such as Metallgesellschaft and Lurgi on nonferrous-metals have also been reported.

Transnational involvement in iron and steel has been made famous by the Baoshan project, an illustration that a giant modern project is hardly feasible without substantial involvement by transnationals. At the same time, the task of evaluation is extremely complicated and haste inevitably makes waste unless serious preparatory studies are made. In addition to major firms such as Nippon Steel, numerous other firms including German and U.S. ones have also been involved. Transnational participation elsewhere includes Kaiser Engineering, in Benxi; Bethlehem Steel, in Suichang; and Scholemann Siemag AG, in Luan.

A number of the minerals and metals projects have either been stretched out or temporarily shelved in line with the readjustment policy. But the long-term outlook remains encouraging, as indicated by the decision to go ahead with the Baoshan project and, more recently, the inclusion of a number of suspended projects in negotiations for a new multibillion dollar Japanese loan.

Manufacturing Industries

The shift of emphasis from complete plant imports to the improvement of existing manufacturing facilities, discussed in some detail in the following chapter, has opened up opportunities for suppliers to a large number of industries. In the textile and garment industries, for example, where the foundations are excellent, cooperation with foreign enterprises has taken place in many forms. The decision to increase production of synthetic fibers to make up for the shortage of domestic raw materials, especially cotton, and to adjust the share of raw materials mix has been accompanied by technology imports, mainly from Japan. China's textile and garment exports have required the supply of materials and designs from transnationals so that the product will meet market conditions abroad. Some of these exports are dyed and finished abroad, since Chinese capacity in this respect is still relatively low and transnationals are reluctant to transfer such technology to China for fear of losing their competitive power. Joint ventures have been established especially with firms from Hong Kong and Japan.[24]

The demand for consumer electronic products has surged with the rise of incomes as well as with the relaxation of restraints on consumption. Television has already become very popular in both urban and rural areas. Domestic production has been aided by cooperative arrangements with firms such as Hitachi, and has been supplemented by imports partly as a revenue measure since tariffs on these products are very high. The use of computers has also leapfrogged in all areas. For example, the processing of the census data taken in 1982 is being aided by IBM computers supplied by the United Nations Development Program (UNDP). Almost all the world's major computer firms have some involvement in China.

Despite the relative de-emphasizing of heavy industries in China's development strategy in the last few years, cooperation with transnational corporations in this area has already shown signs of revival. Energy-related industries have been identified as bottleneck sectors and assigned top priorities. Even machine tools and engineering industries in general, which were hard hit in the early stages of readjustment (affecting especially the Japanese, German, and Swiss suppliers), have begun to recover. The long-run demand for heavy industry is likely to be sustained, since much of the equipment in the enterprises is of the 1960s and 1950s vintage. In some cases, even equipment from the 1930s and 1920s is still in operation, partly because the depreciation allowance has been too low and partly because old equipment discarded by the major enterprises has been picked up by collectives and small enterprises. As the introduction of the responsibility system generates investment funds for enterprises and encourages productivity improvements, re-equipment is likely to be much sought after. This will in turn enhance the export potential of heavy industry products.[25]

The strategic role of transnational corporations in manufacturing is well illustrated by the case of Parker Hannifin in China.[26] A seal for fluid systems (o-ring) may not appear important, but leaks in machine tools and automobiles are highly costly for Chinese manufacturers. A joint-venture arrangement between the manufacturer and Parker Hannifin enables China not only to solve the problem but also to export a part of the o-ring production that is labor-intensive.

Transport and Communications

Although progress has been made in the last three decades in transport and communications, traditional means of both are still highly visible everywhere in China. Animal- and human-drawn carts and sampans continue to provide fascinating local color for the tourists. In line with China's development strategy in the past, priority for the development of the modern sector was allotted to railways. The recent change in the strategy from a basically self-sufficient economy into a more open one, not only nationally but also regionally, has greatly strained the existing facilities. The movement of bulk materials for export has been slowed by inadequate rail and other means of transport. Consequently, the Japanese have been especially interested in assisting this sector.

The development of shipping is more recent. Its importance has been elevated by the discovery of offshore oil, by expanding overseas trade, and by defense considerations. Although the Chinese have bought ships from foreign yards, they are also beginning to export ships. These exports are frequently fitted with imported engines and other equipment so that the local contribution is largely limited to the shell. Development in shipwrecking or repair facilities will also increase the role of cooperation with foreign enterprises. Joint ventures with Poland and Tanzania have facilitated ship movement in areas still hostile to China. The partnership of the China Corporation of Shipbuilding Industries, the National Charting Corporation, the Hong Kong Shanghai Banking Corporation and Worldwide Shipping Groups (Sir Y.K. Pao's) forms a truly international United Shipping Investment Company.[27]

The congestion at China's major ports reflects the lack of deep-water facilities and the rapid growth of waterborne commerce. The need for modernization of port facilities becomes more urgent as ships increase in size.[28] Improvements in these facilities, together with rail connections at Qinhuangdao and Shijiusuo, are being aided by the Overseas Economic Cooperation Fund, of Japan.

Perhaps the most noticeable phenomenon in any developing country is the difficulty of communications. A telephone call can take forever to be connected. Chinese purchases of telecommunications equipment have so far concentrated on Japanese, Hong Kong and European pieces.[29] China's plan to develop satellite telecommunications has prompted discussions with a number of U.S. transnationals, including Varian; Scientific Atlanta; Harris, Inc.; Hughes Aircraft; Radiation Systems; and MACOM. Orders have been received by U.S. firms such as Land Resources Management Corp. for a land-satellite ground station. A joint venture has also been formed with Hong Kong's Cable and Wireless to construct a microwave system. The potentials for the future, especially for the role of U.S. transnationals, depend very much on home-country policies as much as on Chinese willingness and preference, since much of the technology of interest to China may be subject to U.S. export controls.

Agriculture

The scope for transnational-corporation involvement in agriculture has greatly increased with Chinese reforms in that sector. A move toward more specialization in China has meant greater willingness to import in order to ease domestic shortages and has increased the availability of a variety of products for export. The expansion of the grain trade should benefit the major grain companies, which account for the bulk of the trade since a large amount of capital is required and a considerable degree of risk exists owing to unforeseeable fluctuations. The trade in specific agricultural commodities is less certain. The development of animal husbandry in China, for example, is stimulating demand for feed imports. On the other hand, the relaxation of the grain first policy reduces the need for foreign cotton.

Another major effect of agricultural reforms is the keen interest in grass-roots technological improvement. Hopes for massive exports of combines and tractors for the instant mechanization of Chinese agriculture have been dashed, since most Chinese farms remain small and the pace of mechanization is much slower than was first expected. Indeed, the short-run effect of decentalized agricultural management has been a reduced demand for some agricultural machines, especially large ones, since households under contract prefer to obtain their own draft animals to ensure the timely cultivation of the fields they manage.[30] This phenomenon will probably be reversed as machinery management is improved under the new system. Moreover, the development of state farms, partly for experimental purposes and partly to suit local conditions, as in the northeast or in Hainan, should stimulate demand for foreign machinery. Generally, the demand for most inputs such as seeds, breeding stocks, fertilizers, insecticides, as well as certain farm machinery, is increasing rapidly. In Hainan alone, officials have targeted thirty-four projects to bring in some one billion dollars in three years. A number of these projects are in agriculture, and include the development of cashew, coffee, oil-palm, coconut, fruit, herbal medicine, forestry, and rubber production. In addition, some of the light industry projects are related to agribusiness. A greater degree of sophistication in the use of fertilizers has meant a shift in emphasis from nitrogen to phosphorus and potassium fertilizers, for which the domestic resource base for production is limited. Success in agricultural development has stimulated the development of numerous agri-industries and cooperation with transnationals in that sector.

Services

The service industries have been conspicuously absent from the official Four Modernizations. Their importance has not, however, eluded the new Chinese policymakers. The involvement of transnationals in tourism is traditionally one of the first foreign ventures to emerge in socialist countries. First, transnationals are in a good position to know the requirements and tastes of tourists from abroad. Second, compensation, especially in foreign exchange, to the transnationals is facilitated by the self-liquidating nature of the industry. It is not accidental that numerous joint ventures should have been established with transnationals in this area. A notable example is the $22 million Jianguo Hotel, patterned after the Holiday Inn. So far it is the only hotel in China that will make advanced confirmed reservations. Another example is the $75 million Great Wall Hotel, negotiated by E.S. Pacific.[31]

The rush of transnational banks to China has long been observable. In addition to the correspondent relationships of a large number of foreign banks with the Bank of China, major transnational banks have established representative offices in China.[32] Among the first was the Hong Kong and Shanghai Banking Corporation, which is based in Hong Kong and is sensitive to Chinese requirements. First National Chicago is the pioneer on the U.S. side. Most of the banks have regarded China as a good credit risk. The Chinese have, however, been slow to draw upon the line of commercial credit, amounting to some $30 billion at the end of 1982, partly because alternative financial resources have been available from governments and international financial institutions at easier terms and partly because some of the commercial lines do not involve high commitment fees. In 1982 and 1983, the Chinese also enjoyed an accumulation of foreign-exchange reserves.

As is well known, the overseas activities of transnational banks are very much diversified. The commercial banks have no inhibitions about engaging in the functions of investment banks and other financial services. These services should pave the way for greater involvement of other transnational corporations and should in turn be stimulated by the activities of the corporations.

Apart from its use of banks as consultants, China's use of consulting firms has so far been limited. An inhibiting factor is the apparently high cost of consulting services. A major feasibility study, for example, frequently runs to hundreds of thousands of dollars. Another reason is that the Chinese have been in the habit of extracting free information. One notable mechanism is the holding of technical seminars at which competitive suppliers are invited to present detailed information on a particular industry, the firm as well as the technology. No charge is generally made to the Chinese even though the cost to the firm may run from tens of thousands to hundreds of thousands of dollars. The situation is not expected to last. Indeed, some firms are already charging fees for training services. The recent arrangement for exchanges of company information between China and Dun and Bradstreet suggests a quid pro quo relationship.

Increasing Chinese use of the services of international accounting firms and law offices has been evident in recent years. This development is obviously related to the expansion of transnational-corporation activities. The accounting system is an essential tool in cooperation with transnationals, and is also basic to the reform of the Chinese enterprise system. A number of the major international accounting firms, including Coopers & Lybrand, Price Waterhouse, Deloitte Haskins & Sells, and Ernst and Whinney, have representative offices in China and conduct training courses.

The international law firms chiefly serve the transnationals involved in China. The Chinese have recently found it necessary to engage these firms to handle cases abroad; firms include Sherman & Sterling for the menthol case, Baker and McKinzie for mushrooms, and Arter, Hadden, and Hemmendinger and Weil, Gorshal and Mengers for ceramics.[33]

So far the Chinese have not made much use of transnational advertising companies in direct advertising.[34] Most of the advertising costs for Chinese products have been paid by the importers. This reluctance will disappear as the Chinese gain more experience of the costs and benefits of such activities.

The engagement of some financial services by the Chinese has continued to be hampered by ethical notions. For example, trading in the futures market, especially for selling short, is generally regarded as speculative and has bad connotations. When it is realized that the same mechanism can be used to hedge, it should become obvious that the aim is to minimize the risk of speculation against future market developments rather than the reverse. The active use of the futures market by the Chinese can therefore be anticipated, especially as China is already a major trader in such commodities as wheat, soy beans, cotton, tin, and so on.[35]

Types and Sources

In addition to the general role assigned to transnational corporations and industry differences already discussed, there are many reasons why particular firms have special advantages or disadvantages in their relationship with China. In this section, five considerations are singled out for analysis: the political dimension, the state-of-the-art, firm size, its origin, and its Chinese connection.

The Political Dimension

In the early days of the People's Republic, political considerations predominated. The relationship with transnationals depended very much on whether the home country was friendly or not. Transnationals based in the same country were likewise distinguished. Japanese firms trading with Taiwan were especially boycotted, although this was often evaded by cosmetic organizational changes separating the units that dealt with Taiwan from those dealing with the People's Republic.[36]

More recently, with the new emphasis on economic considerations, the political dimension has become less prominent. Firms based in countries with which China has as yet no diplomatic relations enjoy businesslike treatment. Many firms trading with Taiwan have no difficulty in maintaining good relations with China. Even the Hong Kong and Shanghai Banking Corporation has a new office in Taiwan, apparently instituted after checking with the People's Republic. This is probably influenced by the fact that the attraction of Taiwan remains strong for many transnationals; it is not practical to force the transnationals to make a choice between the People's Republic and Taiwan. At the same time, a number of transnationals, such as First Chicago and ARCO, which made political gestures in favor of the People's Republic, have apparently won many friends in China to the benefit of their business relations.

A fine line must be drawn, therefore, between political considerations that might affect business and those that do not. When the Dutch government contracted to sell submarine equipment to Taiwan, the People's Republic not only downgraded diplomatic relations with the Netherlands but indicated that business would also be affected. The continued arms sales to Taiwan by the United States have exacerbated official relations between the United States and the People's Republic, though not as much as in the Sino-Dutch instance. Apparently the Chinese took into account the historical background of the U.S.-Taiwan relations as well as the importance of their own business relations with U.S. firms. This does not preclude a less-favorable attitude toward U.S. firms if alternative sources are available. For instance, at a time when U.S.-Chinese relations were strained, purchases of grain were made in other countries, as much as possible, although this was not as explicitly stated by the Chinese as it was by Soviet officials when the Soviets were unhappy with the U.S. government. Once the fine line is overstepped, the reaction may appear to be precipitous because of pent-up grievances.

The State-of-the-Art

The Chinese preference for the most advanced technology is well known. Article 5 of the Joint Venture Law stipulates, for example, that "the technology or equipment contributed by any foreign participant . . . shall be truly advanced and appropriate to China's needs."[37] This preference arises mainly from the predominance of engineering rather than economic considerations. A preponderant number of Chinese in leadership positions in economic affairs and business have engineering backgrounds. Another reason stems from China's unfortunate experiences with transnationals who promised to supply the most modern equipment but delivered something that they were ready to discard.

Transnationals are thus frequently ranked in the order of their technological advancement. The major Japanese firms enjoy the best reputation in such areas as the manufacture of steel and its products, automobiles, and consumer electronics. The major U.S. firms are recognized to excel in such fields as advanced electronics, telecommunications, space technology, and petroleum. German and Swiss transnationals are admired for precision machinery and instruments.

More emphasis has recently been placed on considerations of appropriateness. It has been found that the most advanced technology or equipment may not only be uneconomical because of its high cost but also technologically unsuitable for lack of the complementary inputs. A clear indication of such considerations is the Chinese willingness to accept secondhand equipment provided the price is right. An examination of a list of firms that have business relations with China reveals many second-string or less technologically renowned ones. Other considerations include differences in transnational strategies and negotiating postures and skills.

Size

The choice between large and small firms is affected by conflicting considerations on the part of the Chinese. Many of these considerations, such as the level of technology, are associated with the size of the firm. A large firm is sometimes presumed to have correspondingly large capabilities, but it has been found that advanced technologies are not necessarily concentrated in these firms. Yet large firms are often easier to negotiate with, since information about them is more readily available. They are also in a better position to absorb the cost of negotiations in terms of personnel time as well as possible risk of failure. A relatively small firm often does not have a Chinese division, as many large firms do. The latter can send their staff on frequent trips to China or even station them there to conduct negotiations and follow-through. Nevertheless, small firms may be more flexible and willing to make concessions. Moreover, some small firms may have special connections, as illustrated in chapter 7.

Origin

The political, technological, and size considerations are sometimes related to the origin of the transnational corporation. As a general policy, the Chinese seek a degree of diversification among home countries so that no single country will dominate. This practice tends to mitigate some of the other considerations. For example, firms from various home countries are frequently lined up so that they will compete with one another. In the case of offshore-oil exploration, the award of contract bids is not necessarily limited to the lowest bidder; this is apparently intended to achieve some distribution between the majors. In coal exploration contracts, U.S., U.K., German, and Japanese firms all have a piece of the pie.

On the whole, the Japanese transnationals have the clearest advantages over other transnationals, especially those based in the United States.[38] First, there is the cultural advantage. The cultural distance between China and Japan is relatively small as compared to other countries. Many Japanese can speak fluent Chinese and are well versed in Chinese affairs. Their research workers often know more about China than do many of their Chinese counterparts. They can rightly claim that they understand the Chinese.

The second is the geographical advantage. The relatively high transactions cost of doing business with China enhances the advantage of geographical proximity. Unlike U.S. and European firms, Japanese firms are able to field a mission to China at almost a moment's notice. The major firms maintain a large resident staff in China and an even larger staff at home for rotational purposes and for backstopping. In contrast, U.S. and European transnationals are satisfied with a much smaller staff or with the use of Hong Kong as a staging ground, partly because their executives consider China a hardship post after they have made the compulsory trips to the Palace Museum, the Ming Tombs, and the Great Wall.

The third is the negotiating advantage, which is related to the first two. The Japanese negotiating style is flexible. They are willing, for example, to sweeten a deal with special prices or loans at concessionary terms. Their patience matches that of the Chinese. They are also more careful about Chinese sensibilities and are less concerned with legal technicalities. Their people maintain a greater degree of continuity than their foreign competitors, whose negotiating-team members change frequently.

The fourth is the strategic advantage. The Japanese corporate strategy generally coincides with the strategy of the Chinese. Japanese firms regard business with China as vitally important for their long-term survival rather than as something of peripheral significance. They are committed.

The fifth is the organizational advantage. Japanese transnationals are generally responsive to particular requirements and more willing and able to deliver than many of their competitors. This is related to the capabilities of the Japanese *sogoshoshas* (general trading companies) and *keiretsu* (group company).[39] These organizations are able to deliver complex or huge packages as required. For example, if the Chinese require quotations on specific commodity prices, these transnationals can tap the global-information network instantaneously. If a project requires a comprehensive line of products or services, they can find virtually all the ingredients within the firm or the group. There is no need to go to numerous other transnationals to put the project together. The Chinese can thereby greatly save on administative costs and fill their information gaps. In the case of countertrade especially, what the other transnationals cannot do the Japanese can handle with ease.

The sixth is the governmental advantage. The relationship between government and business in Japan is more cooperative than adversary, a condition aided by mutual understanding fostered by years of working relations. The informal ties of government and business are strengthened by the practice whereby senior-official retirees join the higher echelons of business. This relationship is also fortified by a set of institutional arrangements, such as the use of government credit and aid to foster business. For example, even though the terms of export credit may be limited by OECD guidelines, a financial package that combines export credit and aid would be difficult to compete with.

Although the above advantages are formidable, as emulation spreads and countermeasures are devised the edge tends to lessen. Moreover, some of the advantages may turn into disadvantages, which can best be illustrated by a comparison of Japanese and U.S. transnationals. U.S. transnationals can progressively reduce the cultural distance through education and better communication. The open society and multiracial makeup of the United States have a unique attraction. In China there is a craze to learn English, or more correctly American, as most of the instructors and texts are connected with the United States, but there is no similar enthusiasm for studying Japanese. Japanese firms may have Chinese-speaking personnel, but U.S. companies can produce Chinese-Americans who can claim that blood is thicker than water.

The geographical barrier tends to be overcome as communications improve. It will in any case become less important after the initial phase is over as representative offices or permanent lines of communication are opened up in China, Hong Kong, or the United States by both sides.

The negotiating advantage may also be altered with time. The U.S. practice of putting all the cards on the table may be appreciated by the Chinese. In contrast, the Japanese willingness to incur losses on particular items, for example, may raise the suspicion that there may be hidden features. Special price discounts may be accompanied by old machinery and equipment billed as new, or a high cost for peripherals, spare parts, and maintenance once the customer is hooked.

The strategic advantage is also shifting. After the initial euphoria of U.S. business about China, most of the fly-by-night firms that sought a big kill without much effort or commitment have been discouraged or weeded out. Those that remain are oriented toward the long term. Moreover, many U.S. transnationals are increasingly internationalized so that the traditional concentration on the domestic market is becoming less predominant.

The organizational advantage of the Japanese transnational is more difficult to overcome. Yet, the Chinese may prefer to deal with individual transnationals that are less cohesive and less likely to present a united front in negotiations that may smell of collusion or monopolistic manipulation. This is all the more significant when combined with governmental backing. The notion of Japan, Inc. naturally evokes caution against possible domination. Support given to the transnationals by the Japanese government, for example, may be interpreted as a power play.

The above discussion has implications for transnationals based in other countries. The Chinese desire for diversification, partly for risk aversion and partly to ensure the best choice of a mix of products, technologies, or partners, should benefit transnationals elsewhere. Even transnationals based in developing countries have some advantages. Inasmuch as China considers itself a member of the Third World, the political consideration is generally favorable except for a few countries closely allied with the Soviet Union. Another advantage is that these transnationals tend to be more sympathetic to host-country concerns, since their home country is predominantly a host to transnationals. They are thus likely to accede to Chinese demands for domestic control and regulations. Moreover, the technology may be more appropriate because the home country's stage of development is closer to that of China. The capabilities of these transnationals are still limited, however. Most of them, such as Indian firms, do not have much to invest and concentrate on technical assistance.[40]

The Chinese Connection

Transnationals based in Southeast Asia, notably in Hong Kong, Singapore, Malaysia, the Philippines, and Thailand, often have a special affinity with the Chinese through local Chinese business groups. Although overseas Chinese are no longer considered by the People's Republic as having dual citizenship, they are treated as "married daughters" whose loyalty to their country is unquestioned but whose roots are not forgotten. Many overseas Chinese are bilingual and can converse in the dialects of the localities they originated from, especially Guangdong, Fuqian, and Shanghai, which have traditionally been and continue to be important areas for foreign business activities. They frequently have relatives, schoolmates, and personal friends in key positions in China. The atmosphere of business is thus friendly and relaxed rather than confrontational.

Many overseas Chinese have nonbusiness motives. Most of them or their ancestors left China because the country was weak and disorderly and life was intolerable. They would like to make a contribution to the prosperity and stability of present-day China. Some factories are in fact established in China mainly to aid particular localities or clans. The aid element can be more important than the busines element.

A number of the overseas Chinese, especially those in Hong Kong, fled the communist regime earlier. Although their political attitudes may be unchanged, their business sense permits them to engage in business relations with China. The Chinese understand this complex psychological makeup and give them a red-carpet treatment. A similar treatment applies to many overseas Chinese from Taiwan, especially in the United States. Those who are willing to engage in business with China are treated especially favorably. The added consideration is a symbol of unity.

The Chinese connection is sometimes used by foreign firms. Chinese staff members frequently act as intermediaries between their principal and business and government in China. Their effectiveness is discussed further in chapter 6.

Similarly, the China connection is sometimes used by transnationals as a showpiece rather than for direct profit. This was especially true when media attention to China was high. In such cases, long-run viability may be in doubt unless the transnationals have real expertise in business in China. Publicity and entry into the higher echelons of the Chinese government are of little lasting value if there is no follow-up in the form of real business. A long-term relationship must eventually depend on what the transnationals can offer in the way of products, services, or technology. Superficial relations at the top cannot by themselves be translated into concrete business.

4 The Choice of Forms of Cooperation

The previous chapter demonstrates the content or substance that transnational corporations may contribute to China's modernization. Basically, the process of modernization requires the use of many ingredients: capital, technology, management, and marketing. Transnational corporations are an important source of all of these. The precise role played by transnational corporations and their relationship with the host country depends not only on the particular ingredient or combination of ingredients involved but also on the form of cooperation. Although a multitude of forms have appeared in practice, most of the literature continues to deal with a few extreme modes such as licensing and foreign direct investment. The purpose of this chapter is to examine the considerations governing the choice of forms, of which there is a rich array. Before the Chinese case is examined, a more general theory of choice must be developed to provide the necessary framework.

Toward a Theory of Choice

The Background

Implicit in the preceding discussion is the assumption that transnational-corporation involvement is not limited to direct investment. This is based on theoretical considerations as well as empirical observation. In theory, in response to varying circumstances, transnationals may choose to engage in direct foreign investment or in noninvestment activities such as export, licensing, and management contracts. The host country may also have a set of preferences for these activities, though they may not be the same as those of the transnationals. The various activities exist side by side, to a greater or lesser extent, in many countries including China.

In spite of the conceptual distinction between transnational activities and foreign direct investment, the two are often taken to be identical. In the first place, the theoretical consideration of transnational corporations is often limited to industrial corporations, particularly with regard to their decision making in international production. Consequently, foreign direct investment has been singled out for investigation. Second, and related to the first matter, the object of the theorizing is often not to explain why a particular form of activity takes place but what it is that determines foreign direct investment. Third, in empirical studies of transnational corporations, the flow and stock of foreign direct investment is often viewed as an indication of their activities.

The shortcomings of such a narrow definition of transnational-corporation activities are many. First, the true picture of transnationals is distorted. The importance of their foreign direct investment activities is in particular exaggerated out of all proportion. The results can be misleading from the point of view of the role that may be assigned to them by a host country; for example, transnationals can play an important role even if no foreign direct investment is contemplated or allowed. Secondly, a host of important transnationals is neglected. They include trading corporations, transnational banks, and service corporations, such as accounting and consulting firms. The growth of these firms has been especially rapid in the last few decades. Moreover, the product mix offered by them tends to be increasingly complicated. Also, direct and indirect linkages have often been established by nonindustrials with industrials so that it becomes increasingly artificial to exclude the former from consideration.

Another limitation of the existing literature on the question of choice is that choice is envisaged from either the transnationals' viewpoint or from host country's viewpoint. The interrelationship between transnational and host is hardly ever considered. Many theories of transnational corporations implicitly assume that the choice is theirs. Even when certain conditions, such as tariffs, are explicitly allowed for, they are often viewed as background facts rather than as the result of interactions. Consequently, transnational-centered solutions often fail to meet the requirements of the host countries. At the same time, host countries often impose conditions to suit their own purposes, not realizing that the transnationals' most powerful weapon is refusal to deal. As the adage has it: you can take a horse to the water but you cannot make it drink.

A cooperative arrangement must therefore be considered from both sides. A satisfactory arrangement requires an understanding of transnationals on the part of the host country and an understanding of the host country on the part of the transnationals. In the case of China, this is difficult. As far as the transnationals are concerned, China remains a mystery to most decision makers. The picture is not always clarified by the old China hands, since memories of the past may overshadow their perspective on the present and the future. To many of them, China is still characterized by the old stereotypes. The new China hands focus on the contemporary scene, but in doing so they have frequently suffered from two major difficulties. First, many intellectuals were forced to make judgments and predictions on the basis of very flimsy information, often secondhand and biased, but because they have been identified with their past views, it is difficult for them to retract. Secondly, the personal experiences of the new China hands are often misleading. They are usually treated so royally by the Chinese that they develop a soft spot for them. Others have experienced deep frustrations, especially in business dealings. These frustrations tend to be cumulative as is shown in chapter 6. At the time of this writing, the major frustrations may be summed up as the unprofitability of conducting business in China. The best indication of this is that most of the China divisions of transnational corporations are contracting rather than expanding. Although this may be temporary, and correct itself as the total volume of foreign deals expands with progress in China's modernization, it will be difficult for some time to induce promising business to concentrate on China.

On the Chinese side, an understanding of the transnationals has been hampered by a long period of virtual isolation. Contact with transnationals was regarded almost as poison. But recent experience of actual contact can also be misleading. A common assumption has been that the transnationals based in the capitalist countries are all eager to do business with China. Personal experience tends to reinforce this hunch, as transnational-corporation executives spend lavishly and are willing to provide many free services, such as technical seminars, visits to the headquarters of transnationals, training, and the like. A banquet for Chinese officials may be held at a cost that can only be matched by dining in a two- or three-star French restaurant. The Chinese predilection for risk avoidance and their eagerness to strike a good bargain further reinforces the difficulty of doing business. In the circumstances, the promotion of mutual understanding is essential to alter the existing relationship.

Toward a Theory of Choice

The inadequacy of traditional theories to explain the activities of transnational corporations has become increasingly clear as the study of transnationals develops.[1]

First, international trade theory[2] is obviously too narrow, since trade is only one of the possible choices of activity open to transnationals. Many of the basic assumptions in that theory do not even correspond to the trade activities of transnationals. They include a competitive-market situation that is not fulfilled, either because the firms involved are oligopolistic or because at least part of the transaction is intra-trade, or conducted within the firm.

Second, international-capital theory[3] is no more satisfactory than international trade theory, since the transfer of capital by transnationals is often combined with the transfer of other resources such as technology, management, and market access. The return to the transnational thus refers to the complex package rather than to capital alone. As far as capital itself is concerned, the distinguishing feature is that the transnational corporation retains control after the transfer, while the transferrer in portfolio investment does not.

Third, the application of industrial-organization theory[4] removes the assumption of perfect market conditions. The reason why transnationals are able to overcome their disadvantages in competing with local firms is explained by their advantages in market power, through the ownership of intangible as well as tangible assets. It is the failure of the market that prompts firms to "internalize" the markets for inputs and outputs. However, this market-failure explanation neglects the fact that within a country where barriers to entry or between localities are insignificant, a "national" firm may operate in different parts of the country. Moreover, unlike transnationals based in the United States, other transnationals, including those based in Japan and even in some developing countries, may be relatively small and their numbers relatively large such that the oligopolistic character of transnationals may not be the whole story.

Fourth, reasons for the engagement of transnationals in activities in more than one locality are offered by the extension of location theory.[5] Transnationals can save transport costs by establishing subsidiaries in various markets. This saving is more important for market-oriented industries than for industries where transport costs are unimportant. This explanation of locational advantage remains to be integrated with other explanations such as firm-specific advantages of transnational activities.

Fifth, attempts have been made to integrate the various approaches[6] in order to explain why firms choose a particular form of activity. A distinction is made between different forms: export, licensing, and foreign direct investment. A comparison is then made of several cost considerations. The initial cost of export as well as the difficulty of negotiation is relatively low when compared to licensing or foreign direct investment. Similarly, the risk of failure is also low for export as compared to foreign direct investment. The risk of diffusion of knowledge, however, is low for foreign direct investment but high for licensing.

The risk of host-country policy change is especially high for foreign direct investment. As far as the difficulty of administration is concerned, a distinction must be made between operations and dispute resolution. In foreign direct investment, the former is relatively low but the latter is high. In licensing, pricing and policing are especially difficult.

Reasons for a transnational's choice of a particular form of arrangement are to be found in all these considerations. For example, for small firms export may be preferable since the initial cost of foreign direct investment may be prohibitive. On the other hand, despite the cost considerations affecting licensing, the lack of resources to exploit technology through foreign direct investment will induce small firms to engage in it. In some industries, however, research and development activity is intensive and the number of innovations as indicated by new patents very large. Even a large firm will find its resources inadequate for utilizing all the new technology in different parts of the world through direct investment. Licensing is therefore resorted to.

From the point of view of host countries, the relative ease of negotiating and administering imports (transnational exports) as compared with foreign direct investment and licensing also applies. As is true of many other considerations, the host country's immediate concerns are frequently the opposite of those of the transnationals. For instance, host countries are interested in gaining control over the activities of transnationals in their territory, while transnationals seek to retain control. Host countries favor the diffusion of knowledge, while transnationals are afraid to do so. There are evident possibilities of conflict. When the conflict is sharp, no arrangement can be reached. Compromises are often possible, although neither side may feel fully satisfied.[7]

The modern theories highlighted above go a long way toward explaining the behavior of transnational corporations, but they remain oversimplified. They fail to consider the interaction between the parties in question. Moreover, they overemphasize the alternatives and neglect the complementarities. These shortcomings can best be illustrated by the defects in the theory of depackaging, and the reasons why the Chinese case is not adequately explained by existing theories.

The theory of depackaging arises from criticism of the foreign direct investment package, especially criticism from the host country. It is maintained that a foreign-investment package, containing all the ingredients of capital, technology, management, and marketing, is like the tying of purchases in a department store. If one wishes to buy shirts, one must also buy ties, socks, cuff links, and so on. A better solution would be to let the purchaser decide on each item separately, in other words, depackaging.

There is no doubt that markets should exist in which each item could be purchased. In the case of transnationals, it would mean that finance, technology, management services, and export access should be obtainable separately. Empirical studies have found that when a purchaser shops around and picks up items from different sources, the cost can be reduced or the quality improved.[8] On the other hand, the theory of depackaging is sometimes invoked to condemn all forms of packages. Such a narrow interpretation is misleading.

In the first place, packaging is a matter of degree. Consider the department store. Many items are actually packaged. Tea may be available in loose leaf form or in tea bags. To the gourmet tea drinker, the bag is not only unnecessary but adds an undesirable taste; to the average consumer, however, it is a convenience. In Chinese hotels, only loose tea used to be left in the rooms. Some foreign tourists complained that Chinese tea was too bitter because they did not know the proper amount of leaves to use to make their own tea. Recently, tea bags have been made available. Similarly, if one was a decorator, one might prefer to pick up different pieces of furniture from different places. For a bride whose sense of aesthetics is not well developed, however, it may be safer to buy a complete set of furniture; otherwise the colors, shapes, and textures may clash. In industry also, the knowledgeable purchaser for a textile factory might obtain one piece of equipment from the United States, another from Italy, and others from Japan, Switzerland, and so on. If the buyer is not experienced or sophisticated, however, the pieces may be difficult to coordinate and appropriate adjustment may be troublesome.

In practice, then, even items that are not fully packaged are not completely depackaged either.[9] Although packaging may be entirely unnecessary or even undesirable for the few sophisticated purchasers, some degree of packaging may be convenient for the less sophisticated. The issue is not simply packaging or depackaging, but is repackaging or optimum packaging so that the degree and mix will suit the particular purchaser.

In the case of relatively underdeveloped countries, some degree of packaging is often needed. Even exports to these countries are not entirely depackaged. Machinery may be fully assembled rather than in knock-down form. An element of technical assistance may be included in the export package, since the instruction manual may not be enough to ensure proper use. The much-publicized sinking of an imported oil platform in China was caused, for example, by misuse. The manual of operations was not translated and proper safety measures were not observed. With Chinese exports as well, foreign firms used to supply management and marketing expertise. Pig bristles were not exportable unless they were well washed, sorted, and graded according to world-market requirements. More recently, the range of foreign contribution has greatly increased for manufactured articles.

It becomes clear that various degrees of packaging are needed, precisely because the ability to put the complex set of parts or ingredients together differs among purchasers or countries. In developing countries, even the simplest form of packaging cannot be taken for granted. For example, there used to be a street in Hong Kong nicknamed "Stinky Street" the reason being that duck eggs imported from China in large baskets had a high percentage of breakages. Even recently, China used to export jingsen (a valuable herb for medical purposes) in twenty-five-kilo crates. The buyers wondered whether it was genuine.

For developing countries especially, therefore, both the complete package of foreign direct investment and the pure forms of depackaged items are extreme cases. As applied to China, these forms and mixes and their theoretical and dynamic implications are evaluated in the following sections.

Emerging Forms

Complete-Plant Imports

The import of complete plants under turnkey contracts implies the packaging of plant and equipment with some ingredients of know-how and occasionally also patented technology. This was the predominant form of the 156 Soviet-aided major projects during the first Chinese Five-Year Plan (1953-1957).[10] The Soviets generally assumed the major role in the design and construction of the plants, in the supply of equipment, and in operations until starting difficulties were overcome and the Chinese were able to take over. Even in the early 1970s, when Soviet aid was discontinued and contact with Western enterprises was kept at a low level, such imports were an important form of major industrial projects. Among the better known examples are the fertilizer plants of Pullman Kellogg. The main advantages of importing complete plants are four. First, foreign expertise helps to determine the feasibility of particular projects. Second, foreign experts also see to it that the package is complete and fits together. Third, these experts will make trial runs and show the local people how to operate the plant for some time before they leave. Last, unlike foreign direct investment, they will disappear when their function has been performed, and the Chinese will have complete control.

Since 1979, the diadvantages of major reliance on this form have surfaced. First and most important, such reliance was related to the nature of planning and management prior to the current reforms. The single-minded pursuit of quantitative-output targets put a premium on increased capacity. The easiest, and perhaps the lazy, way of increasing capacity was to import complete plants—and the state could be asked to allocate the necessary foreign exchange and other inputs. Cost was not a serious consideration since the state would absorb any profit or loss, which was also the reason for extensive rather than intensive development.

Second, feasibility studies by foreign experts under such circumstances tended to concentrate on the engineering rather than the economic aspects. The Chinese were preoccupied with the expansion of output rather than cost minimalization, and the foreign experts had a similar bias since they had a vested interest in securing the business, no matter what it took.

Third, some of the imported items in the complete plant might be readily available from local suppliers, but when the assembling of the package was left mainly to the foreign experts or contractors, they were unfamiliar with these options and it was usually much simpler to rely on the usual foreign suppliers. This was true especially when speed was emphasized. For example, with hotels, some furniture could obviously have been supplied locally but it would have taken time to identify sources and in many cases to develop them. When there was a shortage of hotels, there was little time to explore such possibilities.

Fourth, the Chinese ability to operate the facilities independently might be superficial; when there was a real difficulty, they might not be able to handle it. This is because they have not gone through the process of learning-by-doing. Foreign technology is not thoroughly absorbed and indigenous technology is not developed.

A number of features or ingredients can be added to the complete plant package (or turnkey contract). These may include financing, and may also involve sustained servicing and maintenance or technical assistance. Such an extended package is sometimes referred to as "turnkey plus," and is sometimes referred to as *produit en main* (product in hand) when the technology transfer is extended beyond the start-up stage. The extended transfer enables the Chinese to meet various contingencies long after the complete plant has been set up. It does not even have to be limited to complete plants. Even for imports of specific products, continued technical assistance may be provided by the supplier. In recent years, the Chinese have also allowed the setting up of service centers for a number of foreign suppliers and products, ranging from machinery to watches. Indeed, the lack of these facilities abroad for Chinese products is a major constraint on Chinese manufactures export.

Purchase of Technology

The acquisition of technology as such by simple purchase not embodied in other forms, such as complete plant imports and joint ventures, is still sparsely utilized by China. A main reason for the little use made of consulting firms for the purchase of know-how is unfamiliarity with such services. In the West, these firms have played an important role as advisers to enterprises, especially at the senior executive level. They are able to provide all sorts of expertise that an enterprise cannot find internally. Often such expertise is very specialized, while at other times it may be required for a particular task and the demand may not be sustained. It would therefore be uneconomical for an enterprise to permanently acquire such expertise internally. The most important reason for engaging consultants is perhaps the independent stance that can be taken by an outsider who is unaffected by hierarchical and personality considerations. The chief executive may have to maintain a distance from his subordinates. Likewise, line managers in charge of defined functions may be unwilling to look over the shoulders of others in order to avoid bad feelings among colleagues. Independent and frank advice for the good of the enterprise as a whole is thus appreciated.

Another reason why the Chinese do not make much use of consultants is the apparently high cost of such services. The cost of one day's work by a foreign consultant may be as high as several months' pay for a Chinese counterpart. It seems difficult to justify, especially since the usefulness of consulting services cannot be readily demonstrated. The Chinese have also been somewhat spoiled by offers of free services by those who seek a foothold in China. Notable examples of free services include training of Chinese by major accounting firms and law offices. As noted in the previous chapter, the Chinese have recently been more willing to make use of services and to pay for them.

Since China is not a signatory to the Paris (Patent) Convention, it has a reputation for copying patented products or processes without paying licensing fees, although trademarks are protected by a new law. During the period of isolation from the world economy, the import of spare parts of existing foreign equipment was difficult, but the Chinese were able to duplicate many parts themselves.

In recent years the Chinese have sought licensing for advanced technology, which is evidently hard to duplicate. Examples of licensing agreements include aircraft engines from Rolls Royce and truck trailers and container chasses from Fruehauf. Some of the more successful arrangements have been part of the joint ventures package with foreign enterprises. The patents may in fact belong to a third party. Many firms have, however, been reluctant to license key technologies, such as integrated circuits and computers,[11] since they prefer to exploit them internally and are afraid that the knowledge may be dissipated.

The Chinese are actively considering a draft patent law.[12] One school of thought is opposed to any move in this direction. It maintains that technology is a common human heritage and should not be monopolized by the patent holder. It also regards the cost of royalties as too high, especially since there are many restrictions on the use of the patented technology.[13]

The human heritage argument does not, however, alter the fact that an important part of modern technology is a direct result of conscious research and development expenditure. The return on successful cases must defray not only their own cost but also cost of those that yield nothing. In addition, there is an element of uncertainty about the commercial value of a patented technology, especially since a new and better version may displace the one in question without warning. In any case, if there are no patents, transnationals may exploit the knowledge internally and reap profit from exports or foreign direct investment. Moreover, although the Chinese deficit in technology trade is expected to continue in the near future, there is already some licensing of Chinese technology, such as rice varieties and coal-dust blowers, to foreign firms. As more new technology is developed in China, it becomes doubtful whether China should simply give it away.

Where patents do exist, the practical possibility of copying by the Chinese has been exaggerated. The description in a patent document is usually not one hundred percent complete, precisely in order to prevent easy copying. The chemical and mechanical analyses of imported products are likely to miss some minor yet crucial element. As a result, a duplicated product may not last as long, may be less efficient, or may simply not work. Even though copying is possible technically, the lack of experience and scale considerations usually make the cost prohibitively high.

There is, moreover, room for possible retaliation against Chinese patent infringements. Chinese exports suspected of involving infringement may be challenged, and the import of other technology from the patent holder may be denied.

It is likely that a new patent law will be promulgated by the Chinese soon. A possible compromise between the two schools of thought is that some of the features often found in Third World patent laws, may be incorporated into the Chinese draft—for example, the rule that drugs, chemicals, and computer software should not be patented. Like other Third World countries, China may also voice a demand for revision of the Paris Convention.

Whatever arrangement is made with respect to patent law, Chinese purchase of foreign technology or licensing presumes an ability to understand it and make use of it, which in turn depends on domestic technological and managerial capabilities. These capabilities, ironically, may also enable China to adapt patented foreign technology, using new features so that neither patent infringement nor the purchase of such technology ensues. They will also prompt corporations to seek exchanges of advanced technology that may not be available for simple purchase.

Export Processing

The processing of foreign inputs for export purposes may take the form of the packaging of final products, the assembling of parts, or the processing of customer's materials or intermediate products for a fee. Processing often involves foreign designs, trademarks, or technical assistance such as quality control. The products must naturally satisfy the requirements of the export market. In view of the lack of Chinese experience in these markets, export processing is very prevalent. Since the imported materials, semiprocessed products, or trademarks are supplied by foreign enterprises, they do not raise any foreign exchange issues for the Chinese. Indeed, the processing fees represent foreign-exchange earnings. Most of the purely export-processing projects have been relatively small, reflecting fairly simple products and processes and the major participation of firms in Hong Kong and Macao in the Special Economic Zones. More sophisticated and larger projects also often involve compensation trade[14] or joint ventures.

Compensation Trade

The import of machinery and equipment as well as technology, whether in connection with the processing of imported materials or not, may be paid for over a number of years by the resultant products or by unrelated products. Such compensation trade has been resorted to in the Soviet Union and Eastern European countries in their relations with the West. The Chinese have also made great use of this technique and its variants since the opening to the West. The technique is a variation of barter, which has been used in trade relations (especially with Third World countries) to overcome problems of currency convertibility. In some cases, it also facilitates granting indirect aid by offering favorable terms of trade to the partner country. For example, in barter deals between China and Sri Lanka, the latter's goods are usually priced at higher levels than those prevailing in the world market. From the point of view of transnational corporations, barter deals may pave the way for more meaningful arrangements. An example is the supply of $300,000 worth of diesel engines to China by the General Motors Trading Company in exchange for an equivalent value in cutting tools and other products. A closely related arrangement is counterpurchase, in which a Chinese purchase is balanced against a foreign purchase in a separate contract. In contrast, the balancing in a barter arrangement is accomplished in the same contract. Sometimes the dividing line between the two is hardly perceptible. Since counterpurchase has the semblance of normal trade and payments relations, it is more frequently used. Examples of counterpurchase are aircraft products in exchange for hams, lightbulbs and woodburning stoves from China by McDonnell Douglas, and electronic products for arts and crafts by Control Data.

There are numerous variations of such arrangements. Basically, once machinery or equipment for China has been paid for by the export of products, it will be owned by the Chinese over a number of years. This is a variation of deferred or installment payment or leasing with purchase provisions. An example of such a compensation-trade arrangement is the $110 million deal by Container Transport International to build a container manufacturing plant and to purchase the entire output at a reduced price for five years.

A third party may be involved in compensation trade in order to provide credit to the supplier. It may also be called upon to dispose at a discount of the product that the Chinese have put up in payment for imported equipment. An example of such an operation is the performance of the Noble Trading Company. The company may be involved in financing the inventory of countertraded products, or it may take over these products for companies not experienced in marketing them. It may also assist in the market study of perspective countertraded products to make sure that they can be marketed.

All the above varieties can of course be combined to a greater or lesser extent. Some materials may be supplied locally. Part of the payment for the imports may be in the form of cash, processed products, or other goods. Likewise, the processing may be paid for partly in fees and partly in kind.

Compensation trade of different varieties is very popular in China. A familiar reason is to conserve hard currency. A related reason is that in compensation trade, the Chinese can minimize the size of foreign debt in order to avoid the debt problem of many developing countries. Moreover, to the extent that Chinese relative-price levels do not correspond to international levels converted at official exchange rates, indirect barter facilitates the calculations. Furthermore, from the administrative point of view, compensation trade greatly simplifies the central supervision of local decision making in foreign deals. A rule of thumb is that local autonomy in decision making is usually permitted in foreign business transactions as long as the central authority does not have to provide more than a stated sum of foreign exchange. Compensation trade is especially attractive when both parties have balance-of-payments problems. In such circumstances, there is a tendency to restrict the import of nonessential items. Through compensation trade, the exchange of nonessential items can benefit both sides. Another reason for favoring compensation trade is China's unfamiliarity with foreign markets. Transnationals can be recruited for export promotion through this device.

Nevertheless, some of the disadvantages of compensation trade that have been recognized in Eastern European countries are also beginning to be appreciated in China. As far as the promotion of exports through this technique is concerned, some exports already have a ready market and do not benefit from a semibarter deal. For example, primary commodities such as oil and coal generally belong to this category. Many textile items are subject to quota restrictions in the importing countries. The problem is not that the Chinese are unable to penetrate the market but that artificial limitations are imposed by the importing countries. To the extent that Chinese exports are thrust upon foreign importers, the quality of export promotion may be low since the importers themselves may not possess the expertise either. They may be willing to engage in a complex deal only because they can pass on the added cost, most likely to the Chinese. The question arises whether both sides might not be better off with an alternative arrangement, such as a concession in the price for imports and a fee for export promotion.

Inasmuch as the ability to handle such transactions differs among transnationals, the impact of insistence on compensation trade on them is also different. Some firms such as Japanese *sogoshoshas* or *keiretsu*, as shown earlier, are experienced in dealing with transactions in different product lines. Similarly, Hong Kong trading firms and a number of European firms accustomed to doing business with East Europeans will be favored. In contrast, most U.S. firms will find the transaction costly and inconvenient, except for a few companies such as General Electric or General Motors, which have their own trading arms. This is one of the reasons why a new Export Trading Corporation Act has been enacted by the United States Congress. Under the act, international trading companies and banks are encouraged to cooperate in export promotion without violating antitrust provisions.[15]

A related disadvantage is that, when Chinese exports are in the hands of inexperienced compensation-trade partners, the market may be spoiled by erratic behavior of the partners in regard to pricing and supplies, thereby disrupting the normal channels of trade and damaging the image of Chinese products.

Still another disadvantage of compensation trade is the uncertainty surrounding the implementation of such an arrangement.[16] There may be delays in taking delivery of Chinese exports when the foreign market is faced with recessionary conditions. There have also been cases in which the quality of Chinese exports was considered unsatisfactory by China's partners in compensation trade.

Furthermore, the Chinese have little chance to gain firsthand knowledge of the users of their exports through learning-by-doing. Short-run export may be at the expense of longer-run access to foreign matters.

The true effect of a compensation-trade arrangement on foreign exchange is not, of course, zero. There are indirect as well as direct effects. For example, some activities may yield import-substituting products that are not exported. Others, such as transport or electricity, may help exports but are not themselves exported. These projects may be neglected when foreign exchange is denied to them because of their inability to engage in compensation trade.

Finally, as in some Eastern European countries, the insistence on compensation trade—especially counterpurchase—may come from the transnationals. When transnationals are asked to take Chinese products, they may require the counterpurchase of their products, which may not be products the Chinese prefer.

Joint Ventures

The dividing line between compensation trade and joint ventures is frequently imprecise. This is especially true in China, since joint ventures in the broad sense simply means that the ventures are in cooperation (are joint) with foreign enterprises. Thus, the example of compensation trade between Container Transport International and China is sometimes also referred to as a joint venture.

At least two kinds of joint ventures are distinguished in China. One is joint venture proper, in which the profit is distributed in accordance with equity shares. The other is contractual joint ventures, in which the profit and other rights and obligations are negotiated in the contract not necessarily in proportion to equity holdings. Indeed, the foreign enterprise may not hold any equity at all, and the agreements struck may therefore be nonequity joint ventures. In this sense, coproduction can be considered as part of a contractual joint venture. Examples of coproduction, in which a foreign enterprise contributes equipment or technology to a Chinese plant for producing specific products, include the joint production of McDonnell Douglas DC-9 jets and Bell Helicopter Textron helicopters. Many coproduction arrangements also involve compensation trade, since the equipment supplied by foreign enterprises is paid for by the export of the product to the supplier. Some coproduction arrangements are organized as equity joint ventures. For example, the agreement between American Motors Corporation and Peking Auto Works provides for an American Motors investment of $8 million in cash and $8 million in technology for a 31.4 percent share of the $51 million joint venture. Initially, American Motors will update the existing Chinese 212 model with new engines and other engineering improvements. Subsequently, a new vehicle, based on American's basic model, will be developed. The agreement also provides for export sales to be made by American so that there will be no net drains on China's foreign exchange.[17] The above illustrations demonstrate that the various forms of joint ventures are frequently combined in a single arrangement.

While the existence of equity joint ventures in a socialist country represents a quantum leap away from ideological constraints on the choice of forms for cooperation with foreign enterprises, these ventures are still Chinese entities and are therefore subject to Chinese law. This is not limited to the joint venture law,[18] even with subsequent interpretations and detailed regulations. Joint ventures are also subject to many other laws still on the books in China. Consequently, some of the major advantages of joint ventures, such as the retention of control by the transnationals, do not fully apply in China. On the other hand, there are also special advantages of joint ventures with China.

The joint-venture law states that "each party to a joint venture may contribute cash, capital goods, industrial property rights, etc., as its investment in the venture" (Article 5). As shown earlier, not all joint ventures under the law involve foreign-equity investment. The joint ventures in hotels, for example, which constitute a large proportion of those approved thus far, are a case in point. The foreign joint-venture partner often does not itself contribute the finance but merely arranges it. The party that alternately contributes the finance is only a lender and has no equity investment.

Most foreign observers find it extremely difficult to negotiate a joint venture. How are the technology, land, and existing plants contributed by the parties to be valued? What proportion of the product will be for domestic and what for foreign sales? What prices should be charged for final sales? How much profit can be remitted abroad? What happens if the joint venture is to be liquidated? All these questions and more do not lend themselves to easy solutions.

Even after a joint venture is established, the foreign partner is unsure about its degree of control. To be sure, an innovative feature of the Chinese joint venture is the principle of consensus. Although the foreign partner is a minority shareholder, his consent is required in all major decisions. There will not therefore be a tyranny of the majority. The experience of existing joint ventures indicates that the consensus principle is observed. Usually, the Chinese chairman of the joint venture does not attempt to dictate, and the views of the foreign partner, especially over technology matters, are highly respected. At the same time, the consensus method is extremely time-consuming. It is often exasperating to executives of transnationals who are used to assuming responsibility and making quick decisions. There is also uncertainty in the interpretation of the joint-venture law, as there are gaps in it. For instance, Article 6 provides that "procedures covering employment and discharge of . . . workers . . . shall be stipulated according to law in the agreement of contract concluded between the parties to the joint venture." Doubts persist as to how much autonomy the venture really has in selecting its workers or in firing them. Instances have been reported in which a large number of candidates have been recommended to a joint venture by influential organizations and people. If these recommendations are ignored, can it be assumed that there will be no retaliation? In principle, the Chinese side permits the joint venture to fire incompetent workers, but in fact it may still be difficult although it is becoming less so with the progress of enterprise reform.

The calculation of the net profit of a joint venture is also uncertain. At the time of the promulgation of the joint venture law, the tax laws of China were still being drafted. Subsequently, the income tax law on joint ventures and the individual income tax law were promulgated and detailed rules and regulations were also issued. Yet, foreign lawyers have complained that the Chinese tax authorities sometimes insist on their own interpretations, which appear to differ from the texts of the laws or regulations. Such is also the case, of course, with tax authorities in other countries, including the United States. The difference is that in China there is little precedent to look to; the procedures for appeals is not well-established either. Indeed, what is more unsettling is that many laws and regulations issued before the current modernization drive have not been repealed and may still be invoked. These were drafted when the guiding ideology was very unfavorable to foreign enterprises. In any case, they are obscure to outsiders, especially in their interpretation. Further, unlike other countries where internal rulings are made public, in China they are often not, at least for some time. As a result, these rulings are not known to foreign enterprises. When foreigners are informed of the unpublished rulings, they are never sure that the information is authentic.

Despite all the uncertainties from the point of view of the foreign party, a joint venture has important advantages over other enterprises in China. This is especially true in that the enterprise-responsibility system has not as yet been fully effected. In order to attract foreign enterprises to China, a great degree of autonomy is allowed in joint ventures, a condition provided for in the agreements or contracts and confirmed repeatedly by policy statements by senior officials. In a statement at the China Investment Promotion Meeting, in June, 1982, Wei Yuming, China's Vice-Minister of the Foreign Economic Relations and Trade, spelled out the rights of joint ventures. These included: (1) the right of joint ventures to decide on their own development program, production management plan, and labor-wages plan; (2) the right to buy inputs directly from the domestic and international markets; (3) the right to sign various economic contracts with domestic and foreign companies and enterprises; (4) the right to raise RMB (Chinese currency) and foreign currency funds from internal and external financial institutions; (5) the right to establish their own financial management and other management systems, and to determine their own profit-distribution program; (6) the right to hire and fire employees and to adopt the system of pay scale, wage-form, bonus, and allowance appropriate to themselves for rewarding and punishing employees; and (7) the right to innovate and reform production techniques.[19] While these rights are all within the framework of Chinese society and the provisions in the contract, they give more flexibility than in the case of other Chinese enterprises.

It has been found that in some cases a major reason for organizing a joint venture is to gain the autonomy it enjoys rather than the import of technology or finance as such. It has also been found that the reported increase in an enterprise's production and profit after foreign involvement has nothing to do with the investment as such, since the imported equipment and foreign technology have not yet been introduced during the period in question. The increase is mainly due to the change in the status of the enterprise to a joint venture, which enabled it to have greater latitude in arranging manpower, finance, material, production, supply, and sale, thus also resulting in a general improvement in management.[20]

Another advantage of a joint venture is the show of commitment by both sides. This is especially true of equity ventures, since it is unlikely that the foreign partner will withdraw once it has made the decision. The Chinese are therefore especially interested in entering into joint-venture arrangements with leading transnationals.

From the point of view of foreign enterprises, the organic relationship established with the Chinese constitutes a firm basis for a continuing relationship. Although most joint ventures have a fade-out clause limiting the life of the arrangement, the Chinese have shown signs of flexibility concerning the duration of the fade-out. Moreover, the Chinese participation may be a welcome feature to the foreign partner since Chinese cooperation is required in virtually all phases of operation.

A further advantage of a joint venture is the continuous flow of technology and management expertise, as in the case of foreign direct investment, discussed earlier.

In some instances, transnationals may insist on 100 percent ownership. This is especially the case with U.S. high-technology firms. When compared with transnationals based in other home countries, U.S.-based firms have more affiliates with 100 percent ownership,[21] a form of ownership permitted in China in the Special Economic Zones. There are indications that it is also becoming possible in other parts of China, in exceptional cases. It is reported that Minnesota Mining and Manufacturing Company, now engaged in negotiations to process and market electrical insulating tape in China, is interested not in a joint venture but in sole proprietorship. The reason for the preference is that is does not want to transfer technology, nor does it want to export the products made in China. From the Chinese point of view, 100 percent foreign ownership of domestic production may still be preferable to having to import the product. Allowing sole ownership may pave the way for cooperation in other products.[22]

The degree of flexibility and latitude ascribed to foreign investment is already noticeable in the Special Economic Zones (Shenzhen, Shekou, Zhuhai, and Xiamen). These zones are specially designed to attract foreign enterprise. There are concessions in such areas as taxes, and foreign enterprises are the main actors. Their treatment can be tailored to fit their requirements, without fear that the tail may wag the dog as in foreign enterprises elsewhere in China. These zones are also showplaces. Every effort has been made to make their administration as efficient as possible. In Shenzhen, for example, virtually the entire administration has been changed. The majority of the workers have been recruited from all over China. Those who prove unsuitable can be sent out of the zone. Furthermore, the forms of cooperation are more flexible than elsewhere and much of the uncertainty that surrounds control and administration by foreign investors may be removed.[23]

A further increase in the degree of flexibility accorded to foreign enterprises operating in the Special Economic Zones may be expected in the near future. The removal of the main customs and immigration control services of Shenzhen from the border between Shenzhen and Hong Kong to the boundary line between Shenzhen and the rest of China, expected to be effected shortly, should permit a greater degree of influence by the management style of Hong Kong and integration with activities there.

The introduction in the new Chinese constitution at the end of 1982 of the concept of special-administration areas in which the capitalist system can be maintained points to further possibilities for flexibility, with respect to not only these areas but also the Special Economic Zones, especially Shekou and Shenzhen since they are contiguous to Hong Kong; this innovation is connected to the desired eventual unification of Macao, Hong Kong, and Taiwan with China. A consequence of these developments is that in China not only is the precise nature of foreign investment different from that in other countries but also that it is going through a process of change. The factors that influence the choice of the particular form of cooperation, such as joint venture, are also in a state of flux. There is therefore no substitute for up-to-date analysis of each particular case.

Reverse Flows

According to the traditional theory of international capital flow, there should be no Chinese investment abroad since China is capital poor. There are in fact many reasons why such investment takes place. First, while a joint venture or direct investment is difficult to negotiate and operate in China, Chinese investment abroad is not. The former becomes an entity in China and must operate within the Chinese institutional and legal framework; the latter is an entity within the country concerned and is subject to its laws and regulations, which are generally relatively liberal in market economies.

The main obstacle to such activities was a lack of reciprocity, before diplomatic relations were normalized and trade agreements signed. Once the political hurdles had been overcome, Chinese involvement did not arouse much concern or resentment, as in the case of foreign takeovers or domination by Arab investors, since the scope and scale of Chinese operations is still very limited.

An immediate reason for Chinese investment abroad is that in some industries the Chinese possess certain comparative advantages. A notable example is the provision of Chinese food. A number of Chinese restaurants have been established in New York, Washington, and Tokyo, where Chinese food is already well known and numerous restaurants specializing in Chinese food have long been established. The most common restaurant arrangement is a joint venture, in which the Chinese provide the chefs and native ingredients while the local partner provides the capital and management. The Chinese do not actually make any investment abroad although they do sometimes receive a portion of the profit. These restaurants are not in direct competition with other local Chinese restaurants, since they specialize in regional cuisine complete with regional produce shipped in quantity directly from China in containers. They also concentrate on the high-price segment of the market. Such restaurants are being established in other cities of the world.[24]

Another area of Chinese investment abroad is wholesale and retail vending of Chinese-food products. While most of these activities are still in the hands of foreign enterprises, some are beginning to be established by the Chinese or in cooperation with local entrepreneurs, especially overseas Chinese. These ventures may be extended to food packaging and processing.

Inasmuch as tariff rates in the importing countries escalate with the degree of processing, the shipment of certain Chinese goods for further packaging, assembling, or processing in these countries can reduce tariffs. This should apply to engineering products as well as consumer items. The use of free-trade zones in the importing countries in this connection should also reduce costs.

Another reason for the Chinese to engage in joint ventures abroad is to gain direct contact with the users of Chinese products. One joint venture in the United States in textiles intended to bypass middlemen has recently been dissolved, however, since the entrenched forces proved too strong to overcome.[25] It should be possible to retain the Chinese tradition of not abandoning old friends and at the same time have a more direct understanding of the nature of end-users.

A further reason for Chinese investment abroad is the acquisition of technology. This is an alternative to licensing or foreign direct investment in China. It is especially applicable to technology in the hands of inventors or individuals without much capital or business experience, in which cases the Chinese provide most of the capital as well as managerial expertise.

As far as service industries are concerned, many are global in character. With the expansion of the Chinese economy, the global activities of Chinese shipping, banking, and insurance concerns have also expanded. The Bank of China has overseas branches in London, Singapore, Luxembourg, and Hong Kong.[26] It has actively participated in loan syndications.[27] A joint venture in insurance has been established in the Bahamas, which has been chosen for reasons of convenience.[28] As the Chinese develop their exports of manufactures, the establishment of service centers abroad will be greatly needed. The importance of these centers for foreign manufactures in China has already been recognized, and many such centers established there.

Although Chinese investment in Hong Kong and Macao is strictly speaking not foreign investment since China considers both territories to be Chinese, it is certainly different from investment in other parts of China. The Portuguese have officially renounced their sovereignty over the territory of Macao but at the request of the Chinese continue to administer it. It is well known that on major issues the Chinese view is decisive, although it is communicated to the Macao administration through informal channels.

So far, the economy of Macao remains a satellite of Hong Kong. Most of the tourists and the investment originate in Hong Kong, and the few industries in Macao are closely related to Hong Kong as well. A main reason for locating some textile industries in Macao is to overcome quota limitations imposed on Hong Kong exports.

Following the official Chinese stand that Chinese sovereignty over Hong Kong is nonnegotiable, the status of Macao should in the future converge with that of Hong Kong. In the meantime, Macao is not subject to the same political uncertainties as Hong Kong. There are already signs of greater economic activity there, which should be accompanied by increased investment from China.

The active participation of China in virtually every aspect of economic activity in Hong Kong is evident. Many Chinese firms and joint ventures have long been established.[29] Indeed, the transformation of Hong Kong from what was predominantly an entrepôt into an industrial center was spearheaded by the Bank of China. The bank was the first to recognize the potential of Hong Kong as an industrial base. It was instrumental in the establishment of textile firms in Hong Kong in the 1940s before other banks saw fit to depart from the traditional short-term loans of the commercial banks.[30]

The Chinese retail outlets are also well established in Hong Kong. They serve not only the local population but also tourists from all parts of the world. They therefore act as indirect exporters to other areas as well as advertisers of Chinese products.

What is significant is that the Chinese have given clear signs in favor of continued and increased use of Hong Kong. The claim of Chinese sovereignty and the prospective change in the administration of the territory have not diminished the role of Hong Kong as seen by China. Evidence of China's intent has been forthcoming time and time again in various activities. The rail, road, and shipping links between Hong Kong and China are being constantly improved. Expensive land has been purchased by the Chinese for the expansion of office facilities and real estate development. Joint ventures for industrial activities, such as cement, have been established. All these activities provide a stepping stone for extended operations elsewhere in the world as well as a training ground for modernization in China. At the same time, because of the peculiar relation between China and Hong Kong and the inevitable change in this relationship, the precise meaning and implication of the many forms of cooperation in Hong Kong is also subject to reinterpretation.

The Choice Matrices

The refinements of theory and the complications of Chinese practice may appear unduly complex and diffused. It is useful, therefore to recapitulate the central themes so that the principal lines of argument will stand out. This can best be accomplished in a matrix presentation.

The Matrix of Substance and Form

The matrix in table 4-1 shows the matching of substance and form. The substance or the principal ingredients provided by transnationals are listed in the row and the forms of cooperation are enumerated in the column. It should be noted that the forms are worded from the point of view of the host country, appropriate conversion should be made if the matrix is to be looked at from the corporate viewpoint. For example, host-country import of plant and equipment is equal to transnational-corporation export of the same, and so on. These categories are not unique nor exhaustive. Some economists, for example, would prefer to list production and process technology in substance. Design may be a separate category from both trademark and know-how. Franchising can be added to the list of forms.

Two points are evident in the matrix. First, both depackaging and complete packaging are extreme cases. The former refers to a form of cooperation that has only a single ingredient, as in the upper portion of the matrix; the latter refers to the classic case of foreign direct investment in a branch office, which has all the ingredients. Even this presentation exaggerates the purity of the forms. As has been shown, even simple export or import, especially for a developing country like China, often involves some other ingredient such as foreign know-how. At the same time, foreign direct investment may not involve all the ingredients. For example, finance may be obtained locally. Access to export markets may be irrelevant for import-substituting industries. Moreover, in less pure forms, the presence of particular ingredients is not only variable but also differs in degree. Many variants of the matrix can thus be presented to reflect these variations. Both the possibilities and the degree of presence can, for example, be denoted by probability coefficients or size indicators (for example, they can be graphically represented by different sizes or numbers of stars or periods).

Second, many forms of cooperation are mixed packages, which are neither completely depackaged nor completely packaged; that is, they involve more than one ingredient though not all the ingredients, as shown in the lower middle portion of the matrix. There are many variations of the theme, as indicated by the possible presence of certain ingredients to a greater or lesser extent. Many of these possibilities are not explicitly shown in the figure. For example, processing of imported materials or intermediary products may also involve foreign finance and know-how. If all these possibilities were shown, the mixed packages would be very numerous and would predominate in the figure. Furthermore, because of the numerous

Table 4-1
The Matrix of Substance and Form

Host Country	Capital	Finance	Patent/Trademark	Know-how	Management	Access to Export Market
Import of plant and equipment	*					
Foreign credit		*				
Licensing			*			
Consulting				*		
Management contract					*	
Export						*
Processing of imported material for export			...		...	*
Processing of imported intermediate products for export			...		...	*
Export of goods with foreign designs			*			*
Export of goods with foreign trademark			*			*
Counterpurchase	*					*
Compensation trade	*	*				*
Leasing	*	*				
Import of complete plant	*		...	...	...	
Produit en main	*	...	...	*	*	
Coproduction	*	*	...	*	*	
Joint venture	...	...	...	...	...	...
Foreign branch office	*	*	*	*	*	*

Note: An asterisk, *, denotes the presence of a particular substance (capital, and so on).

Three dots, . . . , denote possible presence, or presence in some degree, of a particular substance.

possibilities of combinations of different forms, the dividing line between individual forms is not clear.

The policy implication for the host country is clear: concentration on a particular form or a few forms of cooperation is generally unwise. Sometimes the concentration is self-imposed, and sometimes it is a result of interactions. To illustrate, the host country may prohibit certain forms. It may consider certain other forms particularly desirable while the transnationals do not. For instance, India was interested in direct investment by IBM provided IBM would transfer the technology, and by Coca Cola if Coca Cola would disclose its secret formula for making the syrup, but the transnationals were not interested under these conditions and decided to liquidate their investments there. These considerations are further brought out in the following section.

The Matrix of Costs and Benefits

The matrix in table 4-2 shows the costs and benefits of each form from the point of view of transnational corporations. In order to facilitate comparison with table 4-1, the wording of forms is unchanged; a mental conversion of the descriptions into corporate viewpoint may be helpful (host-country import is equivalent to transnational export, and so on). The assigned costs and benefits are for illustrative purposes only, since they would vary with the host country, the industry, the technology, and the scale of operations concerned, as well as with the strategy and skill of the corporation. For example, in the early days of the opening up of China, even simple trade was difficult to negotiate because of difficulties of communication and in securing visas. The operating cost to the transnational corporation of any arrangement is directly affected by host country's administrative practices. Vulnerability to disputes may be especially high in the case of natural resources if national control and the environment are serious concerns in the host country. Risk of the dissipation of standard technology has a meaning different from the same risk for new proprietary technology. Various rates of return can be found in individual cases for any form.

Nevertheless, the matrix in table 4-2 illustrates a host of cost and benefit considerations associated with each form. It also suggests the effect on the choice of forms if the costs and benefits are altered, especially by host country policies. Obviously, if costs are lowered and benefits are increased for a particular form, that form's attractiveness to the transnational corporation will be increased.

From the point of view of the host country, apart from the fact that the perspective of the transnational corporations should be taken into account,

Table 4-2
The Matrix of Costs and Benefits[1]

Host Country	Cost			Risk of Loss	Risk of Dissipation	Return
	Negotiating	Operating	Dispute			
Import of plant and equipment	L	L	L	L	L	L
Foreign credit	L	L	L	L	L	L
Licensing	H	H	M	L	M	M
Consulting	L	L	L	L	L	L
Management contract	L	L	L	L	L	L
Export	L	L	L	L	L	L
Processing of imported material for export	L	M	M	M	L	M
Processing of imported intermediate products for export	L	M	M	M	L	M
Export of goods with foreign designs	L	M	M	M	L	M
Export of goods with foreign trademark	L	M	M	M	L	M
Counterpurchase	L	M	L	M	L	M
Compensation trade	L	M	M	L	L	M
Leasing	L	L	L	L	L	L
Import of complete plant	L	M	L	L	L	M
Produit en main	L	M	L	L	L	M
Coproduction	M	M	M	M	M	M
Joint venture	H	H	H	H	L	HL
Foreign branch office	H	L	H	H	L	HL

Note: H denotes high; L denotes low; M denotes medium; HL denotes either high or low.

[1] Transnational-corporation viewpoint.

most of the considerations in the matrix are also relevant. Some considerations are similar. For example, negotiating difficulties apply both to the host country and to the transnational corporation. Their deterrent power differs, however, between corporations with a long-term strategy and those with a short-term strategy. A transnational may be more patient or less patient with these difficulties than the host country. Some costs and benefits may have the opposite effects for the host country and the transnationals. The dissipation of information on technology by the transnational, for instance, is a gain for the host country. But it should not be assumed that a loss for the transnational corporation is necessarily a gain for the host country since the cooperative arrangement is hopefully not a zero-sum game.

The considerations in the choice of the particular forms of cooperation and thus the relative importance of each form in China will change as the modernization process proceeds. As suggested earlier, the usefulness of some forms, such as compensation trade, will decrease as the Chinese gain more knowledge about export marketing. Licensing of high technology will increase when China has a greater capacity to absorb it or to offer cross-licensing. Yet it is unlikely that China will revert to the use of only a few forms, such as the turnkey imports of the early days, and deprive itself of the benefit of many other forms. Nor is it likely that the dynamics will result in a definite phasing, as postulated in the product life cycle, since, even if the theory operated, the aggregate situation in China for numerous product groups would permit the coexistence of numerous forms. Many new forms will evolve to enrich the variety of arrangements and will suit better with the requirements of the time.

5   The Policy Framework

The definition of the role of transnational corporations in China's modernization and the choice of forms of cooperation with those corporations imply certain policies. China's relations with transnational corporations reflect not only the strategies of the transnationals or of the entities directly concerned but also the policy framework, which is shaped by many actors. Obviously, the transnationals do not operate in a vacuum, they are influenced by host and home-government policies as well as by the general external environment. The present chapter describes the most notable features of these influences.

Chinese Policies

The first task in the formulation of policy toward transnationals is to determine the boundary lines within which they are permitted to operate and the priority areas. A decision must also be made on the organizational arrangements for implementing the policy. In terms of method, a choice must be made between laying down general guidelines and case-by-case negotiations, although in practice the dividing line tends to be blurred. The former method is the concern of this chapter, while the latter is dealt with in the next.

The Love-Hate Stance

China's stance toward transnational corporations, like that of most developing countries, is neither unequivocally positive nor uncompromisingly negative. The former posture would mean that all transnational activities were regarded as beneficial, while the latter would be based on a diametrically opposite conclusion. The middle ground constitutes an acknowledgement that both positive and negative elements may potentially be present. It is a love-hate stance, that reflects the intensity of feeling about possible opposite effects. To the Chinese, the positive side is a new discovery, while the negative side is rooted in a generation of Marxian persuasion.

As is true of most developing countries, a chief concern of China is sovereignty. Transnationals are excluded from certain activities that are reserved for nationals. In China, the exclusions are not explicitly stated in a code for transnationals or in similar laws and regulations such as an investment code, but are revealed chiefly in actual practice. This is largely because any dealing with transnationals comes under the purview of some government agency, so that internal guidelines are generally adequate. As relations with transnationals grow more extensive and more complex, however, the guidelines tend to be spelled out, as is shown later. Another explanation of the relative lack of concern for drawing a sharp demarcation line for transnationals is that the Chinese are in a better position to be flexible than other host countries, since the activities of transnationals can be carefully controlled or monitored. Even industries normally considered sensitive, such as defense and natural resources, do not necessarily have to be off limits to all transnationals.

As far as priorities are concerned, administrators of a planned economy have the advantage of knowing its strategy and where transnationals may fit into it. Yet events in the last few years have shown that priorities may be drastically changed. Current slogans on priorities are often adopted in order to correct existing imbalances, and should not be interpreted too literally. For example, the stated priorities in the order of agriculture, light industry, and heavy industry do not necessarily imply that the degree of preferred involvement of transnationals will be in that order. Indeed, by 1982, when readjustment between light and heavy industries had already achieved much of its goal, heavy industry was again growing at a faster rate than light industry.

Even more detailed statements of policy emphasis should be interpreted flexibly. For example, the sectors identified for cooperation with foreign enterprises by the Vice-Minister of Foreign Economic Relations and Trade in June, 1982, are as follows: (1) energy development; (2) light industry, textile industry, food industry, pharmaceuticals, telecommunication, and electronics industry; (3) building materials, machinery, iron and steel, and chemical industry; (4) agriculture, animal husbandry, and stock-raising and -breeding projects; (5) tourism.[1] Although the list covers much ground, it is by no means exhaustive. Numerous cooperative projects, such as in nonferrous metals, aircraft, and shipping as mentioned in chapter 3, are not meant to be excluded.

The 1982 announcement of the long-postponed Chinese Sixth Five-Year Plan indicates the renewed importance attached to planning. An important implication for transnationals is that their activities must be coordinated with the Plan. That does mean a certain order of priorities. It also means that decision making on the Chinese side may involve a large number of people. In cases involving transnationals, especially in large projects, the effect on the plan may be far-reaching. Failure to implement these projects once approved will have disastrous results for the performance of the entire plan. This is one reason why the Chinese bureaucracy is perceived as being reluctant to accept responsibility and take risks. Bureaucratic delays in dealings with transnationals are often more serious in China than in many other economies where there is less emphasis on national planning.

Streamlining the organizations responsible for dealings with transnationals is one way of alleviating the bureaucratic impasse. The establishment of the Ministry of Foreign Economic Relations and Trade, combining the functions of two ministries and two commissions, is a step in this direction. The services offered by the China Council for the Promotion of International Trade (CCPIT) and the China International Trust and Investment Corporation (CITIC) in helping transnationals to make appropriate contacts also facilitate the procedure. At the same time, in light of the vast geographical span of China, a truly one-stop organization for transnationals is hardly appropriate even though it has proved very popular in small countries. In China such an organization would have to be very large; it would need to be extremely centralized and capable of constant communication with the various parties concerned. Local initiative might be stifled and lines of communication would remain weak. The Chinese answer to conflicting demands for centralization and decentralization is a compromise. In general, the local authorities are given autonomy for relatively small projects. A few regions, notably Guangdong and Fuqian, and the Special Economic Zones are granted certain powers to make decisions in foreign dealings. Other areas such as Shanghai and Hainan may be added from time to time, though they may not be endowed with the same powers. In addition, the organization of national corporations along industry lines, such as shipping and automobiles, has facilitated the coordination of activities between regions. A few corporations, such as Capital Iron and Steel Corporation and Wuhan Iron and Steel, have been given authority to deal directly with foreign enterprises.

The Screening Criteria

The criteria for screening foreign trade and investment proposals are couched in very general terms. This is in contrast with many developing countries, where such criteria are spelled out in detail. In Colombia, for example, the criteria include sector priority; contribution to balance of payments, employment, and technology; the promotion of local participation, competition, and Latin American integration; the stabilizing impact on prices of consumer goods; the location of industry outside the city; export diversification; and contribution to fiscal resources.[2] Spelling out the criteria in this way has the advantage of guiding transnational corporations into activities that are considered useful and welcome. It helps them to avoid wasteful preparations that will ultimately be rejected. The criteria also serve as a guide to the bureaucracy in administering the screening of the transnationals, minimize the degree of arbitrariness in foreign trade and investment, and avoid inconsistency.

In practice, though, not all the above advantages are realized. First, there is the index-number problem. The Colombian case illustrates the difficulty of weighing a host of criteria. A transnational's contribution to the balance of payments, for example, is difficult to weigh against the choice of a desirable location. Furthermore, the contribution may be thousands of dollars or hundreds of thousands of dollars. Second, the precise extent to which a given project conforms to the criteria is often difficult to measure. The quantification of contribution to Latin American integration is a case in point. Even for such quantifiable criteria as balance-of-payments contribution, the administrators usually concentrate on direct foreign-exchange earnings and outlays and neglect the indirect effects. Serious distortions may therefore arise. Even if the indirect effects are explicitly taken into account, there is still considerable uncertainty as to exactly how they should be estimated since different models and assumptions will yield differing results. Last, in view of the lack of sophistication of the administrators in most developing countries, actual administration is likely to be guided by rules of thumb. The possibility of errors can be cumulative. For this reason, even in the case of a relatively developed country, such as Canada, the criteria for foreign investment may simply be reduced to the overall contribution to the economy. Thus, the process has come full circle, from generality to specification and back to generality.

In the Chinese practice, several principles have of course been clearly stated. One is equality, and another is mutual benefit. It is argued in the next chapter that equality does not imply equal bargaining power. Nor does mutual benefit imply that the division of gains is fifty-fifty. The principle of equality does, however, indicate the willingness of the Chinese to be fair. Simultaneously, the Chinese believe in a united front in dealings with foreign enterprises. At the Canton Fair, for instance, when the Chinese discovered that several Chinese suppliers were bidding against each other, they recentralized the bidding process. They are at the same time wary of the monopolistic possibilities when foreign enterprises combine in their dealings with China. Even the passing of information on the negotiating experience from one transnational to another is considered unfair.[3]

A corollary of the principle of mutual benefit is the recognition that foreign enterprises must be permitted to make a reasonable profit. This is in itself significant, since profit was a dirty word in China until recently. But the Chinese are certainly not about to guarantee the profitability of foreign enterprises; nor will they make up losses. There is, however, a uniquely Chinese practice whereby the loss of the foreign partner is compensated indirectly if the Chinese feel they are somehow responsible. If a loss were to be caused by a delay in the shipment of Chinese produce, even if the contract does not specify a penalty, the Chinese often volunteer compensation through various forms of concession such as price discounts in subsequent transactions. The

Chinese are reluctant to pay a specific penalty since that would place explicit blame on those involved.

Following the ill fate of some poorly prepared projects, the Chinese now insist on conducting feasibility studies for foreign projects. This is of course the normal procedure followed by private corporations and international lending institutions, as well as by government planning agencies elsewhere. The concept is still relatively new in China; in fact, only two or three years ago, such studies were regarded as capitalist country practices. The major problem now in carrying out these studies is lack of basic data and trained personnel. The absence of basic conditions for serious feasibility studies in turn makes it difficult to evaluate the soundness of these studies.

The Regulatory Framework

Prior to the current reforms, the regulatory framework was fairly simple and straightforward. Transnational corporations were virtually nonexistent in China. All foreign trade was under the control of the foreign trade corporations. These corporations were under the jurisdiction of the Ministry of Foreign Trade and the division of responsibility was by the product. The product groups are:

staple foods

processed foodstuffs

chemicals

packaging materials

photographic equipment, printing equipment, domestic appliances, sporting goods, and other light industrial goods

machinery of all kinds

metals and minerals

cottage-industry products, beverages, and miscellaneous agricultural and foodstuff products excluding staples

process licenses, turnkey imports

fabrics, yarns, garments, and other textile products.[4]

The foreign-trade corporations were the exclusive channels for communication and business arrangements with foreign enterprises. The policies and rules governing their operations were rarely made public and could only be guessed at from limited experience.

The movement towards greater reliance on legal institutions has taken place recently, especially in areas affecting foreign enterprises. This has been necessitated by the increase in the volume and variety of dealings with these enterprises. No longer limited to imports and exports, dealings take many forms including joint ventures, coproduction, compensation trade, and so on, as discussed in chapter 4. Many of these forms are new and more complicated, and some are controversial domestically. Even after the Chinese government has made a decision in principle, many details still have to be specified. For example, although joint ventures with foreign enterprises are permitted, exactly how they should be treated remains to be defined. From the point of view of foreign enterprises, questions of predictability naturally arise. These enterprises like to know what is involved before they plunge in. A series of laws and regulations have thus been promulgated. They include:

law on joint ventures

regulations on the registration of joint ventures

regulations on labor management in joint ventures

income-tax law on joint ventures

law of economic contracts

regulations on the exploitation of offshore petroleum resources in cooperation with foreign enterprises

laws of Special Economic Zones

regulations on Special Economic Zones in Guangdong.[5]

In spite of the proliferation of new laws and regulations relating to foreign enterprises, their adequacy has often been questioned.[6] First, many proposed laws are not as yet in existence. A patent law is still in the drafting stage, while other laws may not even be drafted for a long time.

Second, even where laws already exist, many questions are unanswered until detailed regulations are issued. The Chinese consider the answers self-evident, while the legally minded foreign enterprises do not. On March 8, 1982, for example, the Foreign Investment Commission was absorbed into the newly created Ministry of Foreign Economic Relations and Trade. But the joint-venture law was not amended to reflect the reorganization. Foreign enterprises raised questions as to the legal authority of the new ministry to exercise the power of the commission provided for in the joint-venture law. It was not until about a year later that an explicit ruling was made by the Standing Committee of the People's Congress to reflect the change.[7] Many problems of omission or lack of clarity are being remedied by specific provisions in contracts. The Chinese have in fact advised foreign enterprises not to wait until all laws and regulations are completed before acting. Contractual provisions will be enforced during the lifetime of the contract even if they should conflict with subsequent laws and regulations.

Third, the way in which new laws will be implemented is largely unknown. Foreign enterprises often find the wording too imprecise. Even where it appears to be clear, the Chinese may interpret it in their own way. According to the individual income-tax law, for example, tax liability is limited to persons residing in China for a minimum period. The Chinese have ruled that an individual who has been issued a visa for longer than the minimum period is a resident and is subject to the tax even though he has been in and out of China during the period and the total number of days of actual residence is below the minimum. When this was disputed, the Chinese were able to cite internal rulings to support the interpretation, but the rulings were not publicized and were known only to the tax authorities.

Fourth, disputes can, in theory, be settled in court. The United States government has, for example, advised U.S. individuals or corporations to make use of the Chinese courts. There have actually been few cases, however, and there remains a great degree of uncertainty as to how courts will rule in any given case.

The above again illustrates that where new arrangements are made, new problems emerge. Most of these problems are inevitable. The theoretical solution that all the relevant laws and regulations should be enacted simultaneously is not feasible. Neither is it desirable, since without actual experience or precedent the implications of specific provisions are little known even to the lawmakers. Many questions can be raised with respect to the relationship with transnational corporations. How are their activities to be monitored? By whom? What are the disclosure requirements? What is the definition of restrictive business practices? In what way are they controlled? Evidently, answers to some of these are extremely involved and require very detailed procedures. A declaration of general principles is hardly adequate.

Partner-Country Policies

Although China's opening to the rest of the world has generally been greeted with enthusiasm by its partner countries, including the home countries of transnational corporations, the policies adopted by these countries have been uneven. Many measures have been introduced by partner countries to facilitate business relations with China. Most of these are bilateral, such as agreements on trade, on export credit, and on political risk insurance. Bilateral economic or trade and commerce commissions have been set up to review developments and air views. Some instruments are still being negotiated, for example, investment agreements and tax agreements. Of increasing concern to Chinese business, however, are restrictive policies of partner countries, especially those concerning the export of technology and nontariff barriers. These obstacles raise major issues for the entire international-trade regime and the international monetary system, as well as the rules concerning international investment.

Trading Arrangements

Bilateral trade agreements have two major functions. One is to provide a general framework within which trade may take place. This is often supplemented by a series of specific agreements. The United States, for example, has agreements with China on consular activities, civil aviation, shipping, technology, and the like. The second function is to set specific targets for mutual trade. This is prevalent with partners that have planned economies. For many developing countries, especially where foreign exchange is scarce and currencies not convertible, the setting of specific targets for exchange may amount to a barter agreement. The Chinese have also used this vehicle to extend indirect aid to some developing countries by specifying terms of trade more favorable to the partner than those prevailing in the market. This has been the case, for example, with the supply of oil to Thailand and the Philippines.

For countries with multicolumn tariffs, bilateral trade agreements usually provide for most-favored-nation treatment. Most developed countries have, in addition, accorded preferential tariff treatment to China in line with the Generalized System of Preferences (GSP).[8] The United States has not yet accorded such preference to China. The Sino-U.S. trade agreement does provide for this eventuality by classifying China as a developing country, but preference is contingent upon China's membership in the General Agreement on Tariffs and Trade, to which China has recently become an observer.

The value of the preferential scheme to China depends on four variables. The first is the margin of preference. This margin has tended to decrease as a result of a series of tariff cuts, especially among developed countries. When the tariff reductions negotiated in the Tokyo Round are fully implemented, by 1987, the average tariff rates will be further reduced. This erosion should not be a general argument against preference, since without preference the Chinese as well as other developing countries will be disadvantaged in comparison with many countries which have regional and other special arrangements. Certainly the Chinese will be discriminated against if they do not enjoy preference while other developing countries do.

The second determining factor is the capacity or potential to utilize the preference. In comparison with most other developing countries, the Chinese are in a relatively good position since their manufacturing sector is relatively well established. Even for less-industrialized developing countries the benefit of preference should not be underestimated, since it is the potential that is important in the process of development. The potential can be augmented with the help of transnational corporations or other external infusion of necessary ingredients in strategic scarcity.

Third, and for the same reason, numerous categories in which the Chinese have comparative advantage are either excluded from the scheme or severely limited. This is done sometimes by tariff quotas, whereby imports above a certain amount do not enjoy preferential rates.

The fourth consideration is price elasticity. It is true that major obstacles to exports from China do not arise simply from price considerations because others, such as supply bottlenecks, quality, design, and delivery, are often more important. Yet many of the manufactures and semimanufactures that the Chinese are capable of exporting are standard medium or low-price items. They are usually price competitive. The sharp rise of exports to the United States following the application of the most-favored-nation clause is indicative of the importance of price competition.

On the whole, despite a certain erosion in the value of preferential schemes, the Chinese will continue to benefit from them. This is especially true if the services of transnationals are used to overcome supply rigidities in utilizing the schemes.

Export Credit

Most of China's major partner countries extend official export credit at rates below market.[9] In order to avoid competitive export credit wars, the countries in the Organization for Economic Cooperation and Development (OECD) have agreed on guidelines for a floor rate and other terms. In fact, strict adherence to the floor rate is in some doubt. It is sometimes argued that the terms of export credit from different OECD countries may differ because the exchange risk is different since some currencies may be expected to appreciate in relation to others. In any case, when official export credit is combined with more concessionary development loans, the total package can be on easier terms than the OECD guidelines. This is the case with Japan.[10] The government-to-government loans from such countries as Belgium and Denmark are in fact interest-free. United States Export-Import Bank credit was made possible in April, 1980, by a presidential determination that such credit was in the national interest as required by the Export-Import Bank Act. However, at the time of this writing, Export-Import Bank facilities to the People's Republic are still subject to an annual waiver, despite attempts to remove the requirement. Moreover, a special national-interest determination

must be obtained from the President and reported to Congress for any transaction in excess of $50 million.[11]

Political Risk Insurance

The possibility of political risk in doing business with China is readily
recognized. Opinions differ with respect to the degree of likelihood of specific
risks and the effect. Various probabilities may be attached to leadership
stability, policy disputes, and trends in Chinese bureaucracy and society at
large.[12] Such risk is increasingly evaluated by business analysts,[13] and some of
the results are regularly published.[14] When this analysis is applied to actual
situations, account will have to be taken of differential effect on types of activity and on industry. For instance, equity investment may be more vulnerable than trade, and natural resources more than consumer-goods industry.
In addition, risk may be mitigated by precautionary measures.

Political-risk insurance for doing business with China is available from
private and public sources. In the private sector, Lloyds of London and the
American International Group both offer a full line of export and investment
guarantees against political risk.[15] In the public sector, export guarantees are
generally made by official export-import banks. In the United States, export
credit risk can be covered by the Foreign Credit Insurance Association, which
is composed of some fifty insurance companies in cooperation with the
Export-Import Bank of the United States. Investment risk in China is in-
surable by the Overseas Private Investment Corporation (OPIC) since the
signing of an agreement between the United States and China in 1980.[16] In
contrast to private insurers, OPIC does not differentiate between degrees of
political risk in setting its insurance premiums. The People's Insurance Company of China (PICC) also writes political risk and contract-failure insurance. Inasmuch as PICC is itself a government corporation, some analysts
have raised questions about its suitability for covering political risk incurred
through its own government.

Political risk may also be reduced by an intergovernmental bilateral investment agreement. Such an agreement was signed between Sweden and China
in 1982, and negotiations for one are currently under way between the
United States and China. This demonstrates China's intention to protect
foreign investment, not only with respect to questions of expropriation and
nationalization but also with respect to mutually acceptable procedures for
settling disputes.

Nontariff Barriers

Offsetting the trend toward liberalization of tariffs, nontariff barriers to
imports from China have tended to become more severe. The main excep-

tion is Japan, which has responded to strong pressures from its major partners to ease the barriers. The nontariff barriers range from buy-national provisions to customs procedures, labeling requirements, food and drug regulations, and import quotas. In part, this tendency reflects the long-run structural problem of some industries that have lost their competitiveness in these countries. In recent years, it has been aggravated by serious short-term unemployment problems and the general attempt to export unemployment to other countries. Many of these barriers have a long history and are little noticed. In the United States, many agricultural commodities are subject to import restrictions. No seeds can be imported, for instance. The new variety of rice that Occidental Petroleum licensed from China has to be produced in the United States.

Some of the long-standing nontariff measures can be eased or tightened by administrative measures in order to convey a particular message. When the Japanese refused to reduce exports of cars to Canada, Canadian customs began to inspect one car out of ten instead of the usual one in a hundred. Although the new procedure was temporary, the Japanese acknowledged that the point had been made.[17] France's requirement that documents must be in French may be so administered as to refuse clearance for any product with English markings.[18] The French procedure that all imports of videotape recorders should clear customs at a small and distant place, Poitiers, was clearly aimed at the Japanese. The object was not so much to protect domestic industry as to convey the message that the Japanese must soften their nontariff restrictions such as import inspection and certification requirements.[19]

The Chinese are especially vulnerable to nontariff barriers for three reasons. First, because of the state trading system in China, critics often maintain that China can export without reference to actual cost. Moreover, the Chinese market can be closed to foreign competition through state control. Consequently there are questions about what is fair competition. Second, Chinese exports are relative newcomers to most of these foreign markets. Their recent successes in penetrating these markets often appear alarming. Some competitors are undoubtedly being affected. When quotas for Chinese exports are negotiated, they are usually based on the historical record, which does not reflect present capability or future potential. Third, the Chinese are unfamiliar with nontariff barriers and even less experienced in overcoming them.

These problems are amply illustrated by recent developments. In the United States, several antidumping cases have involved China.[20] Antidumping procedures can be brought by anyone who complains that imports are being sold in the United States at less than fair value. Escape-clause action—Section 201(b) of the Trade Act—and injury to domestic industry action—Section 406(a)—have also been invoked.

In one case involving clothespins, the domestic producer filing the complaint of injury was a small enterprise. The proceedings against the Chinese imports resulted in the imposition of quotas.[21] The work-glove case illustrates the nuisance value of a complaint even though there was little merit in the case.[22]

The menthol case was the first to give the Chinese cause for serious concern about the implications of an adverse decision under the antidumping law. Accordingly, the Chinese engaged a law firm, Sherman and Sterling, to represent them, as well as consultants to do research on the case. This practice set the pattern for subsequent antidumping cases.

The U.S. International Trade Commission (ITC) unanimously decided[23] that there was no material injury to United States industry, despite the Department of Commerce finding that menthol from China was sold in the United States at less than fair value. The decision was aided by convincing arguments put forward by the attorneys for the China National Native Produce and Animal By-Products Import and Export Corporation.[24] Their arguments pointed out that the petitioner, Haarmann and Reimer Corporation, began production of synthetic menthol in 1978 using an expensive technology. The Chinese exports to the United States were natural menthol. They were not at the expense of synthetic menthol, but represented a partial substitution for Brazilian and other imports in the United States market. The Commerce Department finding was countered by the fact that the Chinese export price was higher than China's home-market price, and the small margin relative to the Paraguayan price—a surrogate for domestic price—disappeared in the second quarter of 1980.

In May, 1982, the American Dinnerware Emergency Committee petitioned the ITC for relief from increased imports from China.[25] Importers of China porcelainware, in cooperation with the China National Arts and Crafts Import and Export Corporation, argued that imports of Chinese earthenware sales in the United States, that the procelainware imports had not significantly affected total U.S. imports in that category but had merely substituted for the low end of Japanese imports, and that the domestic earthenware industry had not been injured by Chinese porcelainware. These arguments persuaded the ITC to reject the petition.

In June, 1982, the American Mushroon Institute brought a petition to the ITC claiming injury of domestic industry by Chinese imports. United States mushroom importers joined with the China National Cereals and Oils Import & Export Corporation to argue the case. The ITC was split on the decision; thereafter, the President denied the imposition of quotas against Chinese imports.[26] In October, 1982, an antidumping petition was filed against Chinese mushroom imports. In addition, the American Mushroom Institute called for an orderly marketing arrangement.[27]

In July, 1982, the American Textile Manufacturers Institute requested an antidumping investigation of Chinese piece-goods imports. Action is also possible on a variety of products, including ammonium parantungstate, manhole covers, steel nails, jewelry, and footwear. These cases, whether strong or weak, have an unsettling effect on the expansion of U.S. imports from China. The possible imposition of an antidumping duty on Chinese products poses a significant risk for U.S. importers and users.

It is the imposition of import quotas, however, which is most clearly restrictive. The most important instance is textiles and garments in the major developed markets. On this U.S. position has recently hardened.[28] From the U.S. point of view, imports of textiles and garments have long been an exception to the general tenet of free trade. Import-quota restrictions have been imposed for over twenty years under a series of multilateral fiber arrangements (MFAs) under the auspices of GATT. The main reasons for this posture are, first, that the U.S. textile industry is on the whole labor-intensive. It is a major provider of employment. Unlike some industries such as steel and automobiles, wage levels are relatively low. There is little margin for cost reduction without further unfavorable effects on employment. Second, the industry and the workers are important domestic political forces. Third, the share of imports has tended to increase, affecting especially manufacturers in certain categories. This has continued even after the imposition of import quotas that do not cover all exporters and categories. Fourth, China has rapidly become one of the major exporters. Import restrictions are generally concentrated on these exporters. They are more stringent in other major importing countries, notably the continental countries and the European Community, which accentuates the concentration of imports in the U.S. market.

From the very beginning the Chinese saw no justification for U.S. restriction on imports of Chinese textiles and garments. Apart from the general principle that developed countries should remove obstacles to market access by developing countries, the Chinese drew attention to the relatively small share of Chinese exports in the total U.S. market.[29] The high rate of growth was considered meaningless in view of the very low levels prior to the normalization of relations. Moreover, not only did the United States enjoy a substantial overall export surplus with China, but it also had a surplus for textiles since it was a major source of Chinese natural and synthetic-fiber imports. The negotiations were thus difficult and protracted. It was not until the United States imposed unilateral quotas in 1978 and additional ones in 1979 that the Chinese reluctantly assented to an agreement in 1980.

The agreement set quotas for seven categories, far fewer than those specified for other major suppliers. However, under the consultation clause, the United States may limit Chinese exports to a specified level pending final agreement on a quota.

Negotiations for a new agreement prior to the expiration of the first agreement, at the end of 1982, were even more difficult. This time, the

United States asked for an expanded quota scheme covering twenty-eight categories. It also proposed rates of growth significantly below those of the first agreement, and sought to change the consultation procedure into an automatic mechanism triggering quota restriction. After four rounds of negotiations without an agreement, the United States announced unilateral restrictions on January 15, 1983. Four days later, the Chinese retaliated by banning further purchases in 1983 of cotton, soybeans, and chemical fibers from the United States. An official statement also hinted that China would reduce its planned imports of other American agricultural products. Although the retaliation was more a reflection of anger and frustration than it was an effective counterblow, the acrimonious atmosphere could have broad implications unless it is soon reversed. One difficulty is that the Chinese are afraid that concessions to the United States on textiles and garments may trigger a hardening of positions in other industrial countries. On the other hand, the United States is mindful that a softening of its major position could create difficulties in dealings with other major exporters. After several rounds of negotiations, a new textile agreement was reached in 1983 between the United States and China.

Control of Technology Exports

Exports from the West to communist countries of technology that may be used for military purposes are controlled by the Coordinating Committee on Communist Trade (COCOM) as well as by the national administrations. In exports to China, such control has been influenced by complex forces. China continues to be regarded as a potential adversary because it professes to be a communist nation. At the same time, it is sometimes regarded as a potential ally because of parallel interests as regards the Soviet Union, especially since the invasion of Afghanistan, in December, 1979. In the United States, China was transferred from the Warsaw Pact Country Group Y to a New Country Group P for purposes of export control. The tilt toward China thus became formalized. Selected equipment and technology with possible military applications may be approved for export to China.

Despite the easing of restrictions, China's ambivalent status is reflected in current discussions on U.S. arms exports. On the one hand, an offer has been made allowing China to purchase weapons from the United States. On the other hand, the Commerce Department has approved only a small proportion of the categories in which the Chinese have expressed interest.[32] This reflects the fact that numerous agencies are involved in foreign trade policies. Suggestions have therefore been made for the creation of a single office responsible for such policies.[33]

Apart from the ambivalence of policy, a further complicating factor lies in its administration. Since export control concerns several government departments, especially Commerce and Defense, the need for coordination means that the more stringent department usually has the last word. Inordinate delays in approval have frequently been reported. The IBM computers to be used in the Chinese census, originally scheduled for 1980, were not approved for about two years. This restriction was one reason for the census being delayed until 1982.

A related complication is coordination among the members of COCOM. In most cases, the position of the United States is known to be more stringent than that of other members. Sometimes, however, other members have retaliated against U.S. transnationals because the United States had blocked exports by their transnationals. This raises a series of issues concerning interaction. In the case of nuclear technology, the Chinese decision to go ahead with work on a 300-megawatt nuclear power project outside Shanghai and an 1,800-megawatt station in Guangdong has raised hopes of multibillion dollar business among foreign suppliers.

The Guangdong nuclear-power project was conceived as a joint venture between Guangdong Province and the China Light and Power Company, in Hong Kong. The United Kingdom General Electric Company is being considered as a major supplier of equipment, but it only produces the pressurized-water reactor that the Chinese are interested in under license from Westinghouse. It will not be able to export the reactor without the consent of the United States government.

U.S. officials have initiated discussions with the Chinese for a bilateral nuclear cooperation agreement. Obstacles have arisen in the negotiations because the United States wants an assurance that nuclear exports to China will not get into the hands of nonnuclear or near-nuclear countries. However, China is not a signatory to the Nonproliferation Treaty of 1968. Moreover, China's willingness to permit the inspection of Chinese nuclear installations by outsiders is uncertain. Allegations that the Chinese have failed to keep strict control over the re-export of their nuclear materials to near-nuclear countries have heightened political opposition in the United States to an agreement that does not include strict safeguards against proliferation.

The French involvement in the Chinese nuclear program dates back to 1978. In October, 1980, an agreement in principle was announced for a turnkey project using French finance on concessionary terms. Although the turnkey project has been shelved, French interest in participation in the Guangdong project remains active. The French are apparently more eager to promote their nuclear exports and less concerned than the United States about imposing special safeguards.[35] The issue of U.S. control of technology exports has complicated Sino-American relations. The Chinese have increasingly expressed displeasure over inordinate delays in control procedures, insisting that U.S. firms should be responsible for obtaining export release. The United States government has reported an upsurge in surreptitious Chinese efforts to obtain Western computers and microelectronics technology restricted by COCOM.[36] In June, 1983, the United States announced that technology exports to China will be further eased by treating China on the same basis as other friendly and nonallied countries, such as India and Yugoslavia.

Tax Policy

A basic problem in the taxation of transnationals is that income derived from different countries is subject to different tax jurisdictions. Consequently, a given income may be claimed, or neglected, by more than one tax authority. Among the developed countries, double taxation is usually avoided by bilateral tax agreements, specifying exactly what is to be taxed and by whom. A common measure is that corporate income tax paid to one country, such as by a foreign investor to the host country, may be credited in the home country.[37]

In the absence of tax treaties between China and developed countries, investment decisions by transnational corporations are naturally influenced by tax creditability considerations. Thus, when the Chinese draft their tax laws, they have to see to it that Chinese taxes on transnationals can be credited in the home countries. This has been achieved by informal consultations with U.S. Treasury officials rather than by formal treaties. The Chinese have also sought the advice of tax experts from the transnationals.[38] As a result, the Chinese corporate income taxes generally fulfill the condition of creditability in most developed countries, although questions of interpretation remain. Tax issues will be further clarified when bilateral tax treaties are negotiated between China and the major home countries of transnational corporations. The tax case again illustrates the interdependence of the policies of host and home countries. The influence of the policies of major powers, such as the United States, is striking.

The International Environment

The international environment is more than the sum total of bilateral relations; it also interacts with and shapes these relations. The behavior of countries, which affects transnationals, depends on the nature of the international trade regimes, the international monetary system, and the absence or presence of an international code of conduct on transnationals. China's entry onto the international scene as an important actor raises a host of fundamental issues that demand new attention.

From the point of view of China, also, although the main thrust of the modernization drive must necessarily continue to be national rather than international in orientation, it will be argued that increasing attention must be paid to the implications of, and China's role in, the entire international system. This will be all the more necessary as the system is revamped and the relative weight of China in the international arena increases with the fruits of its modernization efforts.

The International Trade Regime

The international trade regime is at a crossroad. On the one hand, the major trading nations continue to advocate trade liberalization and to uphold the principles of GATT. On the other, the actual implementation of these principles is being questioned more and more. The China factor has introduced two new elements, the first arising from China's socialist system and the second deriving from the recognition that China is still a very poor country and therefore rightly belongs to the developing world.

This dual character raises a series of fundamental issues.[39] In the first instance, the existing regime is predicated mainly upon the existence of three blocs. The first is the developed countries. Despite increasing exceptions, the cardinal rules of trade liberalization apply, by and large, to trade within the bloc. The main reason is that the domestic economies are still dominated by market forces. While beggar-thy-neighbor policies can benefit individual countries, they are increasingly being challenged and prevented from developing into a vicious spiral of trade wars because too much is at stake if seriously interrupted. This applies especially to Western Europe and Japan, whose dependence on the world market is very great.

The second bloc consists of the socialist countries of Europe. Trade among themselves is governed by bilateral arrangements and bloc coordination under the leadership of the Soviet Union. This bloc's relationship with developed-market economies is subject to numerous special arrangements, which include higher tariffs and nontariff measures designed to guard against unfair competition or market disruption in the West.

The third bloc is the developing countries. The relationship between these countries and the developed-market economies is influenced by the spirit of the United Nations Conference on Trade and Development (UNCTAD). Despite numerous exceptions, the developed countries recognize the principle of nonreciprocity in this relationship. The developing countries have great leeway in invoking the infant-industry or balance-of-payments arguments for trade restrictions on their part even while tariffs in the developed market economies are lowered. The developing countries are accorded not only most-favored-nation treatment but also preferential tariffs for their exports. Special treatment for developing countries is also increasingly accepted by GATT.

China, however, is in a class by itself. As a socialist country, its trade relations with the developed market economies are vulnerable to discriminatory treatment. As a developing country, it is eligible for specially favorable treatment. This duality is not unique to China, since there are other developing socialist countries. What makes it special is China's size. As long as China's volume of trade remains limited, the developed-market economies are willing to regard it mainly as a developing country. In a dynamic context, as China's trade relations continue to expand, it will be impossible for them to be as conveniently ignored as trade relations with some smaller countries. Consequently, there is increasing likelihood that attention will be focused on the socialist nature of the Chinese economy.

China's unique qualities pose a new challenge to the design of the future world-trade regime as well as to the policies of individual countries. From the point of view of the major trading nations, a policy of increasing differentiation is likely to be applied in their relations with developing countries. This intention has already been voiced in connection with the newly industrialized economies and is likely to apply more and more to China because of its socialist economy and its size. Thus, China is likely to be called upon to make comparable concessions if it is to enjoy access to the markets of the major trading nations. It will be more difficult, in other words, for it to have a free ride.

In these circumstances, there are a number of helpful policies that the Chinese may pursue. First, it should be recognized that Chinese trade policy, like tax policy, can no longer be formulated without reference to the international regime. The Chinese should therefore seriously consider membership in GATT, even though the immediate entrance fee may be high. The membership would not be aimed primarily at such obvious advantages as qualifying for U.S. preferential treatment, but at long-term participation in a multilateral setting in the formulation of principles concerning trade relations between developed-market economies and developing socialist countries. The current Chinese participation in the deliberations of UNCTAD is inadequate for this purpose, since the agenda there is crowded with items of major concern to other developing countries. At the same time, in comparison with bilateral negotiations, a multilateral setting has the advantage of protecting the party with a relatively weak bargaining position, althouth the solidarity of the Third World becomes tenuous when issues go beyond general principles.

Another policy initiative is to avoid serious charges of market disruption through careful precautionary measures. Changes in market share in particular countries should be monitored. Sudden dramatic increases in these shares should be largely avoided by orderly marketing. For the same reason, export categories that are less sensitive to possible charges and market disruption should be emphasized in the long-term plan. These categories include natural resources such as petroleum and coal, noncompeting goods such as rare earth and traditional Chinese ware, and items with insignificant Chinese share. Intermediate products sourced by transnationals, especially in connection with processing, coproduction arrangements, or compensation trade, are also likely to be less sensitive to market restrictions.

The International Monetary System

The international monetary system is also under new scrutiny. Questions have arisen about fixed or floating exchange rates, the role of the International Monetary Fund in development finance, the conditions imposed by the fund in its lendings, and the distribution of voting rights.

Chinese participation in the IMF as well as in the World Bank has no doubt had an important effect on China. For one thing, it has influenced Chinese policy about the disclosure of financial information. Much of the information required by the world organizations has found its way into Chinese publications.[40] Efforts are being made to bring about improvements in areas such as trade and balance-of-payments statistics. In terms of finance, the Chinese have already made use of these institutions as an important source of foreign exchange, especially on concessionary terms. Further resources from the world financial institutions would inevitably mean their scrutiny of Chinese policies and practices.[41] In the IMF, conditionality tightens with each credit tranche. Even with the World Bank, project appraisal for economic sectors is likely to be more stringent than for the educational projects that predominated in the initial loans.

On the other hand, Chinese impact on the international monetary regime is often ignored. First the Chinese hold a permanent directorship in the IMF and are thus in a position to exert an influence on shaping the future of the world monetary system.[42] The system has already evolved beyond the original conception of the Bretton Woods Agreement. The IMF has not only served as the world's central bank, as originally envisaged, but it has also become a major force in development finance. A proliferation of facilities, notably the oil facility and the compensatory facility, have sprung up as new needs arose. In early 1983, the IMF teamed up with private banks, formally and informally, in arranging sizeable credits for the rescheduling of debt for a number of countries such as Mexico, Brazil, and the Philippines, without which the entire international monetary system might have been faced with a crisis of major proportions.

Second, in the future evolution of the international monetary system the Chinese are likely to be sympathetic to Third World suggestions for strengthening the system. Although the developed countries as a group still currently possess a veto power on all important issues, the position of the United States will become increasingly isolated unless it too pays more attention to the needs of the Third World. This is all the more important since the position of the United States' traditional allies, such as Western Europe, has already shifted in a number of issues. A notable example is the current debate on the appropriateness of linking the creation of Special Drawing Rights (SDRs) with development finance. The U.S. opposition is receiving less and less support from other developed countries.

Third, the future evolution of the world's monetary system will in turn affect China's relationship with transnational corporations. In the past, finance from the IMF and the World Bank was considered an alternative to private sources. This remains true for China, inasmuch as such finance strengthens its position in negotiating with the transnationals. On the other hand, as cooperative arrangements have multiplied between these institutions and the private sector in cofinancing and monitoring the financial health of member countries, China's relationship with the one cannot but affect the other in the same direction.

The Code of Conduct on Transnational Corporations

Unlike the international trade regime or the international monetary system, there are no accepted rules of the game for dealing with transnatioanl corporations or corresponding international institutions.[43] With the establishment of the United Nations Commission on Transnational Corporations at the intergovernmental level and the United Nations Centre on Transnational Corporations at the secretariat level, following the recommendations of the Group of Eminent Persons,[44] a start has been made on filling the institutional void.

The United Nations is currently negotiating a code of conduct on transnational corporations.[45] Although a number of important issues remain to be resolved before a final code can be adopted, years of deliberations have clarified most of the disputed areas and resulted in a general consensus. China, which joined the commission in 1980, has exercised a moderating influence rather than a divisive one, as some had feared at first. The Chinese regard the code as a useful instrument rather than mere whitewash, as it is viewed by some cynics on the left, or destructive of the transnationals, as feared by critics on the right. For the same reasons, the Chinese can hardly ignore principles established by the international community to which they have made an active contribution. These principles would include appropriate behavior by the government towards transnational corporations. As the Chinese influence the shape of international regimes, their policies and institutions are at the same time being increasingly molded by the international framework.

6 The Negotiating Process

In contrast to general policies or specific performance requirements laid down by a government with respect to a whole range or class of activities of transnational corporations, negotiations are carried out on a case-by-case basis. The contrast is sometimes blurred in developing countries.[1] Before making a commitment in a host country, a foreign investor may ask the government for special favorable treatment such as protective tariffs. The tariff rate may be negotiated between the investor and the government. Even though the rate is ostensibly applicable across the board, the party under protection may in effect be a single firm. Similarly, performance requirements such as local content for a foreign automobile plant may apply to no more than one or two cases.

The negotiating process differs according to the parties concerned as well as according to the form and content. For instance, a high-level negotiation is not quite the same as a working-level negotiation; the former is likely to be concerned with broad issues rather than specific details. A government-to-government negotiation has peculiarities not exactly duplicated by a company-to-company negotiation, the former being frequently intermingled with political considerations. A multilateral negotiation has its own dynamics of interaction that are not present in a bilateral negotiation; the former may exact compromises or concessions from the recalcitrant by applying the pressure of public opinion. The differences between the negotiation of a trade arrangement, a joint venture, and other forms of cooperation are amply illustrated in chapter 4. Some industry differences can also be gleaned from the case studies in chapter 7.[2]

The purpose of this chapter is not to review all the issues involved in negotiations, but to single out the peculiarities in the negotiation process between China and transnational corporations. First, an attempt is made to answer the question of why China often resorts to case-by-case negotiations rather than laying down general principles or specific requirements for a class of activities. Next, the gaps in negotiations between the parties concerned are identified. The third area dealt with is relative bargaining power, followed by a discussion of the division of benefits. Last, some advice is offered for the promotion of understanding on both sides.

Reasons for Negotiation

Little negotiation is needed in the world of pure market forces. This is true in a marketplace where neither the seller nor the buyer acting alone can influence the aggregate demand or supply. Each side takes the market price as given in the transaction. In contrast to a bazaar situation, there is no bargaining, for if a supplier were to charge a higher price than the prevailing one, he would price himself out of the market. Conversely, if he is willing to offer a price lower than the market level, his influence will soon disappear since his supply will quickly be exhausted as all the buyers will flock to him. The free-market situation may also be approached in cases of foreign direct investment when a country welcomes all comers with open arms. No negotiation is needed between the investors and the host government provided there are many investors. Even here some negotiations with domestic suppliers or labor groups may still be required to the extent that these relations are not entirely governed by free-market forces.

At the other extreme of complete governmental control or regulation, no negotiation is permissible. Here the government clearly forbids specific activities and stipulates all the conditions for permissible operations. For instance, if munitions are not allowed to be imported by traders or manufactured by foreign investors in the country concerned, the matter is not negotiable. If a foreign investor is required to use a given percentage of local workers or raw materials, he can either take it or leave it.

As is true of many governments, the Chinese do not rely on either of the two extremes. In particular, general policies and regulations are regarded as too blunt to suit special situations. The case of oil in China is a good example. In the first place, since oil is an important natural resource, it is treated separately from other sectors in connection with joint ventures. The income tax regime for foreign oil companies is also different from that for others. Also, in the bidding for offshore exploration by the oil companies, despite the terms laid down in the model contract,[3] the Chinese do not commit themselves to accepting the lowest bid but reserve the right to negotiate with the oil companies. This enables the Chinese to evaluate the capabilities of the competing oil companies in depth and take into account subtle considerations. The Chinese may wish for instance to involve a large spectrum of the world's oil companies in offshore explorations, while only a few would succeed if mechanical means for accepting the bids were adopted. Each major oil company has its particularities, which may be regarded for certain purposes as desirable. Some companies may have more experience than others in dealing with socialist countries. Some others may deserve a reward for their longstanding participation in cooperation with China. Yet others may be of help in strengthening the Chinese position in territorial disputes with neighboring countries.[4]

The negotiated solution usually yields maximum benefit to the party with the superior bargaining power, as is illustrated in the success of a discriminating monopolist. A physician of incomparable skill may adjust his fees to rich and poor patients rather than charge a uniform rate. The same applies to patent holders with discriminatory licensing fees. For the same reason most companies do not wish to disclose the fees charged for licensing to various users. When both parties possess some monopolistic (or monopsonistic) power, the process of negotiation is likely to be involved or protracted because a large area of indetermination exists. An example is collective bargaining between transnational corporations and labor unions.

Relative bargaining power is not, however, fixed. It changes over time and varies with particular situations, as is discussed later. The position arrived at through earlier negotiation may appear totally untenable under new circumstances. Renegotiation is sometimes called for, which raises fundamental principles. Western enterprises are influenced primarily by the doctrine of the sanctity of contracts and do not favor renegotiation. Many developing countries, including China, retain traumatic memories of having been taken advantage of in early negotiations. The concession contracts of the colonial or semicolonial period, which granted the transnationals enormous powers of control and opportunities for profit with very little return to the host country or environmental protection, appear to be unfair. Some of the original negotiations may have been flawed by willful deception, as in the case of numerous contracts signed during the Nkrumah regime in Ghana. There is therefore a large gray area in which even under the doctrine of the sanctity of contracts, renegotiation is considered appropriate. A number of important contracts have actually been renegotiated in China, mainly in response to the need for retrenchment. Here the issue is generally not whether the Chinese have the right to renegotiate but whether a renegotiation will be acceptable to both parties. A cancellation of contract would mean large penalties for the Chinese and a loss of business for the transnational corporation concerned. Compromises have been worked out to prolong the contract period or to trim the scale of operations. In most cases, additional elements such as new credit have been made available to the Chinese so that the new package differs considerably from the old.

There are many other reasons—cultural, informational, legal, and administrative—why negotiations are needed between China and transnational corporations. Many problems of negotiations arise from these aspects, and are discussed below.

Gaps in Negotiation

Experience in negotiations between China and transnational corporations has revealed special difficulties. Four important gaps appear most significant and warrant attention. These are the cultural gap, the information gap, the legal gap, and the enforcement gap.

The Cultural Gap

The cultural gap is perhaps the most obvious, yet its implications are not always understood and mistakes made because of ignorance are often repeated.[5] The Chinese language remains a mystery to most Westerners. Despite the current craze of the Chinese for learning Western languages, especially English, the demand for English-speaking personnel still far exceeds the supply. Consequently, the language gap persists and is aggravated by the fact that many technical terms have no equivalent in Chinese; when they do they are not in common use. The quality of technical presentations is thus more a function of the ability of the interpreter than of the caliber of the speaker. To some extent the speaker's awareness of the problem can narrow the gap. He can pause frequently to give the interpreter enough time to catch up and to insert explanations. He can also avoid excessive use of technical jargon with no definitions and explanations.

The Chinese language is especially rich in shades of meaning inherited from millenia of use. When these terms are translated they may convey different nuances, and vice versa. A now-celebrated example concerns the key word "acknowledges" in the Shanghai Communiqué of February 28, 1972, issued by the United States and China. The English version states that "the United States acknowledges that all Chinese on either side of the Taiwan Strait maintain there is but one China and that Taiwan is a part of China."[6] This has been interpreted by the United States side to mean that it merely takes note of the Chinese position without necessarily agreeing to that position. In the Chinese version, the word "acknowledges" is represented by a term that implies U.S. agreement. While the discrepant implications of the two language versions may in this case have been deliberately ignored in the course of the negotiations in order to facilitate an agreement, there are many other examples of discrepancies that arise from inexact translations or intrinsic ambiguity in the Chinese or the English language.[7] A comparison of the English and Chinese versions of contracts reveals frequent discrepancies in shades of meanings.

Body language also often gives rise to a great deal of misunderstanding. Many Chinese who have some acquaintance with English continue to use the affirmative when a negative is required.[8] The frequent nod by the Chinese, reinforced by "yes, yes," is often used to signal "I have heard you" rather than "I agree with you." Even smiles do not imply "I am happy with your statement." It is reported that when Secretary Marshall attempted to mediate between the dispute of the Nationalists and the Communists in

China after World War II he was furious with Chiang, the Nationalist leader. When Marshall made a proposition in meetings, Chiang would say "yes, yes" in Chinese and nod. Marshall reported his mission's great success in winning Chiang's acceptance of his proposals, only to find later that Chiang raised questions in subsequent sessions. He did not understand that Chiang was merely being polite to him and indicating that the proposals had been heard! This is not an isolated instance. In general the Chinese regard saying "no" as something negative and undesirable. A disagreement is frequently not explicitly stated. Silence can therefore have a double meaning and negotiators with the Chinese do not know where they stand.

Despite the effect of the revolutionary style on manners, the Chinese are likely to be upset if the other side appears rude or impolite. Chinese good manners, on the other hand, may sometimes be misinterpreted by outsiders. A case in point is the Chinese practice of not looking into the eyes of the opposite side in face-to-face negotiations. This is a sign of respect inherited from the past. Indeed, in the early days, it would have been very impolite for a subordinate to look straight into the eyes of his superior. Sometimes he had to be specifically requested to do so or even to raise his head. The Westerner would interpret such a mannerism as evasiveness or lack of confidence.

The Chinese also have a preference for subtlety. This probably stems from a thousand years of veneration for poetry, as every scholar must practice this form of art. In Chinese poems, little is expressed directly. The feeling of love is expressed without the word ever being used. The accent is not on what is said but what is implicit. Similarly, most great painters of the classic style prefer black and white to color because the former will give more room for imagining many more shades than can be conveyed by the actual use of colors. Yet, in some cases, the Chinese appear to Westerners to be too direct. They will ask your age, your weight, or even your income without realizing that this is not done in the West.[9]

An important point in regard to subtleties is that the effectiveness of communication depends as much on the context of what is said as on the content. In other words, who says it, and when and how it is said, is very important. On a recent lecture tour in China, I stayed in a building for foreign specialists. The towels were not changed every day as they were supposed to be; the breakfast toast was cold and the milk had a burnt taste. All the foreign inhabitants complained about these deficiencies but felt that the management had generally been cooperative and friendly. A complaint might affect the friendly atmosphere. When I was asked by the head of the institution to suggest management training, I took the opportunity to make the point that some improvement in management would be possible even without a lengthy process of sophisticated management instruction. For example, the deficiencies enumerated above could be remedied immediately if someone was put in charge and periodic inspections made and systems of checking introduced. All three problems were not particularly the fault of the personnel directly concerned. The room steward might regard a daily change of towels as wasteful from his personal experience. The cooks and waitresses had no idea what toast and milk should taste like because these items were not in their diet. The next day all the towels were changed, the toast was warm, and the milk was not burned, although it is not known how long this improvement lasted. This surprise success was followed by numerous other requests to me to intervene on behalf of the experts. With each request, two considerations immediately entered my mind. One was whether the request was reasonable. For example, one expert wanted to be given the key to the gate so that he could come back late at night without waking up the gatekeeper. I did not convey this request because it would have raised serious questions of security if allowed. The other consideration was whether one ought not to exercise great restraint in telling the Chinese what to do, and whether the time was opportune.

The Information Gap

There is a Chinese proverb that says: In warfare, know thyself and know thine enemy. This underlines the importance of information. The same importance should be attached to information in negotiations, even though that activity is not altogether warlike. Although the marketplace may be compared to the battlefield, the purpose of a business negotiation is first to maximize the total gain and then to secure a large share of the pie. In warfare, while each side expects to win, the objective is to inflict a loss on the enemy. One side's victory is another side's defeat. Objectively, it is possible for both sides to lose; consider the possibility of mutual destruction in a global atomic conflict. A business negotiation aims at a positive-sum game, while warfare can be zero-sum or even negative-sum.

Whether a business negotiation will yield a positive sum depends a great deal on the soundness of the project as the tenor of negotiations. Literature on project analysis abounds, and the Chinese are now insisting on feasibility studies as a precondition for foreign project proposals. The purpose of the present section is not to review the issues relating to feasibility studies but to draw attention to the lack of information on the part of the transnational corporations as well as the Chinese. A well-managed transnational corporation can be expected to know its own objectives. At the same time, these objectives may be based on misconceptions about China. The old China hands are no exception since their image of the past may be stronger than their ability to absorb new developments. As acknowledged experts, they may be bent on defending their views even though those views are outdated and unsupported by fresh evidence. These people are sometimes resented by the Chinese, in particular because they perpetuate the myths about the Chinese in stereotypes reminiscent of the bad old days. Archetypes of the old hands can be found, for example, in the representative offices of some of the major transnationals in Beijing. A revealing trait of their arrogance and complacency is that, despite their long residence in China and their profession, they have still not learned Chinese and are thus ignorant of the main sources of information on developments in China.

The new China hands are more eager for knowledge and are less condescending. Most have not found their way into the higher echelons of the transnationals because the volume of business is as yet too small and erratic. Where corporations are organized along geographical lines, the China desk or division is still small and is often subsumed under the Asian or Southeast Asian unit. It is very difficult for the few new China hands to learn enough about the company's business and follow what is going on in China.

One solution to the cultural gap is for transnationals to make use of ethnic Chinese personnel. This is a relatively new development even in the United States, the nation of immigrants, since the older generation of Chinese have hardly graduated from their traditional occupations. While the rise of ethnic Chinese up the business ladder is to be applauded, both for the resourcefulness of the Chinese and for the social mobility and equality of opportunity offered in the West, their role should not be exaggerated. In general, relatively few first-generation Chinese have acquired sufficient status in business to make a big impact. For the first requirement in business is "know thyself", meaning expertise is some product or process of the company. Their Chinese background is of limited use unless they have also acquired professional expertise, as well as rank and authority. Second- and third-generation Chinese have the advantage of starting on a more or less equal footing with other citizens. In some cases, they may even have benefited from reverse discrimination, a fallout from the efforts of other minorities. Their climb up the business ladder frequently requires certain acceptable behavioral patterns. Indeed, the very reason why they are liked by their superiors or promoted to positions of importance is because they are as good as the others, meaning that they are well assimilated. Moreover, unlike other minorities who are much more powerful as a group because of their number, entrenchment, and organization, U.S. Chinese can derive little benefit from mutual aid by identification with the group. The incentive to be bicultural is thus relatively weak for the upper-strata overseas Chinese. When they deal with the Chinese on the mainland, the question of cultural distance may arise for them as well. This distance may be magnified because both sides start with contrary expectations. In one case, a transnational representative of Chinese origin was well treated in China until he revealed his ignorance about Chinese sensitivities by asking questions about details of Chinese production plans. The role of ethnic Chinese in transnational corporations depends ultimately on what individuals can do rather than on their ethnic origin.

Another approach to bridging the information gap is for transnationals to engage independent advisors or agents. Advisors can serve the purpose of scale economies since most companies do not have such extended resources or the need to know a great deal about China. Consultants or intermediaries were relatively important when information about China was almost totally absent. They know how to make the initial contact with Chinese institutions such as the CCPIT, the CITIC, the ministries or the foreign trade corporations concerned, and they knew the procedures to be followed in obtaining a visa or presenting a proposal. Their role becomes more limited once the preliminary stages are over and serious negotiations have taken place. Most large transnationals feel that they are the only ones who really know their business, and that they can do without an intermediary except for specific tasks. The exceptions are the relatively small companies, who have especially limited management time in which to deal with the Chinese. They may be able to make one three-week business trip to China involving most of the company's decision makers, but what if the Chinese request another visit and yet another in the unknown future? The opportunity cost in lost business elsewhere may be too great. On the other hand, many small companies are distrustful of outsiders and generally prefer to keep their business secrets within a very small circle.

The transnationals' lack of knowledge about the Chinese is aggravated by the typical negotiation arrangements. The Chinese generally do not reveal their true objectives or intentions during negotiation except in very general terms. The precise identity and role of those who participate in the negotiations is usually unknown. When, for example, a negotiator claims that he has to check with others, it is difficult to know whether the subject matter is truly beyond his authority or whether a point is being rejected or stalled deliberately but politely. At the technical level, the transnationals are not generally hampered by the Chinese reluctance to disclose information. Many agricultural, mining, industrial, and transport facilities have been opened for detailed inspection by potential partners from transnationals. The same openness is rarely extended to research workers, domestic or foreign.

The Chinese lack of information about transnationals is more glaring. It arises from years of isolation from the rest of the world as well as from the compartmentalization of specialist responsibilities. While it is true that many Chinese negotiators are experienced and have done their homework, some of the rudimentary information contained in company annual reports or the financial press, for example, is not known to them. This is reflected in the eagerness of the Chinese to pump information from the transnationals

It is ultimately a very costly way of gathering information, as the transnationals have to send teams to China, where they must stay in hotels.

Unlike their counterparts, the Chinese do not generally know the strategies of the companies with which they are negotiating. In-depth information on these companies is elusive. A case in point is the negotiation with a major transnational on the establishment of a black-and-white television plant in China. The transnational's main motive was to relocate the plant from another place in Asia to China, where costs are lower. Most of the product could be exported, because there is a demand for a second or third television set in developed country households. The Chinese showed an interest in the project but could not make a quick decision, partly because the proposal sounded to be too good to be true and partly because the matter involved more than one ministry. The transnational grew impatient after many rounds of fruitless talks. It gave the Chinese a deadline, as it had to relocate the plant soon. The Chinese felt that this was only a negotiating tactic; when they finally approved the proposal, the transnational was obliged to inform them that the plant had already been relocated in another place.

The Chinese information network suffers especially from the long-term isolation of the academic community from the real world. This is particularly true of social scientists, most of whom had no empirical data to work with nor access to information in the operational units. Unlike their counterparts in the West, who serve as a large reservoir of personnel and knowledge for the practitioners, Chinese academicians are rarely consulted by the enterprises. Partly for this reason, almost all the operational units have their own research units since they have to rely on in-house information. Despite frequent meetings at the interdepartmental and interministerial levels, the flow of information between units is severely limited. Most operational units have hardly any information on transnationals since the units have had very little to do with foreign firms until recently. The information network on transnationals currently being established in China should alleviate the difficulty, but it will take time, especially as the information requires analysis.

The lack of serious analysis of information, other than that directly related to the narrowly defined responsibilities of research workers, is especially evident in connection with the general environment within which transnationals operate. Chinese negotiators are generally not well informed about foreign policy measures that affect the activities of transnationals. Although cadres have access to foreign press information on major political and economic developments, the details are often missing. This deficiency is revealed, for example, in the Chinese insistence in technology negotiations that the transnational should see to it that export licenses are issued. The assumption is that the transnationals can tell their capitalist governments what to do. Although they do lobby their governments at various levels, the truth is that their possible influence should not be confused with an ability to control the action. A related example is the Chinese refusal to submit to inspections in order to satisfy the exporting country's requirement about the end-user of advanced technology. While these actions may either be a deliberate tactical move or a matter of principle, it is a frustrating experience for the transnationals.

Another assumption the Chinese often harbor is that transnationals are enormously rich and reap tremendously high profits. This view is supported by knowledge of the high salaries of transnational executives, which are a thousand times the highest earnings of their Chinese counterparts. It is also reflected in the ostentatious living styles of Westerners and in company spending. There have thus been numerous instances in which Chinese charges for services and price quotations were considered to be exorbitant. What must be realized is that the transnationals are profit conscious, even if they are willing to cultivate the market. The bottom line is that they must make a profit. Whether or not the rate is too high is a matter for detailed analysis rather than assumption.

The Legal Gap

The traditional aversion of the Chinese to the legalistic approaches is well known.[10] This has been accentuated by a long period of insulation from the outside. Transnationals seeking to establish business relations with China are concerned about the lack of a legal basis; China is still, for example, in the stage of drafting a patent law. The Chinese recognize the concern of the transnationals, apart from their own general interest in moving toward greater reliance on law. The number of new laws recently promulgated is impressive. One of the first was the Law on Joint Ventures using Chinese and Foreign Investment, enacted in 1979.

The Law on Joint Ventures illustrates the second concern, namely that Chinese laws appear to the transnationals to be too brief and too vague. They are said to raise more questions than they answer. For this reason laws are followed by detailed regulations, but these also tend to be too brief by Western standards. The rules relating to individual income taxes in the United States run to a thousand pages, for example, while the Chinese rules can be packed into a few pages.

Another question is raised with respect to the actual implementation of the laws or agreements. As the transnationals see it, most of the laws are untested. Lawyers trained in the Anglo-Saxon tradition of case law are particularly worried that there have been virtually no court cases to demonstrate how the law is enforced. In contrast, those trained in the continental tradition of Roman law are less concerned. This difference explains the willingness of many European and Japanese businessmen to go along with the

Chinese and agree to very brief contracts, while the U.S. lawyers feel obliged to make provision for every possible contingency in order to protect themselves. The difficulty with this insistence is that it exacerbates the negotiating process. There are as yet too few Chinese lawyers in a position to digest fifty or a hundred pages of draft contract, let alone translate it into precise Chinese and convince their superiors that there are no hidden problems if the language is accepted.

The scarcity of court cases is also related to the Chinese aversion to lawsuits. Despite recent attempts to remove from lawsuits the stigma of being mean, unfriendly, or even unethical, the traditional perception is slow to change. In foreign-trade relations, for example, the Chinese still try to avoid legal settlement of nonfulfillment of contracts. When a foreign importer receives defective goods from the Chinese, he is often persuaded to accept it as a misfortune and keep quiet. The Chinese will take note of the fact that a "friend" has suffered a loss due to the fault of the Chinese, and the loss will be made up by specially favorable treatment in the next round, whether in the allocation of scarce commodities or in price discounts or priority deliveries.

The Chinese aversion to formal legal steps for the settlement of disputes is also reflected in the relevant contractual provisions. The general preference of transnationals is to make use of third-party arbitration mechanisms. (The International Chamber of Commerce is ruled out as an arbitrator as long as Taiwan continues to be a member.) The Chinese generally insist on the use of their own arbitration institution of the CCPIT, in line with their preference for conciliation rather than adjudication. Another belief, which is shared by many developing countries, is that the objectivity of Western institutions is questionable. It is claimed that these institutions are dominated by Westerners and their judgment is strongly influenced by Western tradition. In practice, though, in some contracts the Chinese have accepted international arbitration by such countries as Sweden.

Despite the legal gap identified above, the Chinese have assured transnationals that in the absence of laws and regulations the provisions in the contracts will be honored even if they should contradict subsequent laws. A number of cases indicate that this promise has been kept. But problems may arise from the contrasting styles of doing things between the Chinese and their Western partners.

The Enforcement Gap

Frequently, what has been agreed upon, either explicitly stipulated in a contract or agreed upon informally, is not fulfilled. Mention has already been made of a number of such cases in other connections. The Chinese have experienced misrepresentations by foreign enterprises. In one case, a foreign businessman approached the Chinese for joint venture arrangements claiming he had the financial backing (amounting to several billion dollars) of an Arab prince. The Chinese gave him the red carpet treatment. Subsequently, one cadre tried to check the background of the foreign company and found out from the home country that it had a small office with one secretary and several hundred dollars in the bank. Thereupon the negotiation was suspended. If a joint venture agreement had been signed, the company would probably not have been able to live up to the terms of the contract.

Deliberate misrepresentation by the Chinese is highly improbable. But some problems do exist, the most common of which is production bottlenecks. The quantities contracted for are simply not available for delivery. When they are delivered, they have missed the crucial season such as Christmas. Such occurrences may not even be the producer's fault. The essential materials may not have been allocated for the purpose, or there may have been a general cut-back in electricity supply.

A related problem is that although the quantity of goods may be there, specifications have not been adhered to. In garments, the sizes are sometimes mixed up and the buttons missing. Thousands of cases of Chinese beer are exported without carbon dioxide. These cases reflect deficiencies in quality control in numerous activities.

Another problem one foreign exporter encountered was that its scientific equipment was inspected at the customs piece by piece. Since it was a delicate instrument, the handling spoiled it. This was not a deliberated non-tariff barrier as it might have been in some other countries, but was simply an indication of the curiosity of the customs people. A similar case involved a joint venture in toy manufacturing. When the prospective foreign joint venture partner was invited to visit the Chinese factory with samples, the customs insisted that each had to be taxed, notwithstanding the plea of the Chinese host. In this case, certainly, it was not the fault of the Chinese partner. He also was powerless under the circumstances. The damage done was not the duties paid on the samples but the inordinate amount of time wasted.

The Relative Bargaining Power

A basic principle repeatedly stated by the Chinese in their dealings with foreign business is equality. This must be interpreted in historical perspective. Western enterprises in the past entered China on the heels of military invasions and unequal treaties. They enjoyed special status, such as exemption from the burdensome *lijin* (tax) levied on the movement of goods within China from one locality to another. They were exempt from prosecution under Chinese law since foreigners enjoyed extraterritorial rights. Many of them, in fact, operated in the foreign concessions, which were virtual colonies. The contention now is that the Chinese are independent and sovereign and therefore on a par with foreigners. But obviously the principle of equality does not imply that the bargaining power of the Chinese is now equal to that of the transnationals. The question, then, is: in what respects do the Chinese enjoy strong bargaining power, and conversely.

Factors Favorable to China

The socialist nature of Chinese organization is often considered to be a business asset to the Chinese. Business with foreigners is conducted by state corporations, which were until recently direct arms of the state. The foreign-trade corporations were organs of the Ministry of Foreign Trade. More recently, in line with the introduction of the responsibility system, economic and business organs are increasingly separated in China from political and administrative ones. Even under the new system, the corporations with responsibility for foreign business dealings have the backing of the entire state. Moreover, the Chinese have attempted to eliminate internal competition among their own corporations in, for example, bidding against each other in exports or imports. A number of combines have been organized, so that dealings with foreign business will be centralized. Transnationals, in contrast, generally compete with one another. Collusion is a relatively rare occurrence.

Factors Favorable to Transnational Corporations

It is unlikely that the Chinese are in a position to exercise monopoly power in relations with foreign enterprises. The trump card of the foreign enterprises is that they can go elsewhere. There are very few Chinese export items that cannot be obtained in other parts of the world. Certainly the volume of Chinese imports is still relatively too small to justify any exercise of monopolistic power. As far as foreign investment is concerned, the Chinese are competing with numerous other host countries as well as with the home countries themselves for scarce capital. The Chinese must also be careful in their business behavior, since a bad reputation could implicate all other state enterprises.

The apparent eagerness of transnationals to rush into China is somewhat misleading. It is to be explained mainly by the desire to gain a foothold in China. While it is generally acknowledged that there is a vast potential for business with China in virtually all areas, as indicated in chapter 3, any business that ignores this potential has to find justification and defend its decision. For if steps are not taken early enough in the game, the field may be too crowded later on. Given this consideration, transnationals have been willing to develop business even if there is no immediate prospect for profit. The initial expenditure is similar to an allocation for development or advertisement, and the outlook is for the long haul. Even in actual dealings, transnationals have frequently been willing to tolerate very thin margins if not deliberately introduce loss leaders. This is best illustrated by the terms of numerous bank loans negotiated at the start of the opening of China to foreign trade and credit. They were on a par with the term enjoyed by some of the most creditworthy countries such as France. The interest rate was often only a fraction above the London Inter-Bank Offered Rate (LIBOR). In contrast, most developing countries are paying two percent or more above LIBOR. Commitment charges were also often waived. The Chinese are not in a hurry to draw on such credit, however, when even better terms are available from international institutions and intergovernmental aid agencies.

On the debit side, the Chinese bargaining power suffers from three related considerations. The first is lack of adequate information on the transnationals, as indicated in the previous section. The second arises from their low level of technology, which is closely related to the first. The third stems from the first two, in that the hidden cost is insufficiently perceived. For example, the Chinese side may drive a very hard bargain on price but ignore details of quality and other considerations such as reliabililty of delivery. Indeed, in numerous Chinese purchasing contracts, penalty for late delivery is usually missing. In joint ventures, the gains of foreign partners may not be limited to the share of profit from the venture but may include shift of profit through transfer pricing or the channeling of purchases to related companies. This is especially difficult to monitor when the foreign partners are in control of the technical details of accounting and engineering specifications.

The Division of Benefit

In principle, the Chinese are as insistent on mutual benefit as they are on equality. This principle is a major breakthrough in ideology. If the foreign enterprises were capitalistic, would they not merely be exploiting the Chinese? The new principle admits that the relationship is not between exploiter and exploited but that both parties will benefit. At the same time, the division of benefits is not necessarily fifty-fifty, nor is the benefit limited to a share of the pecuniary profit.

The calculation of who gets how much is not simple. In the case of foreign trade, given the relative isolation of the Chinese market from external commerce, domestic prices often deviate significantly from world levels. The deviation is made up by differential subsidies or paper profits. For instance, the domestic price of crude oil is much lower than it is in the world market. Exports of crude oil thus result in huge paper profits. Those profits do not reflect real gains from a social point of view. Similarly, domestic prices of most manufactured articles are much higher than those prevailing internationally, but the paper loss of these imports does not represent real social loss.

Although detailed statistics are unavailable, a common complaint of the Chinese is that they are not getting a fair share. One indication often cited is that, for roughly the same type of goods (shirts, for example), those of Chinese origin are worth only a fraction of those from other countries. Here the determinant is brand loyalty or quality differential. In order to obtain a higher return, upgrading is required. This, however, takes time, and requires concurrent developments in numerous areas. In textiles, Japan and Hong Kong have succeeded in moving in this direction. Competition is keener as one moves to the upper end of the scale.

A related complaint by the Chinese is that they receive only a small fraction of the retail value of Chinese merchandise in the export market. The Chinese have frequently discovered that what they have sold for one dollar is selling for four dollars on the foreign market. Most of the profit has gone into the hands of the importer, the middleman or the retailer. This is similar to the complaint of other developing countries or United States farmers,[11] and underlines the importance of marketing. In the case of famous brands, marketing is reinforced by vigorous advertisement.

In joint ventures, the division of profit is calculated in accordance with the share of capital invested. To the extent that profit is after taxes, the Chinese also benefit from the taxes levied on gross profits. With petroleum, the formula for the division is more complicated. It involves royalty payments as well as product-sharing and corporate income taxes. As is true of other oil-producing countries, China will certainly get more than fifty percent of the cut, reflecting economic rent (received by the host country) on the natural resource. Moreover, most of the risk here is borne by the transnationals.[12] In other contractual arrangements, the division of profit is not proportional to capital contribution but is negotiated case by case.

One benefit valued highly by the Chinese is technical assistance, which is often provided without explicit charge. Chinese personnel are trained both on the spot and in plants in the home countries or in subsidiaries of the transnationals. These provisions are sometimes used as sweeteners to bargaining since they directly benefit a number of the Chinese involved in the negotiations. In some cases, the Chinese receive more a guided tour than a lesson in technology. Some transnationals have recently begun billing the Chinese for their training activities, especially in some computer technology, which many Chinese are anxious to learn. Other direct benefits include increase in employment, positive balance-of-payments effect, and capital inflow. As is emphasized in chapter 3, the indirect benefit or loss is frequently more important than the direct one. Contribution to the balance of payments, for example, is not limited to the export of the product concerned but includes substitution for imports that would otherwise have to be bought. Some of the indirect effects are negative and, as in instances of pollution or other environmental damage, should be added to the cost side and deducted from gross benefits.

Toward Mutual Understanding

To the extent that the problems encountered by both the transnationals and the Chinese in their negotiations arise from newness and inexperience, signs of progressive improvement along the learning curve are already emerging. Many of the initial difficulties, of a housekeeping nature, for example, have been ameliorated and misunderstandings clarified.[13] Visas for business trips are now easily obtainable. For frequent travelers, multiple-entry visas are issued. Quality control has been introduced in many production units, partly in line with domestic economic reform and partly in response to the demands of foreign business partners. Some of the difficulties, however, are more fundamental or stubborn. For example, an entrepreneurial spirit of assuming responsibility and taking risk is difficult to inculcate among the cadres. Know-how about the world market cannot be acquired in a short span of time. In particular, as in business relations elsewhere, there are always areas of conflict and dispute. A greater degree of contact does not always mean a corresponding degree of mutual understanding and accommodation, otherwise few families would ever have fights and few neighboring nations would become enemies.[14]

There are many manuals and much advice on how to negotiate.[15] Some of the cardinal rules, such as adequate preparation, patience, and perseverance, evidently have universal application. The following concentrates on a few items of advice for transnationals as well as for the Chinese in their future negotiations; these points have either been neglected or deserve special emphasis.

Advice for the Transnationals

The most important knowledge for a transnational to acquire in dealing with China is understanding of what the Chinese are faced with. Transnationals should imagine themselves in Chinese shoes. Since the Chinese are not in a position to change their environment and the institutions within which they must operate, it is not very useful to merely complain that the Chinese are bureaucratic or inefficient. Many of the problems probably do not arise from personal negligence or willful sabotage but are systemic in nature. While they are being tackled by the Chinese at the highest levels, to the extent that they remain the best approach is to try to solve or at least mitigate them for the Chinese.

When Chinese negotiators refuse to borrow money at a rate above a certain ceiling, it is not lack of realism on their part; they are merely following the official guideline. In these circumstances, a way out must be found for the Chinese negotiator. The artificially low rate of interest may be offset by raising the price of exports, or charging other fees that may be acceptable to the Chinese.

Another illustration is the Chinese refusal to agree to inspection of the end-user of dual technology imports. The Chinese are either uninformed about the export control procedures of the supplier country or are deliberately sending a message of protest through the supplier firm. Whatever the reason, the result is an impasse. One way to circumvent the issue is to offer a free periodical product-maintenance service so that the identity of the end-user will be revealed without raising the question of sovereignty.

In solving problems through indirect measures, the transnational must take care to avoid projecting an image of being devious, underhanded, or too clever. Certainly some expedient measures are deceitful or unethical. A reputation for deceit is especially damaging in dealings with China, since information may be shared by many official agencies and a new reputation would be difficult to establish.

Many difficulties can be avoided if the transnational does sufficient homework prior to negotiations. If the locus of decision making for specific projects is known, many wasteful steps can be avoided. Projects that require the joint approval of more than one ministry should be undertaken only in exceptional circumstances, since interministerial coordination, just as in other countries, is laborious. In these cases, allowance for a long lead time is mandatory. Simultaneous contact with different ministries is extremely delicate, as the Chinese wish to do their own coordinating at their own pace. There are frequently subtle jurisdictional issues as well. In one instance, an experienced Japanese steel supplier declined to deal with a new Chinese export-import corporation that attempted to establish new channels of business in competition with the Chinese corporation that had traditional relations with the supplier. To do otherwise might have irritated the traditional buyer and jeopardized further relationships, even though the new buyer offered better terms.

The wisdom of having some twenty copies of any transnational proposal for submission to the Chinese is well known. Obviously, the Chinese do not have the same copying facilities as the transnationals, and the circulation of a limited number of copies through many hands is time-consuming. There is also a Chinese tendency to hoard, since questions may arise concerning the content of the proposal and a document may not be easy for one Chinese decision maker to retrieve after he has passed it on to another unit.

The translation of the proposal into correct Chinese is also a useful time saver. Although the quality of the Chinese translators is generally high, their availability for particular purposes is subject to priorities and jurisdictional limitations. A lengthy document may not be translated for many months.

Whether or not a transnational should place more emphasis on the high or on the working levels of personnel cannot be answered unequivocally. A well-managed firm should involve both its own high executives for the necessary commitment and its working-level people for practical implementation. A dual approach is especially needed in relations with the Chinese. For one thing, the Chinese are hierarchical. They will discuss with the transnationals at the appropriate level. As in diplomatic convention, an ambassador of one country does not normally negotiate with the second secretary of another. Some of the most conspicuous successes of transnationals involved laying foundations at the highest level. Many heads of transnational corporations have been received by Chinese ministers or premiers. It is reported that Dr. Hammer, of Occidental Petroleum, was introduced to Deng Xiaoping during the latter's visit to the United States. Deng was acquainted with Hammer's background, especially his cooperative ventures with the Soviet Union, which reflected the unusual interest of the Chinese in the affairs of the Soviets as relations between these countries were strained. Deng asked Hammer why he did not take a trip to China; Hammer's response was that he was advanced in age, and his trips to the Soviet Union were by special personal plane that allowed him necessary rest during the long journey. He thought such arrangements would be difficult to make for a trip to China. Deng immediately offered to help, and this special treatment marked the beginning of high-level discussions.

A number of China trade firms have suffered from a lack of groundwork in their relations with the Chinese at the working level. These, strangely enough, have even included some of the well-known major firms in Hong Kong. The higher echelons of these firms have rightly cultivated their counterparts in China. They have been well received and vows of mutual cooperation have been exchanged. They have unfortunately neglected to follow through at the working level, so that they are rarely given the opportunity to bid on contracts.

The virtue of flexibility is also well known. To illustrate, when Nestlé first approached China, the first thought was: Wouldn't it be wonderful if one billion Chinese were to eat soup made from the company's bouillon cubes and hot water? Experience in Africa indicated that the potential existed. The response of the Chinese was that they were not so much interested in importing from Nestlé as exporting to it. Thereupon Nestlé negotiated to purchase Chinese spring rolls for the European market. As business expands, opportunities for Chinese imports from the company may very well be explored. Recent negotiations with a number of firms for coproduction mainly for the Chinese domestic market indicate that the Chinese can be flexible in this respect. In this case, the change from the stringent foreign exchange conditions of 1979 and 1980 to the trade surplus of 1982 and 1983, and rising exchange reserves, from the background to this flexibility.

Advice for the Chinese

The discussions concerning structural reforms as well as the need to develop strong points and strengthen weak links in bargaining with foreign enterprises are all relevant to this section. At the present phase on the learning curve, two points deserve special attention by the Chinese. The first is the importance of protecting the China hands of the transnationals. The second relates to China's special need to go beyond a purely nationalistic frame of reference.

With respect to the first point, just as the transnationals should try to understand the problems facing the Chinese negotiators, the Chinese should realize the difficult situation that the China hands in the transnationals are facing today. The China desks or divisions of many transnationals have already been cut down considerably since the days of euphoria. Such trimming is in itself a healthy development toward more realistic expectations. On the other hand, even the trimmed China specialists are often very much on the defensive. They have so far been absorbing resources from other units of the company; they have hosted innumerable Chinese visitors, and they have made several trips to China, in some cases at very short notice. Each trip has cost them several hundred thousand dollars to prepare for. Some of them may even have succeeded in actually signing some kind of contract with the Chinese. To the Chinese, the China hands have been well looked after. Indeed, the ritual of greeting the visitors at the airports and seeing them off, the customary dinner parties showered upon them and the toasts of *mao tai* (an alcoholic drink) all signal warm friendship and good feeling. The trouble is that the China hands are now facing serious scrutiny by their superiors and strategic planners. The question is blunt and simple: When are they going to make some profit for the company? It is granted that the company should take a long view and many U.S. transnationals have begun to take this message seriously. But when will contracts be signed? When will the volume pick up beyond the level of trial shipments?

These are nagging questions that few China hands are in a position to answer. The strategy of the Chinese should not therefore be to concentrate single-mindedly on getting as much as possible from the transnationals, as they might in warfare, but on seeing to it, as the Chinese say, that there is truly mutual benefit. That means that some of the best things, like technical assistance, trips to visit the company plants, and consultations, are not really free. They must all figure into the cost of doing business with China and be reflected in the bottom line. There is no free lunch.

An important change in the Chinese attitude is required. The Chinese should not assume that they are doing the transnationals a favor when they make arrangements to talk business with foreign firms. This old attitude is a transfer from domestic relations in the environment of shortages. It is also related to the separation of the performance of Chinese enterprises from their own position or earnings. The current reforms in enterprise responsibilities should help in the change of attitude.

The second point has broader implications. So far, the Chinese have taken a nationalistic stance. This is natural since China, like many developing countries, is still engaged in nation building. About half of the nation and most of the strategic areas are inhabited by minorities. Divisive forces continue to constitute a potential danger to its cohesion and even survival. This preoccupation explains why the Chinese are virtually unanimous in insisting on the principle of one nation, indivisible, as Lincoln used to do when the United States was threatened by disintegration. At the same time, as China succeeds in modernization its position in the world becomes different from that of most other developing countries. In terms of population, territorial size, and military might, China is already a giant among nations, a fact that will increasingly translate into economic power. What China does or does not do will have a growing impact on the rest of the world. In this context, the Chinese must cease to think only of China's welfare or convenience, but must increasingly frame their policies and actions within the global framework that the Chinese have a stake in helping to form and reform.

There is evidence that the Chinese are keenly aware of their global role. Certainly their increasing participation in the work of the world organizations, their aid to developing countries despite their own poverty, and their interest in the new international economic order point to this awareness. In the field of business relations, however, the orientation appears to continue to be more nationalist than internationalist. While the Chinese rightly condemn the protectionist measures of the industrial countries against their exports, the concern of these countries about possible dumping, market disruption, and unfair competition by the controlled economies cannot be brushed aside lightly. Take, for example, the worst case of a nontariff barrier, such as the French rule that all Japanese videotape recorders had to be cleared at a small inaccessible place. A socialist country can effect the same by simply refusing to purchase any Japanese recorders, no matter how competitive they may be.

Similarly, the costs of socialist-country exports are difficult to determine, as export prices may have little relationship to cost or domestic prices. As long as the size of Chinese foreign trade remains less than one percent of the world total, problems are limited to a few specific items. When the share grows dramatically, it becomes a systemic issue, in which case the fact that the Chinese system is socialist will not be ignored by the others. Consequently, the Chinese will be faced with the danger of incipient demand for reciprocity if not with discrimination. They therefore must do more than simply condemn the industrial countries; they must devise numerous arrangements for allaying their fears. Moreover, they must work with the industrial countries to reform the system by which relations between private-market economies and socialist countries of particular varieties are governed. In other words, it is not enough to be active in the international arena as one of the developing countries, which China undoubtedly is. It must also take the initiative to forestall future difficulties arising from the very size and success of the Chinese modernization program. Negotiations with the transnationals are thus intimately linked with global negotiations for the future.

7 Case Studies

The foregoing discussions have been illustrated by numerous examples in order to make this study more lively and less abstract. There are evidently many more cases that could illustrate different or even contrary points. A great degree of selectivity is implied in the presentation of the examples.

While illustrations have the advantage of bringing home the particular points made, they do not unfold the story of a particular industry or corporation. The present chapter supplements the case illustrations presented earlier by concentrating on specific sectors and firms. Most of the cases have been chosen mainly on the ground that there is something worthwhile to say about them that has not been said before. Some of the materials used here were collected in the course of the author's personal interviews and field visits. Others reflect the research work of members of his seminars in Chinese-International Business Relations or on Transnational Corporations, together with supplementary information from other published sources.

The advantage of having the sectoral and company case studies that follow is that certain peculiarities of individual cases are brought out within the general context and in dynamic sequence. The disadvantage is that some information has to be treated as confidential, which would not need to be true of illustrations that did not reveal the identity of the particular firms or personalities involved. The studies should therefore be interpreted with this limitation in mind.

Industry Cases

Toward More Effective Advertising[1]

Before the current modernization drive, advertising was considered either necessary or repulsive in China. Under conditions of centralized purchase and allocation as well as general scarcity, advertising was hardly required to push sales. During the Cultural Revolution it was linked with capitalistic practices, so that the only advertising company in the country was not allowed to operate. In 1978, the change in policy orientation was signaled by a burst of advertising activity by foreign enterprises in China as well as by Chinese corporations abroad. Because of a lack of basic understanding on both sides, however, the effectiveness of advertising improved only gradually.

The tortuous road to this improvement is briefly charted here, so that future mistakes may be avoided.

Advertising in China. Foreign enterprises have learned that the Chinese, in contrast to the general practice in the West, still prefer to receive information rather than be subjected to hard selling. These enterprises have thus concentrated on the provision of technical seminars, scholarly papers, and exhibitions rather than on advertising as such. What advertising there has been was frequently through industrial and technical literature.[2] This approach was appropriate because the targeted audience was the professionals and specialists who participate in decision making on purchases rather than the average consumer.

The granting of greater decision-making power to end-users in more recent years has complicated the picture, however. Since the relevant decision makers are both diverse and scattered, a narrow target may miss them altogether. For example, some foreign firms have continued to direct their advertising at the foreign-trade corporations, although these no longer take the main initiative without requests from end-users.

When advertising is targeted at a general audience, Madison Avenue's stock in trade has to be applied with great caution. Certainly up-sexing has to be avoided. Even magazines printed abroad that show models in revealing dresses risk embargo at the Chinese customs. The maps and flags used by transnationals to demonstrate their global reach are often fraught with dangerous political implications. Translated into Chinese, puns may be not only meaningless but even distorted or offensive. Phonetic renderings of foreign names, especially company and brand names, however innocent in appearance, may have hidden meanings. Most companies have learned to avoid the derogatory undertones of early translations,[3] while some have invented totally new names that bear no resemblance to the original, apparently to avoid possible embarrassment.[4] Others have used Chinese to advantage in order to convey additional meaning.[5]

Currently, a larger array of media can be used for advertising in China. Means range from direct mailing to newspapers, periodicals, radio, television, and billboards. The rates per page or per second and the effective rates in terms of exposure give little help in choosing a particular medium. The most important considerations, apart from the advertising content, are readership composition and the availability of the goods and services being advertised. For example, while a national advertisement for foreign consumer goods may reach an enormous number of people, most may be without the income to buy them. Moreover, the goods are largely unavailable for purchase. The picture may change drastically in light of the emergence of rich farmers in the rural areas since the introduction of the responsibility system. It is also subject to policy changes, such as the government's decision to import quantities of consumer goods including beverages, watches, televisions, and recorders, partly for fiscal purposes.

The Chinese have also used transnational-corporation advertising in China for acquiring goods or services. A recent example is an arrangement with CBS, where CBS is to sell advertising time on Chinese television in exchange for CBS programs to be shown in China.

Chinese Advertising Abroad. It is difficult for the Chinese to learn about advertising abroad because their lack of any general conception of marketing. Some of the early Chinese exhibitions sent abroad appeared to lack focus. They contained a mixture of museum pieces, goods for domestic consumption, and exportable products.[6] To a large extent, the technical difficulties were solved by relying on foreign merchandizers or agents. Bloomingdales' recent exhibits of Chinese ware and its accompanying 104-page catalog were an example of attractive display. Yet from the Chinese point of view, the effect was limited. It was a one-shot affair, designed to promote general sales rather than Chinese merchandise. At other times, the store's advertising campaign theme would be other nations, such as India and France. In view of this orientation, there was little attempt to project a new image of China. The accent remained on traditional rather than on modern China. Models wearing Chinese-produced clothing were featured in rice fields or in pseudo-Kungfu poses.

The reliance on foreign merchandisers for advertising also reflects the stringency of Chinese direct-advertising budgets. The allocation for advertising expenses is frequently not known until several months have elapsed, so that there tends to be a rush to use up foreign exchange in the second half of the year. This bunching of Chinese advertising of similar products from various Chinese provinces and factories tends to confuse buyers, who cannot tell the difference between them.

The content of Chinese advertising has been influenced more by visual appeal than by market analysis, reflecting the fact that most of the Chinese responsible for advertising have backgrounds in design or packaging rather than in business or economics. Consequently, insufficient attention has been paid to economic effectiveness. For example, in advertising industrial products, emphasis has been sometimes placed on the aesthetics of the designs or photography, with little regard being paid to basic information on specifications. Even the visual layout is not always attractive to Westerners, as it tends to cram too much information into too small a space and contain disparate elements.

Most of the Chinese advertising abroad results from the sales efforts of foreign advertising agents. There is little overall planning or strategy on the Chinese side. Many advertisements are one-shot deals, and have no sustained impact.

Advertising expenditures are considered as part of the administrative budget. There is little relation between these expenditures and foreign sales. In one light-industry export-import company, the advertisement-to-sales ratio might be as low as 1 to 4,000. Such a low ratio reflects the lack of marketing studies. In one case, a Guangdong manufacturer planned to conduct a market study abroad in order to help determine his advertising program. The study was not approved because the cadres refused to make sales-price data available.

One way of improving the flow of information for the purpose of evaluating the effectiveness of advertising was introduced by a tea company. The company requested the export-import corporation involved to supply sales information to the company's development division, thus enabling the latter to conduct response studies. Another method employed by some Chinese advertisers abroad is to introduce a reader-response system, whereby responses could be collected by the advertising agents, by other representatives, or directly by the company.

The unfamiliarity of Chinese advertisers with conditions abroad has especially benefited Hong Kong agents in that publications specially designed to attract Chinese advertisement have proliferated in Hong Kong. Their claims of foreign circulation may have been exaggerated, however. Also, these agents or publications are sometimes given business because of personal relations. Direct advertisement in foreign countries, especially non-English or non-French-speaking countries, is faced with particular difficulties because few Chinese responsible for advertisement have the necessary language skills.

The preceding instances underline the importance of training Chinese advertising personnel. There are currently two primary channels for training. One is to send teams abroad; the tour is usually short so that the Chinese gain a general impression rather than an in-depth understanding. The second is through lectures and seminars by foreign experts in China. A fairly large audience may benefit from these. In some cases, however, the sponsors of ostensibly free seminars have had an axe to grind. For example, a lecture given by a financial daily, engaged in propaganda for its effectiveness as an advertising medium. Moreover, neither the lecturers nor the audience have a systematic program. Many foreign experts lack an understanding of China, and the content of their presentations tends to be too theoretical. The consensus of one group of Chinese trainees on a course on marketing conducted by a university professor from abroad was that the theories were not applicable to China, indicating the need for the long-term training of Chinese advertisers. This can be conducted both abroad and at home, and the major transnational advertising corporations have an important role to play in cooperating in these training programs. They can provide practical training as well as scholarships. The Chinese can also organize in-service training domestically. Such training would start with basics in a systematic fashion and should suit Chinese conditions.

The Chinese may also gain a deeper understanding of advertising abroad through joint promotion efforts. The promotion of Tian Tan carpets by Young and Rubicam, a transnational advertising corporation, is an example. Three importers and Beijing Carpet shared the cost of the promotion. The campaign consisted of five parts: film, print ads, media kits, point-of-purchase materials, and individual catalogs and brochures for the importers. Although it was difficult to achieve a consensus among all the parties concerned, especially since the Chinese approach was different, the negotiations provided the Chinese with an opportunity to familiarize themselves with marketing methods abroad.

Foreign Involvement in Hotels[7]

Hotels are a major link between China and transnational corporations, and their importance is elevated by three special circumstances. First, hotel facilities acceptable to foreign travelers were scarce in China when the modernization program began.[8] When foreign businessmen were invited to the Canton Fair, some of the senior company executives found themselves sleeping in uncomfortable cots in corridors. Not surprisingly, a number of them vowed never to visit China again. Second, even some of the best hotels were below standard from the point of view of foreign travelers used to modern amenities and meticulous attention to personal comfort. There were many stories about the prolonged effect of a seller's market on the attitude of the service personnel, despite their reputation for honesty in returning lost articles. For example, a guest often had to carry his own baggage, messages were unreliable, rooms were not thoroughly cleaned or made up when a new customer moved in, and faucets were often leaking. Third, the proportion of time that a businessman spent in his hotel was unusually high, reflecting in part the lack of alternative places to go to, whether for work or for entertainment. Many businessmen had to work in their hotel rooms; the regular offices or foreign companies are still mostly in hotels. In addition, because of protracted negotiations and uncertainty about their next appointment, foreign businessmen were often confined to their hotels with nothing definite to do.

In response to the need, additional hotel capacity was one of the first targets both for the Chinese and for foreign enterprises once the direction of Chinese policy was clear. By 1978, scores of proposals had been made by transnationals to the Chinese for joint building efforts. Only a few, however, proved to be successful. The reasons for both successes and failures are instructive.

One U.S. company that succeeded in negotiating a joint venture is E-S Pacific Corporation. Their venture calls for the construction of a $70 million, twenty-one story, 1,000-room-plus hotel. A major reason for the firm's success in negotiating was E-S Pacific's ability to assemble the financial package prior to its entry into China.[9] Other factors included the historical friendship extended toward the People's Republic by E-S Pacific's senior executive officers and their experience in dealing with socialist countries. Even in this case, though, there were many disagreements within E-S Pacific and with the Chinese over the implementation of the project. Significant delays were reported.

One way of avoiding constant disagreement is to keep the operation as simple as possible. This principle was apparently applied by Clement Chen, a Chinese-American, who successfully completed the ultra-modern, 500-room-plus Jianguo Hotel, in Beijing. The hotel was a virtual copy of the Holiday Inn in Palo Alto, California.[10] By eliminating hassles over design, Chen was able to concentrate personally on the business and construction aspects of the project. Although the rooms are relatively expensive (costing almost twice as much as those at the Beijing Hotel), the conveniences offered by Jianguo, such as advance booking, are as yet unmatched by most other hotels in China. The hotel is operated under a management contract by the Peninsula Group, which is well known for its international-class hotels in Bangkok and Hong Kong.

The approach of I.M. Pei, a renowned architect, offers a sharp contrast to the replication of Western hotels.[11] Asked to design a hotel in Beijing, Pei chose not to construct a high-rise in the Forbidden City, but instead to create a structure in the Fragrant Hills, in the suburban area. The design was his personal statement, blending the old with the new in harmony with the natural environment. Some of the concepts were inspired by his ancestral gardens, in Suzhou. For example, each window offers a picture from every angle. Notwithstanding tradition, modern conveniences are found in the hotel's 300-odd rooms. As an architect with deep roots in both his native China and the United States, Pei came to the project with an unusual sensitivity and understanding of the environmental context in which he was building as well as the needs of the hotel's future guests.

The concept of developing Chinese-style hotels appears particularly suited to many scenic regions. In the ancient capital of Sian, there are hotels with Tang imperial gardens and central courtyards. There are restorations of Buddhist temples, and tourist accommodations in Uygar architecture and on bamboo stilts.

The initial hopes of some of the major transnational hotel chains—such as Intercontinental, Hyatt, Hilton, and Western International—of engaging in large-scale projects in China have not yet been realized. The lack of success of the major transnationals certainly does not reflect the lack of a fundamental need for hotel development in China and for foreign cooperation in this sector. The successes cited here, as well as numerous other cases involving builders from Hong Kong and Singapore, demonstrate the possibilities. The main difficulty appears to arise out of the transnationals' unfamiliarity in dealing with the Chinese. Most often, they did not foresee the great number of Chinese authorities involved in cooperative arrangements. It was often not enough to obtain approvals from a central government authority; municipal authorities were also crucial. In some cases, the complications of the proposed projects were not appreciated. Where a large number of families have to be relocated from the proposed hotel site, for example, there are often great difficulties. High-rises have proved unfeasible because water cannot be pumped to upper floors without huge new investments by the water department.

Cooperation in Publishing[12]

The relationship between U.S. publishers and the People's Republic of China has been marked by a realistic approach on both sides. By developing business relations with China, the U.S. publishing industry recognizes the long-term potential of China as a market for expanding international sales, even though the short-term prospects are rather limited. As for China, U.S. books are a principal source of quality research in science, technology, and medicine. Relatively easy shipping from the U.S. west coast is an argument for China's dealing with companies in the United States rather than those in Europe. China's interest in importing books stems from a desire to acquire technology and raise the level of education in specialized fields. In addition, China has recognized the need to become well acquainted with Western culture. Beginning with a brief overview of the Chinese publishing structure and the current state of the industry, this section illustrates the nature of the book-trading relationship and the problems encountered. Brief as it is, it should serve as a broad evaluation of the trading relationship and its future prospects.

The Cultural Revolution left a lasting imprint on the publishing industry, through its effects on education, on the development of expertise in industry, and on the modernization of machinery. Scholarly work nearly ceased, and work that did proceed was either unpublished or published at an unsophisticated level. There were also shortages of printing supplies and trained editorial personnel. The arrested development of printing technology meant that the capacity of the printing industry was fairly low just at a time when demand for printed works surged upward. Finally, the lack of retail outlets created a continual bottleneck.

Attempts by the National Publishing Administration Bureau (PAB) to alleviate some of these difficulties have been mostly in the form of reallocation of supplies. The PAB has given priority to the publication of reference books, reallocating paper to those publishers that published reference works, and has held conferences on the need to improve distribution procedures. But administrative measures have been unable to make the increases in paper production necessary to meet the high level of demand for paper by the publishing industry, which is estimated to be increasing at an annual rate of about twenty-five percent.

These shortcomings, combined with a tremendous rate of increase in China's intellectual population, made it clear by 1978 that the time had come to consider importing books from the West on a massive scale. Established in 1972, the China National Publications Import (and now also Export) Corporation (CNPIEC) is the organization primarily responsible for importing books. CNPIEC is organizationally subordinate to the State Scientific and Technological Commission; it acts as an intermediary between foreign publishers and Chinese institutions that are permitted to import books by compiling and distributing a selected book list from the catalogs sent by foreign publishers. CNPIEC has no budget of its own with which to order books, nor does it stock foreign books for subsequent sale; it only processes the orders sent by end-users and provides those permitted to import books with foreign exchange. After the foreign publishers have received the orders and filled them, CNPIEC distributes the orders among the end-users.

To facilitate this process, the CNPIEC has opened a wholly owned subsidiary in the United States called the Beijing Book Corporation. American publishers need only send their shipments to a central depot, where the orders are consolidated for shipment to China. CNPIEC has also opened a New Books Showroom in Beijing and publishes its own magazine, *Shijie Tushu* (World Books). The New Books Showroom carries sample copies of foreign books and publishers' catalogs; those who visit the showroom can place orders for the books with CNPIEC there. *Shijie Tushu*, a monthly, carries articles on Chinese and foreign publishing and has advertisements from foreign publishers, often for books not listed in CNPIEC's distributed list.

China's approach to the U.S. publishing industry took shape largely after the normalization of diplomatic relations. Although individual publishers had already been doing business on a relatively small scale before that time, more extensive business followed the visit of a delegation from the Association of American Publishers (AAP) to China, in April, 1979. Many American publishers participated in exhibitions of their books in China in 1980 and 1981. Most of these exhibitions were limited either to one subject area such as economic management, to a few publishers, or to a single publishing company. But in May, 1981, the AAP mounted an exhibition which featured the books of nearly 600 U.S. publishers.[13] Although it is difficult to gauge the direct impact of these exhibitions in terms of resultant sales, this opportunity to see the variety of U.S. titles left a deep impression upon those who visited the exhibitions.

Whether entry into the China market resulted from personal interest on the part of a senior executive or from a Chinese approach, the publishing companies that have retained a long-term view toward China have emerged with greater success in selling books there. Books on scientific, technical, and medical subjects, especially textbooks, have constituted an overwhelming majority of sales; those publishers that specialize in these areas have benefited to the greatest degree. Of particular interest to the Chinese are the practical sciences, such as engineering, with less emphasis being placed on theoretical topics. The Chinese want to buy the newest materials available, bypassing basic titles. Finally, sales have also covered a broad variety of topics in the social sciences and humanities: business management, English as a second language, literature, and so on.

Although representatives of publishing firms doing business with China speak optimistically, the present level of book exports is only about ten percent of their Asian market.[14] But the amount of sales can be called small only in relation to the tremendous international sales of these publishers, especially those to Southeast Asia and Japan.

In addition to export sales, several U.S. publishers have participated in joint ventures. One of the first copublishing projects was entered into by Litton Educational Publishers, which has a first-option arrangement on all new books to be developed by Science Press for copublication in English.[15] As exclusive distributor, Litton has coproduced eleven works so far. A disappointing level of sales and dissatisfaction with the quality of Chinese research have, however, led to the reconsideration of any future joint venture projects.[16] Time-Life Books has copublished a children's encyclopedia called *The Children's Treasury of Scientific Knowledge* in cooperation with the Chinese Science Popularization Publishing House; previously published by Kodansha, Ltd., the series was revised by the Chinese and translated by Time-Life. Indiana University Press signed an agreement with the Foreign Language Press to exchange personnel and establish a joint imprint in North America for the English translation of Chinese literary classics such as *Outlaws of the Marsh* (also known as *The Water Margin* or *All Men Are Brothers*). Other copublishing ventures include Britannica's agreement to produce a Chinese-language encyclopedia, the translation and compilation of scholarly papers by Academic Press, and an Annual Economic Report published by Eurasia Press.[18]

Though it is by far the majority, not all the trade with China is in scholarly books. The Benjamin Company has been attempting, with no success so far, to send low-cost paperbacks to China; its Books to China program was intended to have U.S. sponsors place advertising in the books and then have them distributed to communes, libraries, and the like.[19] Bantam Books has been more successful. Already some 35,000 paperbacks have been sold, mostly in hotels that cater to foreign tourists and in foreign-language bookstores. Most of these titles are popular fiction. Although they are clearly aimed at earning foreign exchange from tourists, there is some indication that the Chinese have been buying them as well. Also geared to the tourist trade are two successful guidebooks: the *China Guidebook* from Eurasia Press, and the *Official Guidebook of China*, coproduced with China International Travel Service by the Lee Publishing Group.

Various periodicals are produced by U.S. publishers especially for distribution in China. These magazines are either compilations of past material from English-language industry publications, translated and distributed to a controlled circulation, or they are published for China locally or are Chinese editions of American periodicals with no changes; they may also be English-language periodicals with a special supplement. There are several representatives of each of these. For example, *China Computer World* incorporates editorial input overseen by the Computer World Communications Publishing Company with Chinese production. The magazine's contents come in equal proportion from material in the English-language edition of *Computer World*, from international editions, and from original articles written by Chinese.[20] *Scientific American* is virtually unchanged in its Chinese edition. It was already being circulated in Chinese when its editor first went to China in 1979 and subsequently set up a licensing agreement.[21] The Johnston International Publishing Company inserts a special China section in editions of *Modern Asia*.[22] In a category by itself is the Chilton Publishing Company, which produces reference volumes called the *American Engineering and Industry* series, completely paid for by U.S. advertisers. These industry-specific technical volumes are printed and translated in China, then distributed free by the China Council for the Promotion of International Trade (CCPIT) to a controlled circulation.[23] The *International Industrial Report*, in its original incarnation as *American Industrial Report*, was bought by McGraw-Hill from a Hong Kong publisher; unlike other magazines, which depend on CCPIT for distribution, it handles half of its own distribution in China.

In doing business with China, publishers have encountered both logistical and conceptual stumbling blocks. The basic impediment, which is found in other industries as well, is Chinese unfamiliarity with Western business practices, combined with the seemingly impenetrable Chinese bureaucracy that must be dealt with. The importance of acquiring information on who in China can make decisions and of maintaining consistent personal contacts cannot be overstated. Moreover, Chinese end-users may lack information about what is available; the Chinese infrastructure has not been able to keep up with the rapidly growing volume and complexity of details involved in the distribution of promotional materials, not to mention the books themselves. Finally, in both magazines and books, publishers have had to struggle to convey the importance of working within the U.S. industry's schedules and deadlines.

In the course of negotiations, some differences have arisen over contractual terms and pricing policies in copublishing ventures, as well as in procedures to be followed in the event of disputes. The Western partner usually finds Chinese contracts too ambiguous. In pricing decisions, the Chinese partner often has difficulty in grasping all the determinants of retail prices in the United States above the cost of production, and in forming a realistic view of how much it can expect to sell in the U.S. market. The Western partner must take care that the benefits of its business deals really are mutual, in the face of continued Chinese expectation of a special show of good faith.

Of longer-term consequence is the attitude of the Chinese government toward adopting a copyright law. Since China does not have such a law and has not signed the international copyright convention, foreign authors feel that their rights are inadequately protected. It is expected that the copyright law will have to wait until a patent statute has been drafted.

As things now stand, U.S. exporters of books are protected from the re-export of unauthorized copies. Moreover, the 1979 Bilateral Trade Agreement includes a clause on appropriate measures to ensure copyright protection. The agreement, however, does not state whether this clause requires legislative implementation by China or if China's obligation is immediately effective. The understanding on both sides is doubtless that the clause is not "self-implementing."[24]

The question of censorship in the Chinese publishing industry must be considered within the framework not only of the prevailing publication controls, but also of the purpose of publishing as stated by the government. While formal regulations outline what are considered to be illegal publications, control over actual publication has largely been accomplished by self-discipline. The publishing industry is considered part of the superstructure. Increasingly, publication units are being called upon not only to pay attention to the ideological content of books, but also to practice economic accounting. Publication restrictions act to control the substantive content of books that are published—as well as giving priority to works that will aid modernization efforts—in the face of shortages of the materials needed to produce books. Works considered illegal or of poor quality are criticized as being wasteful of resources.

As for imports, while the exhibitors of U.S. books report no prior censorship by the Chinese authorities, they should not be misled into thinking that access to the books they exhibit or sell is unrestricted. Rather than blacking out or excising the offending passages of publications from abroad, the Chinese method is to restrict access to the publications and to limit subject areas to those regarded as scientific, and therefore "objective," in nature.

Company Cases

Monarch Wine and Import Company[25]

Monarch Wine and Import Company is the sole U.S. importer of Tsingtao Beer, which has become one of the most popular imported beers in the country.

Before Monarch came into the picture, Tsingtao was marketed by a number of distributors under arrangements made at the Guangzhou Fair. These distributors made little effort to push sales. Monarch is primarily known for its Manischewitz Wines, and its marketing of Chinese wine in the United States met with little success. It became interested in Tsingtao beer when it was impressed by the amount of Japanese beer served in Chinese restaurants in the United States. In 1978, representatives from Monarch were invited to Beijing to discuss their interest in importing vodka and beer into the United States. At that time, Seagrams, a major transnational in alcoholic beverages, was also competing for Tsingtao. The Chinese, however, liked the idea of working with a small family company. They were impressed by a visit from Monarch's septuagenarian President, Leo Star, and by Chester (Chet) Moss and Marshall Goldberg, who went to the plants and showed them how to improve the product for the U.S. market. Monarch also agreed to sell Tsingtao vodka because the Chinese wanted to compete with Soviet vodka.

In preparation for the trip to China, Moss collected a large sample of Chinese beer and wine through his brother, Warren, who makes frequent business trips to China for Van Heusen. From this sample, extensive testing and research was conducted on both the gas and liquid components. During talks with the Chinese, the first set of questions dealt with Moss's personal qualifications, followed by a discussion of Monarch Wines. Once these discussions had proceeded satisfactorily, there was extensive questioning on beer. Each day, a few experts would participate in discussions on specifics such as machinery, chemistry, and other factors in beer production.

Negotiations took a little over three weeks and in September, 1978, Leo Star signed a three-year contract to import beer and vodka, which was followed by a long-term contract in 1981.

The vodka launched the Tsingtao name into national recognition. At the time of its introduction, Monarch and its advertising agency, Romann and Tannenholz, mounted a political advertising campaign that matched Tsingtao against Stolichnaya vodka. Although the cost of the campaign was not justified by an increase in sales, the secondary effect was significant.

Following the vodka campaign, Tsingtao beer was also introduced by massive advertisement. Commercials were shown on all three major networks for a period of six weeks. The estimated reach was ninety-one percent of the New York adult male population on an average of ten times each.

In the meantime, improvements were made in quality and packaging through a cooperative effort between Monarch's beer experts and the people from the brewery. Crown caps were supplied by Monarch to prevent mold and permit longer shelf life. Quality control was improved. Failing to secure help from U.S. companies for modernizing the plant facilities, Moss obtained trial samples of the newest bottling machinery from its European connection. In August, 1981, Monarch hosted a group of seven officials from China National Cereals, Oils, & Foodstuff Corporation (CEROILS) on a three-week trip through the United States. Over the years, Monarch, CEROILS, and the brewery representatives have maintained close contact, and as a result Tsingtao has become a premium imported beer, priced on a par with Heineken. From the point of view of distribution, the Monarch strategy has been to emphasize as a starting base market all Chinese restaurants holding liquor licenses in the United States.

At the beginning of 1983, Monarch's distributors started a drive for outlets in non-Chinese restaurants and bars. This step is in keeping with Monarch's goal of making Tsingtao one of the ten largest-selling imported brands in the United States by 1985.

An important lesson to be drawn from this case is that the importing of Chinese products sometimes has to start from the production stage, which includes packaging. Even with all the attention to detail, problems often arise unexpectedly. For example, one entire shipment of Tsingtao beer was found to be flat. It was shipped back to China, and subsequent investigations revealed that the beer had been tested in China and found to be deficient, but nothing had been done about it. Another surprise occurred in the spring of 1983, when the entire stock in the United States was sold out. Shipments due two months before had not arrived. Urgent telexes from Monarch were not answered, and no explanation was given for the delay. The danger was that the entire summer season might be missed. Moreover, the reputation for reliable supply might be spoiled. One possible explanation of the delay was a bottleneck in transport in North China. A re-routing through Hong Kong would entail higher costs, which Monarch suggested that the Chinese should absorb, although the price of Tsingtao to Monarch has remained stable over the years even though production costs have apparently increased.

Despite these problems, Moss continued to be enthusiastic about his China connection. He felt that a "small big company" has advantages over giants, because it can make strategic decisions without having to justify them to so many people. He also felt personally secure in the company, so that he could devote a great deal of time to China by delegating authority to other people to take over his other responsibilities during his absence from the United States. Presently, he could sell all the beer he could get, but the volume is still somewhat below the break-even point.

China-Schindler Elevator Company[26]

China-Schindler Elevator Company is a joint venture of China Construction Machinery Company, Schindler Holding AG, and Jardine Schindler. The last-mentioned foreign partner is in turn a joint venture of Schindler Holding, a Swiss company, and Jardine, Matheson and Company, of Hong Kong, with equity holdings of 60 percent and 40 percent respectively. Schindler Holding's contribution to the China joint venture is 15 percent, Jardine Schindler's 10 percent, and that of the Chinese 75 percent of the $16 million capital.

From the Chinese point of view, the joint venture fitted the criteria of (1) the need for domestic use, (2) competitiveness in the world market, (3) transfer of advanced technology and management techniques, and, (4) generation of foreign-exchange earnings.

Schindler Holdings, one of the world's largest manufacturers of elevators and escalators, was interested in China's low production cost and sourcing for Schindler's existing markets. It was also interested in gaining a foothold in the China market. Jardine Schindler is the sole agent of Schindler's products in Southeast Asia. Jardine Matheson was also interested in establishing good relations with China. The negotiations for the Chinese joint venture lasted about eighteen months. Other competitors included Otis, Mitsubishi, Hitachi, and Westinghouse. To date, the joint venture has been profitable.

The joint-venture agreement is one of the very few in China that has been made public. It consists of four parts: a licensing agreement, a consulting agreement, a maintenance franchise agreement, and an export-agency agreement. This composite balances the interests of both parties. The foreign side realized that the joint venture must be a Chinese entity, but through licensing, technology, consulting, maintenance, and market access, it exercised a degree of control. The negotiation process was facilitated by the participation of the Foreign Investment Control Commission, whose personnel were familiar with foreign business functions and which had to approve the final agreement. The potential foreign partners found that the Chinese side did not outline their requirements but preferred to hear suggestions from the other side so that they could evaluate their feasibility.

A comparison of the performance of the Chinese elevator company before and after the joint venture revealed significant improvements. According to Mun's study, the major contribution of the joint venture was not capital or production technology but improvement in management. One of the reforms introduced was a job-assessment system to clarify job responsibility. Bonuses were linked to fulfillment of specific targets. Another measure was strict enforcement of quality control. All these reforms were facilitated or made possible by the special status enjoyed by a joint venture. A joint venture, in spite of its problems as noted elsewhere, is generally able to emphasize the profit objective, has greater autonomy in operations, and receives special treatment from government departments.

Warner-Lambert Company[27]

Warner-Lambert Company is a major worldwide provider of health care and consumer products with headquarters in Morris Plains, New Jersey. Worldwide sales were $3.2 billion in 1982. Its Asian operations are headed by G.J. Figueiredo, president, Asia/Australia, who was born in China and spent nineteen years there and five years in Hong Kong.

Figueiredo's most recent trip to China was in September, 1982. His negotiations with the Chinese have focused on technology transfer, since one of their principal objectives is to improve the manufacturing of health care and personal products. At this time, Warner-Lambert's empty capsules and Shick razor blades are under consideration.

Warner-Lambert is the world's largest producer of empty capsules. Its advanced know-how permits the uniform manufacture of capsules. This is critically important for efficient machine-filling of pharmaceuticals, since uneven capsules will jam the machines and slow the manufacturing process.

Figueiredo estimates the effective Chinese market for most consumer products to be limited to an urban population of some hundred million people. The estimated demand for razor blades is further limited to adult males who generally do not shave frequently. Moreover, blades last longer because the Chinese beard is comparatively light. Although Warner-Lambert's preferred form of overseas operations is wholly-owned subsidiaries, its current negotiations are for the creation of a joint venture whose chairman will be appointed by the Chinese partner. On the operational side, quality control will be exercised by Warner-Lambert. The total capital involved will be between $2 and $3 million, with loan financing made through the China International Trust and Investment Corporation. The project, because of its relatively small size, only needs provincial government approval, but will be immediately communicated to the Ministry of Foreign Economic Relations and Trade. Warner-Lambert's equity contribution is relatively small as compared with loans, which has the advantage of avoiding possible criticism of a foreign firm reaping a large profit.

In his negotiations, Figueiredo was impressed by the good communications among the various Chinese units. He was surprised to find that the people he met during his recent trip to Suzhou were thoroughly familiar with the details on a recent visit of officials from Shandong to Warner-Lambert's headquarters.

The topics for negotiations are numerous. Export-performance requirement for the joint venture is one of the points which needs extended negotiations. Another difficult point is the criteria for an appropriate rate of profit. Chinese authorities are generally familiar with basic international accounting practices, and one possible parameter for defining the level of profit is to relate it to international rates. The cost in expatriates is high. It usually involves a trip to Hong Kong every three months or so, home leave every six months, and a backup person for every important post.

Many issues after the life of the joint venture have to be anticipated. How is the brand name to be protected? What should be done about the special equipment left in China? How should the foreign firm be compensated? To facilitate negotiations, Warner-Lambert has used an interpreter familiar with its business.

Warner-Lambert does not expect immediate profit. It is interested in establishing some investment relationship with China because of long-term real opportunities. It considers investment in China a form of risk capital. It is not pushing for technology sales in certain areas because it does not consider the Chinese to be ready for them. For example, chewing gum that does not stick to the wrapping paper may be of low priority to the Chinese.

Warner-Lambert is not totally new to China, where microscopes are currently manufactured for export under the company's standards. It took less than two years to meet the desired quality standards without further Warner-Lambert direct involvement.

Tyco[28]

Tyco is a newly created private company in the United States specializing in trade with China. K.W. Liu, one of the partners of Tyco, left China in 1949. Before emigrating to the United States, Liu spent four years in Hong Kong in his youth and seven years in South America, mainly in Argentina. After earning the bachelor's degree, he joined United Parcels Service (UPS), and simultaneously earned the M.S. degree in the School of Engineering at Columbia University. He was the engineering manager for metropolitan New York, with a professional staff of thirty that planned the workload for 4,000 employees. He rose to head the Western region and the Eastern region respectively, managing some 300 professional staff, and coordinating the workload for about 30,000 workers in ten district offices. His last assignment in UPS was working on mergers and acquisitions. Two years later, he left to start his own business with a group of friends from several fields.

In 1980, Liu's father, who was in the mineral business in China before the establishment of the People's Republic, received an invitation to visit his homeland. His Chinese hosts included a number of old friends in Beijing, and many friends who now held important positions in Hunan in the field of metal and minerals and had been former staff members of his. They suggested developing possible business relations. Liu's father, who is in his eighties, passed the invitation on to his son for consideration.

Liu's first reaction was not enthusiastic; his life in the United States was comfortable, and he does not like to travel. His main motive in doing business with China stems from his Chinese background. Struck by China's continued need to modernize, he was eager, as an overseas Chinese, to make some contribution toward improving the situation.

Once he made a commitment to the China trade, his first question was what specialty he should pursue. Ideally, he thought, he ought to concentrate on one line. He also tried to maximize the potential by discussing other possibilities while the Chinese side indicated interest in lines not originally contemplated. In the process he became involved in minerals, garments, and porcelain ware. Other lines included starting exports of chemicals from the United States and imports of cashmere from China. There are currently many other lines of business possibilities that cannot be explored because of human- and financial-resource limitations. These opportunities cannot be passed on, owing to the special relationship that the group has established and the trust that has been built up.

All three main product lines have great potential for export to the United States because they are labor-intensive and are based on Chinese raw materials.

For minerals, contacts were established to import ferrochrome, tungsten, mercury, and other metals. Several shipments were made but business has recently slowed down due to the world economy.

As for garments, the company has exclusive use of a silk-garment factory in a Chinese province. Another one is now being contemplated. Management of the factory is left entirely to the Chinese, with a quality-control man from the company making frequent visits to the factory for several weeks at a time. This man has authority to inspect the production processes and has direct access to the factory's top management. The company supplies designs for blouses and dresses. Typically, the blouses retail for around $50 and the dresses for around $110. So far, no major machinery and equipment has been supplied by the company.

The merchandise is price competitive internationally. China is the largest silk producer in the world, and the cost of Chinese silk is lower than that of the competition. The labor cost for garments is much lower than Hong Kong, Taiwan, or South Korea. Translated into retail prices, each garment is substantially lower than the competition.

The main problem is nonprice aspects, especially quality control. For instance, there were hooks missing from some of the garments; belts for dresses of different sizes were of the same length; and delivery was not punctual. There have been gradual improvements, however, as the Chinese have learned the trade. Dyeing has improved significantly in the course of a year. It should be remembered that in garment exports, the Japanese started in the 1950s, the South Koreans and Hong Kong in the 1960s, and the Chinese start will be in the 1980s. China's potential is very great because it is a low-cost producer. Some of the problems will probably take a long time to solve, but eighty-five percent of them can be solved within the next two or three years. This is the reason why some U.S. buyers are willing to get into the very competitive, relatively thin-margin and high-risk China business: they realize that if they wait for years while most major problems are solved, it may be too late for them to get involved on a preferred footing.

In porcelain, the Chinese advantage is legendary. Tyco, through an affiliate company, is talking with two other companies in this business as potential partners. A major distributor will supply the design for porcelain ware. A manufacturing company will supply the technical know-how for production. The potential for Chinese porcelain in the U.S. market is very large since the market is currently dominated by imports from Japan, where raw materials must be purchased and the wage rate is many times higher than China's. In the future, the Chinese ought to be able to compete favorably in the market, provided importers like Tyco can get through this difficult initial stage of laying the groundwork.

In contrast with some other U.S.-China trade companies, Tyco emphasizes personal relations and trust, and the ability of its members to understand both cultures and social habits. It is understood, for example, that as a gesture of good will, Liu financed the visit of a Hunan Opera troupe to the United States under the auspices of the China Institute in America. When a contract is negotiated, it is usually very simple, and has only a couple of pages. No lawyer has been hired to go over the technical details. Nor have the negotiations been protracted. The same operating style applies to relations with the partners in the United States. The division of benefits is rough and ready, and there is no haggling and bargaining over small percentages.

Minor potential problems are not extensively studied for lack of management time. For example, the question of whether the quality-control people in China, who have multiple-entry visas for a year or more but who stay for less than a year in each visit are liable to Chinese personal income tax will be dealt with when the problem arises.

Outside experts or consultants are generally not used. The expertise needed is built through long-term relationships in various forms of partnership. Numerous companies have been formed to suit particular purposes, although the precise structure and arrangement can change with the development of business and individual needs. Flexibility is the key to success.

The company has not explored the use of Export-Import Bank credit or Small Business Administration finance. The main reason is that it is time-consuming to make use of the facilities, and management time is scarce. As it is, Liu is already working fourteen hours a day, seven days a week.

In spite of his own Chinese connection, Liu does not think that the overseas Chinese, in general, have much advantage in the China trade. Most of them do not have knowledge both of U.S. business and how the Chinese operate. Second- or third-generation overseas Chinese may be too Westernized and new immigrants to the West may not know enough about U.S. business. In contrast, major corporations, especially the Japanese, do their homework well. They have the research, finance, and organization to back them up, which a small corporation cannot afford.

Fish Ponds[29]

Because of geographical proximity and ethnic affinity, Hong Kong's businessmen have exhibited unusual interest in China. Many of the ventures have been small scale. The case of investment in fish ponds illustrates some of the pitfalls of reliance on friendship and trust when large margins of error exist in rough-and-ready calculations.

In 1978, a group of eighteen Hong Kong investors with experience in fish ponds in the New Territories obtained a land contract and a supplementary labor contract with a commune in Shenzhen (a Special Economic zone, contiguous with Hong Kong). The land contract authorizes the investor group to turn a thousand acres of farmland into fish ponds. The group has autonomous control in the management of the fish ponds. The commune is to receive thirty percent of the sales revenue for a seven-year period, after which the land will be returned to the commune. The commune will supply workers upon request, but the group has the authority to fire.

The group formed a company with 1 million Hong Kong dollars in capital, which represents 140 percent of the estimated cost of building the fish ponds. The estimated operating costs, mostly land and labor in Shenzhen, compared favorably with those in the New Territories. The size of the fish ponds was about several hundred times larger than the other investors owned. Virtually the entire output was to be shipped to the Hong Kong market.

Fifteen months later, the entire capital was exhausted before the fish ponds were completed. The main reason for the cost overrun was idle-time costs. New capital was called for. As a result, five of the original investor group dropped out. An additional 1 million Hong Kong dollars was raised, and the fish ponds were completed six months later.

Production started soon afterward. However, productivity per acre was lower than expected. The original estimate was that it would be half of that in the New Territories. In actuality it was less than one-quarter as much. Consequently, losses were incurred.

A review of the reasons for low productivity revealed theft and pilferage, which the investors had no effective means of dealing with. It was also found that the local workers responsible for testing the water and taking sample fish to monitor conditions of health and growth were failing to perform their duties according to schedule. Moreover, an agreement with the Water Works Department in the district to supply water in the dry season was ineffective because the water was diverted by the farmers to their fields before it reached the pond. Finally, the general manager stationed in Shenzhen and the director in charge of production were at odds, making management inefficient.

In the meantime, demand for freshwater fish was depressed on account of the economic downturn in Hong Kong at the beginning of the 1980s. This was aggravated by the increased supply of fish from nine other companies that had established similar fish ponds in the area. As a result, the price of fish dropped from an average of 12-13 Hong Kong dollars per pound to HK$8-9.

Faced with unprofitability, two of the investors withdrew. Two new investors put up another HK$0.5 million and took over the management. The land contract was renegotiated. The payment of thirty percent of revenue was replaced by a fixed rental of HK$0.26 million per year, to be revised upward after two years.

The management was reorganized to give central control. Five of the inefficient workers were replaced. The production work was split into two teams competing for performance and bonus. At the same time, production was shifted to the high-price end to cope with the competition. After six months, the five ponds were close to the break-even point.

Sumei Corporation[30]

In the spring of 1978, C.T. Wu, professor of Geography at Hunter College, in New York, was appointed by Governor Hugh Carey to the New York State Advisory Council on Ethnic Affairs. He was sent in late 1978 by the Council to his native province, Sichuan, to establish bilateral state-to-state relations with New York. During the discussions a Sichuan delegate asked what the province could do for New York. Wu's response was that there were many Sichuan restaurants in New York but there were few authentic ones.

The idea of bringing to New York the best cuisine that Sichuan could offer was enthusiastically received by all the participants and approved by the then governor of Sichuan, Zhao Ziyang. The Chinese were very proud of their culinary heritage, and Governor Carey also endorsed the proposal.

Capital needed to start the venture was raised by Wu privately, with little difficulty. The Sichuan government would be a partner in the venture without equity participation.

A location near the United Nations was selected for high visibility in international circles. In addition, Wu was familiar with many people at the U.N., thereby obviating the need for initial advertising.

The Sumei Corporation was formed with the restaurant, the Sichuan Pavillion, as a wholly owned subsidiary. It entered into a contract with the Sichuan government. Under the terms of the contract, Sumei is responsible for the management, marketing, and daily operations of the restaurant. The Sichuan government was to provide the chefs, special ingredients, and decorative items. Ten chefs are to stay for three years in New York, and then return. Sumei is to pay their wages to the provincial government and to take care of their lodging and necessities in New York. Imported ingredients such as specialties like local spices are under exclusive license and are provided by Sichuan at cost. The decor was to be a classical Chinese atmosphere of simplicity and elegance. Many famous calligraphers and painters were commissioned for this purpose.

By the fall of 1979, the restaurant was ready to begin operations. However, bureaucratic delays in the work visas for the chefs kept the restaurant from opening until July, 1980. Sumei incurred losses from eight months of idle capacity, and Sichuan had to contend with the ten chefs waiting for the visas.

Since its opening the venture has been a success. Costs have been kept low, as ingredients from Sichuan are supplied at cost and marketing has been aided by free publicity. Word-of-mouth in the local community, including the United Nations, brought in the initial customers. Local television and newspapers gave good reviews. By 1983, a Chongqing Pavillion, patterned after the New York venture, was established in Washington, D.C.

The Sichuan International Economic and Technical Cooperation Company is now exploring similar ventures in some ten countries. In the meantime, Sumei is also looking into other enterprises such as Sichuan cookbooks, catering, specialty food importing, and consulting.

Residential Construction in Shenzhen[32]

Residential construction in Shenzhen was a favorite vehicle for Hong Kong investors, at least until mid-1982, when the Hong Kong real-estate market collapsed. The present case illustrates the risks involved in dealing with firms whose background has not been thoroughly investigated.

The construction was a 150 million-Hong-Kong-dollar joint venture between the Shenzhen Real Estate Company and a Hong Kong company, with an equity holding of seventy percent and thirty percent respectively. The building was to be located in a new commercial center, with twelve hundred residential units and a ground floor and basement for commerical use. The residential units were priced at about half the level of comparable units in the New Territories (Hong Kong). The Hong Kong Company was the sales agent for the units under construction.

In March, 1982, some buyers saw delays in construction. Their inquiries to both partners in the joint venture went unanswered. They stopped installment payments in May, 1982. In June, the buyers received notice from the lawyer representing the joint venture to the effect that in accordance with the terms of the contract their previous down payments were forfeited. One of the buyers approached the Shenzhen Real Estate Company and obtained an assurance in writing that the construction would be on time, that the downpayment would not be forfeited, and that the Hong Kong Company would not be able to withdraw any money without the concurrence of the Shenzhen Real Estate Company. In the meantime, the Shenzhen Company informed the Hong Kong Company that the buyers should be allowed to continue their installment payments and their down payments should not be forfeited.

In September, the buyers brought the case to the Central Government authorities in Beijing and the provincial authorities in Guangdong. However, the official in Shenzhen expressed the opinion that the forfeiture of the down payments was in accordance with the terms of the contract. The matter should be settled in Hong Kong.

Some buyers informed the press in Hong Kong that (1) the purchase contract of the residential units was not in accordance with Hong Kong legal requirements, (2) the contract did not protect the interests of the buyers, and (3) the Hong Kong's Company's registered capital was HK$500,000, but only HK$48,000 had been paid in.

The Hong Kong Company also informed the press that (1) the delay in construction was due to road repairs and work would be accelerated to complete the construction on time, and (2) the company's paid-in capital had been increased to HK$1.5 million and registered capital to HK$2 million.

At the same time, the Shenzhen Company explained that one reason for the delay in construction was a reconsideration of the overall development of the commercial center at the beginning of the year. The center's area was increased from eight-tenths to two square kilometers, and the road near the building from fifteen to thirty kilometers. It reiterated that the buyers' down payments would not be forfeited.

In October, 1982, one hundred buyers made the following declaration: (1) the contract with the Hong Kong Company would be cancelled, (1) the Shenzhen Real Estate Company should acknowledge receipt of all the payments made by the buyers, (3) the contract should be made directly with the Shenzhen Company, (4) the installment payments would be suspended until a new contract was negotiated, and (5) continued confidence in Shenzhen's development plan was reiterated. In October, over 200 buyers organized

a buyers' association to protect their rights. They declared that the installment payments would be deposited in escrow accounts for each buyer.

At the time of this writing, the case has not been settled. Whatever the
outcome, because of wide publicity the case has served the useful purpose of
improving the understanding of all the parties concerned.

Notes

Chapter 1

1. See Wang, N.T., "Theories of Economic Growth and Stagnation, with Particular Reference to China, 1840-1940," Banca Nazionale del Lavoro, *Quarterly Review* (March, 1960): pp. 3-34; Fairbank, John K., Alexander Eckstein and L.S. Yang, "Economic Change in Early Modern China," *Economic Development and Cultural Change* (Oct., 1960): pp. 1-26; Perkins, D.H., *China's Modern Economy in Historical Perspective* (Stanford: Stanford University Press, 1975); Hou, C.M., *Foreign Investment and Economic Development in China, 1840-1937* (Cambridge, MA: Harvard University Press, 1965); Nathan, A., "Imperialism's Effects on China," *Bulletin of Concerned Asian Scholars* (Dec., 1972): pp. 3-8.

2. Teng, Ssu-yu, and John K. Fairbank, (eds.), *China's Response to the West: A Documentary Survey, 1839-1923* (Cambridge, MA: Harvard University Press, 1979); Ho, P.T., and Tang Tsou, (eds.), *China in Crisis* (Chicago: University of Chicago Press, 1968).

3. The best illustration of this is the case of the court historian. The terms of reference of such an historian were to record exactly what the Emperor did. This was supposed to serve as a deterrent from wrongdoing because it would go down in history. One Emperor beheaded a court historian because he did not like what the historian had recorded. Another historian filled the post; when he did his job in exactly the same way as his predecessor, he suffered the same fate. The sequence was repeated again and again until the Emperor gave up.

4. The Boxers belonged to a secret society, the Corps of Righteous Harmony. Their main aim was to protect the country and destroy the foreigners. They believed that performing certain boxing exercises and rituals would make them invulnerable to modern weapons.

5. Wu, Cheng Huan, (ed.), *The Complete Works of Sun Yat-sen* (Shanghai: 1927); Wilbur, Martin, *Sun Yat-sen* (New York: Columbia University Press, 1976); Zhao, Jing, "Generalization of Thoughts of Modern China on Developing Industry and Commerce," *Economic Research*, no. 7 (July, 1982): pp. 64-71.

6. See, for example, Carlson, Ellworth C., *The Kaiping Mines (1877-1912)* (Cambridge, MA: Harvard University Press, 1962); Feuerwerker, A., *China's Early Industrialization: Shang Hsuanhuai (1844-1916); Mandarin Enterprise* (Cambridge, MA: Harvard University Press, 1958).

7. Chang, John K., *Industrial Development in Pre-Communist China* (Chicago: Aldine Publishing Co., 1969).

8. The purge of the capitalist roaders was also known as "cutting the tails of capitalism." This reflected a simplistic interpretation of the Darwinian theory of evolution applied to social systems. Like man, who was believed to have evolved into a tailless being from tailed monkeys, social systems would attain a higher state of socialism by cutting off the remnants, or tails, of capitalism.

9. Recent disclosures have renewed speculation that starvation was widespread in the early 1960s and still existed in parts of China in the 1970s. However, the general situation could not be compared with that of the war years and earlier.

10. According to World Bank estimates, grain production, on an unmilled basis, was 232 kilograms per capita in 1970, and 239 in 1979, as compared with 234 in 1952 and 248 in 1957.

11. The arable area in 1973 and 1979 was lower than in 1952 or 1957. The sown area in 1973 and 1979 was higher than in 1952, but lower than in 1957.

12. See Lippit, V., *Land Reform and Economic Development in China* (White Plains, NY: International Arts & Sciences Press, 1974); Wiens, T., "The Evolution of Policy and Capabilities in China's Agricultural Technology," in United States Congress, Joint Economic Committee, *Chinese Economy Post-Mao* (Washington, DC: U.S. Government Printing Office, November, 1978); Tang, Anthony M., and Bruce Stone, *Food Industries in the People's Republic of China* (Washington, DC: International Food Policy Research Institute, 1980).

13. Saburo Okita, personal communication.

14. Barnett, A. Doak, *China's Economy in Global Perspective* (Washington, DC: Brookings Institution, 1981); Cheng, Chu-yuan, *China's Economic Development: Growth and Structural Change* (Boulder, CO: Westview Press, 1982); Eckstein, Alexander, *China's Economic Revolution* (London: Cambridge University Press, 1977); United States Congress, Joint Economic Committee, *China Under the Four Modernizations* (Washington, DC: U.S. Government Printing Office, 1982); Xue, Muqiao, *Study of China's Socialist Problems* (Beijing: People's Press, 1979); Ma, Hong, *Economic Structure and Economic Management* (Beijing: People's Press, 1982).

Chapter 2

1. Lardy, Nicholas, and Kenneth Lieberthal, (eds.), "Chen Yun's Strategy for China's Development: A Non-Maoist Alternative," *Chinese Economic Studies*, Spring-Summer 1982 (New York: M.E. Sharpe, Inc., 1983). This volume is a translation of *Selected Manuscripts of Comrade Chen Yun, 1956-1962* (Beijing: People's Press, 1981) together with an

illuminating introduction by the editors. Chen's essays have been recommended for study by all cadres.

2. Liu, Guoguang, (ed.), *Some Theoretical Problems in the Comprehensive Balance of the Economy* (Beijing: Chinese Social Sciences Press, 1981), pp. 15-16. For a similar discussion of the two strategies, see World Bank, *World Development Report, 1981* (Washington, DC: 1982).

3. Ma, Hong, (ed.), *A Dictionary of Contemporary Chinese Economic Events* (Beijing: Chinese Social Sciences Press: 1982), pp. 76-77.

4. Lin, Cyril Chilren, "The Reinstatement of Economics in China Today," *The China Quarterly*, no. 85, (March, 1981), p. 27.

5. In 1979, above-quota prices were raised by 30 percent to 50 percent for grains and edible vegetable oils; new above-quota prices were established for cotton at 30 percent higher than those for quota purchases. See Ma, Hong, *op. cit.,* (1982), pp. 498-99; Wiens, Thomas B., "Price Adjustment, the Responsibility System, and Agricultural Productivity," *American Economic Review* (May, 1983): pp. 319-324.

6. A statistical analysis is contained in Wang, N.T., "Social Expenditure in Economic Development," *Journal of the American Statistical Association,* (Sept., 1956). A broader analysis is presented in Wang, N.T., "Some Problems in International Comparison of Public Social Expenditures," *Indian Economic Review* (Feb., 1955): pp. 23-52.

7. Liu, Guoguang (1981), *op. cit.,* pp. 71-86.

8. This is the reason why the terms presently employed to describe the new arrangements are deliberately different from those used by Liu, such as "three freedoms and one contract."

9. Riskin, Carl, "Market, Maoism and Economic Reform in China," in Seiden, Mark, and V. Lippit, (eds.), *The Transition to Socialism in China* (Armonk, NY: M.E. Sharpe, 1982); Wong, Christine, "The Economics of Shortage and The Problem of Post-Mao Reforms in China," paper presented at the Modern China Seminar, Columbia University, Feb. 10, 1983 (mimeographed).

10. *People's Daily* [Beijing], Oct. 21, 1982, p. 1.

11. The international standards are a useful starting reference point. Appropriate adjustments will have to be made, however. These standards are aimed at the lowest common denominator so that gaps remain respecting the requirements of a particular nation. In the case of China, the requirements are affected by the unique features of the Chinese economic system. As far as accounting standards are concerned, international efforts have only just begun. See Wang, N.T. "The Design of International Standards of Accounting and Reporting for Transnational Corporations," *Journal of International Law and Economics,* vol. II, no. 3 (1977): pp 477-64; "Non-financial Information in Annual Reports," *Maanblad voor Accountancy en Bedrijfshuishoudkunde,* Haarlem (1981): pp. 194-204.

12. An employee seconded from one employer to another may reclaim the post vacated.

13. An additional RMB 20 billion for investment in energy and transport for 1983-85 was to be financed partly by the Central Government and partly by a special contribution from regions, ministries, and enterprises. This contribution will amount to RMB 12 billion and will be assesed in accordance with the size of extra budgetary funds. See *People's Daily,* Dec. 21, 1982.

14. The other consumer goods include watches, alarm clocks, sneakers, color television sets, films, and electric fans. *Official Register of the State Council of The People's Republic of China,* Mar. 15, 1983, pp. 51-60.

15. See *Xinhua Monthly* (Dec., 1982): pp. 163-164.

16. Zhao Ziyang, "Report on the Sixth Five-Year Plan," *Xinhua Monthly* (Dec., 1982): pp. 33, 37.

Chapter 3

1. For a general introduction, see Robock, Stefan H., Kenneth Simmonds, and Jack Zwick, *International Business and Multinational Enterprises* (Homewood, IL: Richard D. Irwin, Inc., 1983). For a review of the literature on transnational corporations in developing countries, see Caves, Richard E., *Multinational Enterprise and Economic Analysis* (Cambridge: Cambridge University Press, 1982), pp. 252-78; Hood, N., and S. Young, *The Economics of Multinational Enterprise* (London: Longmans Group, 1979); Parry, T.G., *The Multinational Enterprise: International Investment and Host Country Impacts* (Greenwich, CT: JAI Press, 1980). The most comprehensive discussion of the issues is to be found in *Multinational Corporations in World Development* (New York: United Nations, 1973); *The Impact of Multinational Corporations on Development and on International Relations* (New York: United Nations, 1974); *Transnational Corporations in World Development: A Re-examination* (New York: United Nations, 1978); *Transnational Corporations in World Development: Third Survey* (New York: United Nations, 1983).

The terms "multinational corporations," "multinational enterprises," and "transnational corporations" are used interchangeably here. "Multinational corporations" appeared most often in the Anglo-Saxon literature until the mid-1970s. A number of recent writers, including those of the O.E.C.D., prefer to use "multinational enterprises" to convey the meaning that they may be incorporated or not. The term "transnational corporations" was adopted by the United Nations in 1974 following the recommendation of Latin American delegates in the Economic and Social Council. The Latin Americans reserve the term "multinational corporations" for corporations created and controlled by a number of nations, as, for example, in a Latin American regional cooperation arrangement. Firms such as Exxon or Nestlé are nationally (U.S. or Swiss) based corporations that extend their operations to other countries (transnationally), and are thus called "transnational corporations."

2. U.S. Congress, Senate Committee on Foreign Relations, *Multinational Corporations and United States Foreign Policy: Hearings before the Sub-Committee on Multinational Corporations* (Washington, DC: Government Printing Office, 1973).

3. The argument of the two-gap model is now familiar in development literature. Basically, it postulates that the growth rate of a developing country may be constrained by a lack of savings or of foreign-exchange earnings. Because of structural rigidities, domestic savings may not be convertible into foreign exchange for purchase of needed imports, and hence the foreign-exchange gap may be a greater constraint than the domestic-savings gap. See Chenery, Hollis, and Alan Strout, "Foreign Assistance and Economic Development"; *American Economic Review* (Sept., 1966): pp. 680-733.

4. See Areskoug, K., "Foreign Direct Investment and Capital Formation in Developing Countries," *Economic Development and Cultural Change* (April, 1976): pp. 539-47; Weisskopf, T.E., "The Impact of Foreign Capital Inflow on Domestic Saving in Underdeveloped Countries," *Journal of International Economics* (Feb., 1972): pp. 25-38.

5. See Bos, H.C., Martin Sanders, and Carlo Secchi, *Private Foreign Investment* (Boston: D. Reidel, 1974); Streeten, Paul, and Sanjaya Lall, *The Flow of Financial Resources: Private Foreign Investment,* (Geneva: United Nations, Document TD/B/C-3/111, May, 1973).

6. For an empirical test, see Bornschier, V., "Multinational Corporations and Economic Growth: A Cross-National Test of the De-Capitalization Thesis," *Journal of Development Economics* (June, 1980): pp. 191-210.

7. Chudson, Walter A., and Louis T. Wells, Jr., *The Acquisition of Technology from Multinational Corporations by Developing Countries* (New York: United Nations, 1974); Wells, Louis T., "Economic Man and Engineering Man: Choice in a Low-Wage Country," *Public Policy* (summer, 1973): pp. 319-342; Lecraw, D.J., "Choice of Technology in Low-wage Countries: A Nonneoclassical Approach," *Quarterly Journal of Economics* (Nov., 1979): 631-654. Numerous case studies may be found in Fund for Multinational Management Education, *Public Policy and Technology Transfer* (1978).

8. See Teece, D.J., "Technology Transfer by Multinational Firms: The Resource Cost of Transferring Technological Knowhow," *Economic Journal* (June, 1976): pp. 242-261; Telesio, P., *Technology Licensing and Multinational Enterprises* (New York: Praeger, 1979).

9. See a series of case studies in working papers of the World Employment Program of the International Labor Office.

10. See Cline, William R., "Distribution and Development: A Survey of the Literature," *Journal of Development Economics*, vol. 1, no. 4 (1974): pp. 359-400.

11. See Lall, S., "Multinationals and Market Structure in an Open Developing Economy: The Case of Malaysia," *Weltwirtschaftliches Archiv*, no. 2 (1979): pp. 325-350; Biersteker, T.J., *Distortion or Development: Contending Perspectives on the Multinational Corporation* (Cambridge, MA: MIT Press, 1978); Newfarmer, R.S., and W.F. Mueller, *Multinational Corporations in Brazil and Mexico: Structural Sources of Economic and Non-economic Power.* (Washington, DC: Government Printing Office, 1975); *Transnational Conglomerates and the Economics of Dependent Development: A Case Study of the International Electric Oliogopoly and Brazil's Electric Industry* (Greenwich, CT: JAI Press, 1980).

12. Sun, Jian, *Draft Economic History of the People's Republic of China* (Jiling: People's Press, 1980); Andors, Stephen, *China's Industrial Revolution* (New York: Pantheon Books, 1977).

13. For the text of the law, see Wang, N.T., (ed.), *Business with China: An International Reassessment* (New York: Pergamon Press, 1980), pp. 126-131.

14. This view was expounded by Xu Dixin in a monthly seminar of the China-International Business Project at Columbia University.

15. For studies of the four modernizations see Baum, Richard, (ed.), *China's Four Modernizations* (Boulder, CO: Westview Press, 1980); Maxwell, Neville, (ed.), *China's Road to Development* (New York: Pergamon Press, 1979); United States Congress, Joint Economic Committee, *Chinese Economy Post-Mao* (Washington, DC: Government Printing Office, 1978); *China Under the Four Modernizations* (Washington, DC: Government Printing Office, 1982).

16. See Xue, Muqiao, *Several Problems Concerning China's Present Economy* (Beijing: People's Press, 1980); "Chinese-type of Modernization," a series of articles in *Beijing Review* (1983), Jan. 3, pp. 14-18; Jan. 10, pp. 13-19; Jan. 24, pp. 14-18; Jan. 31, pp. 16-21; Feb. 14, pp. 14-18; Feb. 28, pp. 12-16; Mar. 14, pp. 15-20; Mar. 28, pp. 17-23; Apr. 18, pp. 15-20.

17. In addition to the relevant parts cited in note 15, see Jencks, Harlan N., "The Chinese 'Military-Industrial Complex' and Defense Modernization," *Asian Survey* (Oct., 1980): pp. 964-89.

18. See monographs issued by Research Policy Institute of University of Lund, Sweden, such as Berner, Boel, *The Organization and Planning of Scientific Research in China Today* (1979); Orleans, Leo A., (ed.), *Science in Contemporary China* (Stanford: Stanford University Press, 1980); Suttmeir, Richard P., *Science, Technology and China's Drive for Modernization*

(Stanford: Hoover Institute Press, 1980); Volti, Rudi, *Science and Technology in China* (Boulder, CO: Westview Press, 1981); Liu Jing-Tong, *On Introducing Technology to China* (New York: East Asian Institute, Columbia University, 1983).

19. The operators that headed multicompany groups are: British Petroleum and Elf Aquitaine in the Bohai Gulf; AMOCO, ARCO, Mobil, Esso, and Chevron/Texaco in the South China Sea.

20. The most comprehensive analysis of the energy issues is in Woodard, Kim, *The International Energy Relations of China* (Stanford: Stanford University Press, 1980). Transnational-corporation involvement in petroleum is reported in a series of articles in *China Business Review*, especially, (Nov.-Dec., 1981): pp. 24-25; (Jan.-Feb., 1982): pp. 53-55; (July-Aug., 1982): pp. 53-55; (July-Aug. 1982): pp. 34-37; (May-June, 1983): pp. 18-25, 42-48. Up-to-date information can be found in current issues of *Petroleum News, China Petroleum, Petroleum Economist* (Nov., 1981); *Petroleum Intelligence, Oil and Gas Journal.*

21. Weil, Martin, "Hydropower," *China Business Review* (July-Aug., 1982): p. 10.

22. *Ibid.*, p. 20.

23. Chen, Jun-Yan, "Prospects for the Metal Mining Industry in China," *China-International Business,* vol. 1, no. 6 (1981): p. 555; Wang, K.P., *The People's Republic of China: A New Industrial Power With a Strong Mineral Base* (Washington, DC: U.S. Department of Interior, Bureau of Mines, 1975).

24. Communication from Leland S. Liang.

25. The lack of appreciation of foreign enterprises of the order of magnitude of this potential is illustrated by the following case. One foreign enterprise was impressed by Chinese machine tools and offered to purchase any amount the Chinese could supply. After considerable canvassing of potential suppliers, the Chinese came up with thousands of units that the enquirer could not possibly absorb.

26. Williams, Jeffrey R., and Wyckoff, D. Daryl, "Parker Hannifin in China," (A) and (B), a Harvard Business School Case (Boston, MA: Harvard Business School, 1982). The importance of o-rings was dramatically demonstrated by the near disaster of one passenger plane in the United States owing to improper maintenance. For other examples, see Bowman, Kenneth I., "Food Processing," *China Business Review* (Mar.-Apr., 1983): pp. 6-9.

27. Wyckoff, D. Daryl, "Chinese Ocean Shipping Industry" a Harvard Business School Case (Boston, MA: Harvard Business School, 1982).

28. Pisani, John M., "The Big Seven," *China Business Review* (Jan.-Feb., 1983): p. 26.

29. Brown, Chris, "Telecommunications," *China Business Review* (July-Aug., 1982): p. 44.

30. Wiens, Thomas B., "Price Adjustment, the Responsibility System, and Agricultural Productivity," *American Economic Review* (May, 1983): p. 322.

31. Boorstin, Robert, "The Great Wall Story," *China Business Review* (Sept.-Oct., 1982): pp. 6-9.

32. Reynolds, Paul D., *China's International Banking and Financing System* (New York: Praeger, 1982).

33. Knight, Robert H., and Lisa Sloan, "Strangers Across the Table: An Overview of the Influence of the Developing Chinese Legal System on Commercial Relations Between the People's Republic of China and the United States," *China-International Business,* vol. 1, no. 6 (1981): pp. 561-571; Richards, J.M., "Protectionism and the ITC," *China Business Review* (Sept.-Oct., 1982): p. 29.

Also see United States International Trade Commission, *Menthol from the People's Republic of China* Investigation No. 731-TA-28 (Final), Respondent's Pre-hearing Memorandum; United States Department of Commerce, Memorandum in Support of the Use of Chinese Home Market Prices of Menthol (New York, Oct. 16, 1980); Statement of Carl A. Riskin, (New York, Oct. 20, 1980); Supplemental Statement of Carl A. Riskin, (New York, Nov. 25, 1980); Supplemental Statement of Hong Jun-Yan (New York, Nov. 25, 1980); Cuneo, Donald L., and Charles B. Manuel, Jr., "Roadblock to Trade: The State-controlled Economy Issue in Antidumping Law Administration," *Fordham International Law Journal,* vol. 5 (1982): pp. 277-317.

35. "Is There a Future for Futures Trading by China?," *China-International Business,* vol. 1, no. 6 (1981): pp. 541-43.

36. Henderson, Dan Fenno, and Tasaku Matsuo, "Trade with Japan," in Li, Victor, (ed.), *Law and Politics in China's Foreign Trade* (Seattle: University of Washington Press, 1977), pp. 28-69.

37. Wang, N.T., (ed.), *Business with China: An International Reassessment* (New York: Pergamon, 1980), p. 128.

38. The following points were first presented in a conference organized jointly by the Asia Society and the Japan Society, May 6, 1983, New York.

39. Yoshino, M.Y., *Japan's Multinational Enterprises* (Cambridge, MA: Harvard University Press, 1976), Tsurumi, Y., *The Japanese Are Coming: A Multinational Spread of Japanese Firms* (Cambridge, MA: Ballinger, 1976); *Sogoshosha* (Montreal: Institute for Research on Public Policy, 1980); Young, A., *Sogoshosha* (Boulder, CO: Westview Press, 1979); Ozawa, T., *Multinationalism, Japanese Style* (Princeton, NJ: Princeton University Press, 1980).

40. Agmon, T., and C.P. Kindleberger, (eds.), *Multinationals from Small Countries* (Cambridge, MA: MIT Press, 1977); Wells, L.T., *Third World Multinationals* (Cambridge, MA: MIT Press, 1983); Kumar, K., and

M.G. McLeod, (eds.), *Multinationals from Developing Countries* (Lexington, MA: Lexington Books, 1981).

Chapter 4

1. Preliminary versions of this section are contained in United Nations, *Transnational Corporations in World Development: A Re-examination* (New York: United Nations, 1978), pp. 48-157; Wang, N.T., "New Forms of Cooperation Between China and International Enterprises," presented to the workshop sponsored by the Subcommittee for Research on the Chinese Economy, Joint Committee on Contemporary China, Social Science Research Council at the East Asian Institute, Columbia University, New York, Feb. 15-16, 1980, and published in *China-International Business* vol. 1, no. 1 (1981): pp. 11-23; Wang, N.T., "TNCs in China's Modernization," *CTC Reporter* (New York: United Nations Centre on Transnational Corporations, summer, 1983).

2. See Dunning, J.H., "Trade, Location of Economic Activity and the Multinational Enterprise: A Search for an Eclectic Approach," in Ohlin, B., P.O. Hesselborn, and P.J. Wiskman, (eds.), *The International Allocation of Economic Activity* (London: MacMillan, 1977), pp. 395-418; "Explaining Changing Patterns of International Production: In Defense of the Eclectic Theory," *Oxford Bulletin of Economic Statistics* (Nov., 1979): pp. 269-95.

3. Rugman, Alan M., *Inside Multinationals,* (New York: Columbia University Press, 1982).

4. Williamson, Oliver E., "The Modern Corporation: Origins, Evolution, Attributes," *Journal of Economic Literature* (Dec., 1981): pp. 1537-68; Plott, Charles R., "Industrial Organization Theory and Experimental Economics," *Journal of Economic Literature* (Dec., 1982): pp. 1485-1527; Leff, Nathaniel H., "Industrial Organization and Entrepreneurship in the Developing Countries: The Economic Groups," *Economic Development and Cultural Change* (July, 1978): pp. 661-675.

5. Horst, T., "The Industrial Composition of U.S. Exports and Subsidiary Sales to the Canadian Market," *American Economic Review* (Mar., 1972): pp. 37-45.

6. See, For example, Dunning (1979), p. 276; Caves, Richard E., *Multinational Enterprise and Economic Analysis* (Cambridge: Cambridge University Press, 1982); Rugman, Alan M., *Inside the Multinationals,* (New York: Columbia University, 1981); Calvet, A.L., "A Synthesis of Foreign Direct Investment Theories and Theories of the Multinational Firm," *Journal of International Business Studies* (spring/summer, 1981): pp. 43-59.

7. Frank, Isaiah, *Foreign Enterprise in Developing Countries* (Baltimore: Johns Hopkins University Press, 1980); Behrman, Jack N., "Transnational Corporations in the New International Order," *Journal of International Business Studies* (spring/summer, 1981): pp. 29-42.

8. Cooper, Charles, and Phillip Maxwell, "Machinery Supplier and the Transfer of Technology: A View of 'Packaging' and Learning-by-Doing," *Development Research Digest,* no. 3, (spring, 1980): pp. 27-30.

9. I have examined packaging, depackaging, and repackaging elsewhere. See United Nations, *Transnational Corporations in World Development: A Re-examination* (New York: United Nations, 1978), pp. 154-56. Some writers prefer to use the terms "bundling" and "unbundling."

10. Eckstein, Alexander, *China's Economic Revolution* (Cambridge: Cambridge University Press, 1977), pp. 103, 203, 238.

11. Based on interviews with company executives.

12. Based on interviews with Chinese officials.

13. For an illustration of numerous restrictions see United Nations, *Restrictive Business Practices* (New York: United Nations, 1971); *Major Issues Arising from the Transfer of Technology to Developing Countries* (New York: United Nations, 1975); and a series of reports on the international transfer of technology issued by the United Nations Institute for Training and Research in 1975 (Sales Nos. E75.XV.RR.1-12).

14. The term "compensation trade" is used here in a broad sense. It includes counterpurchase, barter, and switch, although they can be distinguished. Some writers prefer "countertrade" as the generic term. See Verzariu, Pompiliu, Scott Bozek, and Jeanette Matheson, *East-West Countertrade Practices* (Washington, DC: U.S. Department of Commerce, 1980), pp. 7-14; Dennis, Robert D., "The Countertrade Factor in China's Modernization Plan," *Columbia Journal of World Business* (spring, 1982): pp. 67-75; Markscheid, Stephen, "Compensation Trade: The China Perspective," *China Business Review* (Jan.-Feb., 1982): pp. 50-52; Ehrenhaft, Peter D., (ed.), *Countertrade: International Trade Without Cash,* (New York: Law & Business, Inc./Harcourt, Brace & Jovanovich, 1983).

15. "Export Trading Company Act," *American Banker,* special edition, Feb. 17, 1983: U.S. Congress, Committee on Foreign Affairs, Subcommittee on International Economic Policy and Trade: *Hearings on H.R. 1799,* May, 1981; May, 1982; April, 1982 (Washington, DC: Government Printing Office, 1982).

16. *Investment in China* (Hong Kong: Wen Wei Po, Aug., 1982), pp. 54-66.

17. *New York Times,* May 3, 4, 1983.

18. Lubman, Stanley B., "The Emergence of New Institutions for Trade and Investment in China," *Private Investors Abroad* (New York: M. Bender, 1979), pp. 189-250; Torbert, Preston M., "China's Joint Venture

Law: A Preliminary Analysis," *Vanderbilt Journal of Transnational Law*, vol. 12, no. 4 (fall, 1979): pp. 819-95; Cohen, Jerome Alan, "Equity Joint Ventures," *China Business Review* vol. 9, no. 6 (Nov.-Dec., 1982): pp. 23-30; Stepanek, James B., "Direct Investment in China," *China Business Review* (Sept.-Oct., 1982): pp. 20-27.

19. *Investment in China* (Hong Kong: Wen Wei Po, 1982), pp. 33-45.

20. This is based on a case study of the joint venture with Schindler by Mun, K.C. See chapter 7.

21. *Transnational Corporations in World Development: A Re-examination* (New York: United Nations, 1978); Curhan, J.P., W.H. Davidson, and R. Suri, *Tracing the Multinationals: A Sourcebook on U.S.-Based Enterprises* (Cambridge, MA: Ballinger, 1977).

22. *Wall Street Journal,* Mar. 2, 1983.

23. Based on field trips and interviews with officials in Shenzhen. See also Barson, Joy, "Special Economic Zones in the People's Republic of China," *China-International Business* vol. 1, no. 5 (1981): pp. 461-94; Terry, Edith, "Decentralizing Foreign Trade," *China-International Business,* vol. 1, no. 5 (1981): pp. 445-60; *Investor's Handbook: China Merchants Shekou Industrial Zone in Shenzhen Special Economic Zone of Guangdong Province,* (Hong Kong: China Merchants Steamship Navigation Company, Sept., 1981).

24. See chapter 7 for a case study.

25. In October, 1980, Scheuer International Trading, Inc. entered into a joint venture with the China National Textiles Import and Export Corporation to make sales in the United States of various types of Chinese gray goods. The joint venture, Huafong Trading Co., Inc., was to deal directly with end-users and cut off many traditional intermediaries. The dissolution of the joint venture in October, 1982, indicates that the original purposes were not fulfilled. One explanation is that the traditional intermediaries, who have historical relations with numerous end-users, jointly resisted doing business with the joint venture, especially during the period when the textile business was affected by recessionary conditions in the United States. Information provided by Leland S. Liang.

26. Bank of China, *Annual Report 1981* (Beijing: April, 1982).

27. These include a HK$4 billion loan with fourteen other banks to Hong Kong Land Co.; principal lender in a $175 million syndication for Danish Export-Import Bank; joint lead manager of a $230 million syndication for ENI of Italy; comanager of a syndicated loan for Spain of about $200 million; principal lender in a $3.2 million syndicated loan to the Italian State Railway. Information compiled by Susan B. Levine.

28. The joint venture is organized by the People's Insurance Co. of China and the American International Group.

29. Thirteen banks in Hong Kong are controlled by China. The Bank of China coordinates the activities of the twelve other banks. The deposits of

the twelve banks amounted to HK$37.8 billion, or 43 percent of total bank deposits in Hong Kong. The management of the Chinese banks is very flexible; for example, their interest rates on deposits are more in line with fluctuations in rates in other world financial centers than the rates of their competition. One of the banks, Po Sang Bank, engages in gold trades.

30. Communication from S.K. Fong, of the Bank of China, Hong Kong.

Chapter 5

1. *Investment in China* (Hong Kong: Wen Wei Po, 1982), p. 36.

2. Lombard, F.J., *The Foreign Investment Screening Process in Less-Developed Countries: The Case of Colombia* (Boulder, CO: Westview Press, 1979). For screening criteria in other countries, see *National Legislation and Regulations Relating to Transnational Corporations* (New York: United Nations, 1978, 1983); *Supplement to National Legislation and Regulations Relating to Transnational Corporations* (New York: United Nations, 1981).

3. Lubman, Stanley B., "The Emergence of New Institutions for Trade and Investment in China," *Private Investors Abroad* (New York: M. Bender, 1979), pp. 189-250.

4. Terry, Edith, "Decentralizing Foreign Trade," *China-International Business,* vol. 1, no. 5 (1981): pp. 446-47; Economic Information Agency, *China's Foreign Trade and Its Management* (Hong Kong: Economic Information Agency, 1977).

5. See Chan, Peter P.F., *China: Modernisation and its Economic Laws* (Hong Kong: The Hong Kong Economist Newspaper, 1982); Nee, Owen D. Jr., Franklin D. Chu, and Michael J. Moser, (eds.), *Commercial Business and Trade Laws: The People's Republic of China* (Dobbs Ferry, NY: Oceana Publications, 1982).

6. See Cohen, Jerome Alan, "Equity Joint Ventures," *China Business Review* (Nov.-Dec., 1982): pp. 23-30.

7. *Official Register of the State Council of The People's Republic of China,* Apr. 20, 1983, pp. 171-172.

8. The Generalized System of Preferences (GSP) was the result of the first United Nations Conference on Trade and Development, held in 1964. The concept of preference was put forward in a paper, in the name of the Secretary General, drafted by this author with the aid of a number of staff economists, statisticians, and consultants, for the conference. In preparing the paper, two separate simulation studies were made to determine which developing countries might gain and to what extent if certain preference schemes were introduced. The results were encouraging but sensitive to the models used. The precise results were therefore not presented to the conference.

During the political discussion of preference, the developing countries insisted that it should be applied by all developed countries to all developing countries for all manufactures, hence the term GSP. The author attempted to convince the negotiators that a more flexible scheme was more practical. This view was aired in a signed paper on "Preferential Schemes: A Reappraisal," Banca Nazionale del Lavoro, *Quarterly Review* (Mar., 1967). The actual schemes adopted were in line with the author's conception, since each developed country defined for itself the group of developing countries as well as the list of items to be included in its preferential scheme. In addition, a number of safeguards were also introduced. The term GSP is retained, however.

9. Organisation for Economic Cooperation and Development, *Export Financing Systems in OECD Member Countries* (Paris: OECD, 1982).

10. Baxbaum, David C., Cassondra E. Joseph, and Paul D. Reynolds, (eds.), *China Trade* (New York: Praeger, 1982), pp. 267, 271, 406-07.

11. United States Congress, Senate Committee on Foreign Relations, *United States-China Economic Relations: A Reappraisal* (Washington, DC: U.S. Government Printing Office, 1982), pp. 138-39.

12. For a survey of methodology and application to China, see Nathan, Andrew J., "Political Risk in China," *China-International Business,* vol. 1, no. 2 (1981): pp. 143-95.

13. LaPalombara, Joseph, "Assessing the Political Environment for Business: A New Role for Political Scientists," *Political Science* (spring, 1982): pp. 180-86.

14. See, for example, *Institutional Investor* and *Euro-Money.*

15. Kobal, Daniel A., "Political Risk Coverage," *China-International Business,* vol. 1, no. 3 (1981): pp. 235-39; Greenberg, M.R., "American International Group: A Case Study" in Baxbaum, David C., Cassondra E. Joseph, and Paul D. Reynolds (eds.), *China Trade* (New York: Praeger, 1981), pp. 302-12.

16. See *China-International Business,* vol. 1, no. 2 (1981): pp. 197-99.

17. *New York Times,* Feb. 16, 1983.

18. *South China Morning Post,* Nov. 12, 1982.

19. *South China Morning Post,* Nov. 2, 1982. These requirements have been eased since January, 1983, after Prime Minister Nakasone's visit to Washington.

20. Stoltenberg, Clyde, "U.S. Antidumping and Related Laws and Chinese Exports to the United States," (unpublished paper submitted to seminar in Chinese-International Business Relations, Columbia University, spring, 1983).

21. United States International Trade Commission, Publication No. 902 (Aug., 1978), Investigation Nos. TA-406-2,3,4.

22. United States International Trade Commission, Publication No. 867 (Mar., 1978), Investigation No. TA-406-1.

23. United States International Trade Commission, Publication No. 1151, *Menthol from the People's Republic of China* (Washington, DC: June, 1981).

24. See note 33, chapter 3.

25. Richards, J.M., "Protectionism and the ITC," *China Business Review* (Sept.-Oct., 1982): pp. 28-31.

26. *New York Times,* Dec. 2, 1982.

27. *Ibid.*

28. Liang, Leland S., "Textile Industry and Trade in the People's Republic of China," *China-International Business,* vol. 1, no. 6 (1981): pp. 573-84; Ranganathan, Vember K., "China's Textile Exports to the United States," *op. cit.,* pp. 585-604; Weil, Martin, "The Textile Deadlock," *China Business Review* (Nov.-Dec., 1982): 31-35; *New York Times,* Jan. 14, 1983.

29. Inasmuch as the Chinese exports to the United States are concentrated in the low price ranges, the share in value is smaller than the share in volume. Moreover, the share of the market (production plus net imports) is smaller than the share in domestic production.

30. *Beijing Review,* Jan. 24, 1983, pp. 9-10; *New York Times,* Jan. 20, 1983.

31. United States Department of Commerce, *Export Administration Bulletin,* no. 205, June 9, 1980.

32. *New York Times,* Dec. 3, 1982, reports that the Commerce Department has only approved seven out of fifty-five desired by the Chinese.

33. Senator Daniel Patrick Moynihan, member of the Senate Finance Commitee and its Subcommittee on International Trade, notes eight Cabinet departments with statutory roles in international trade policy: State, Treasury, Agriculture, Defense, Commerce, Labor, Transportation, and Energy. Five independent agencies are involved as well. *New York Times,* Jan. 16, 1983, p. E10. In June, 1983, the U.S. Government sent to Congress a proposal to create a consolidated Department of International Trade and Industry.

34. Weil, Martin, "The First Nuclear Power Projects," *The China Business Review* (Sept.-Oct., 1982): pp. 40-44; Reardon, Lawrence C., "A Bilateral Nuclear Cooperation Agreement with the People's Republic of China," Dec. 16, 1982 (unpublished).

35. This was the case with India. While the United States sought safeguards for the spent fuel from India's Tarapur atomic power plant, the French did not. *Foreign Broadcast Information Service* (FBIS): *PRC,* Aug. 11, 1982, G3.

36. Statement of Lieutenant General James A. Williams, Director, Defense Intelligence Agency, before the United States Congress, Joint Economic Committee, Subcommittee on International Trade, Finance, and

Security Economics, on Allocation of Resources in the Soviet Union and China—1982, June 29, 1982.

37. United Nations Groups of Experts on Tax Treaties Between Developed and Developing Countries, *Guidelines for Tax Treaties Between Developed and Developing Countries,* (New York: United Nations, 1974); OECD Committee on Fiscal Affairs, *Model Double Taxation Convention on Income and on Capital,* (Paris: OECD, revised edition, 1977); Wang. N.T., "Code of Conduct and Taxation of Transnational Corporations," *Georgia Journal of International and Comparative Law,* vol. 8, issue 4 (1978): pp. 809-22; "Towards an International Tax Code," *Intertax* (1977): pp. 194-99.

38. Price Waterhouse, *Doing business in the People's Republic of China* (New York: 1982); *International Tax News,* various issues.

39. See Bergsten, C. Fred, (ed.), *Toward a New World Trade Policy: The Maidenhead Papers* (Lexington, MA: Lexington Books, 1975).

40. The main items are regularly published in *International Financial Statistics.* Much of the data submitted to the World Bank mission has been published in *Chinese Statistical Yearbook, 1981* (Beijing: Bureau of Statistics, 1982), although the nine-volume 1981 Bank report on China has not been released for publication apparently for reasons of confidentiality.

41. In December, 1980, the Chinese introduced an internal exchange rate of US$1 = RMB2.8, applicable to visible foreign-trade activities (except tourism). The official rate then was US$1 = RMB1.5. The Chinese maintained that this was neither devaluation nor a multiple exchange rate system. The IMF's position is somewhat ambivalent in such a gray area. See *Annual Report on Exchange Arrangements and Exchange Restrictions* (Washington, DC: IMF, 1981).

42. For issues concerning the reform of the international monetary system, see Dam, Kenneth W., *The Rules of the Game: Reform and Evolution in the International Monetary System* (Chicago: University of Chicago Press, 1982); Cooper, Richard N., Peter B. Kenen, Jorge Braga de Macedo, and Jacques van Ypersele, (eds.), *The International Monetary System under Flexible Exchange Rates* (Cambridge, MA: Ballinger, 1982).

43. This was first brought to the attention of the Group of Eminent Persons of the United Nations in a study entitled *Multinational Corporations in World Development* (New York: United Nations, 1973). This author headed the international drafting group for preparing this study.

44. See the report by The Group of Eminent Persons entitled *The Impact of Multinational Corporations on Development and on International Relations* (New York: United Nations, 1974).

45. The official term is simply "code of conduct," since it may address both transnational corporations and government policies relating to transnational corporations. For an early conceptualization of the code, see

Wang, N.T., "The Design of an International Code of Conduct for Trans-national Corporations," *Journal of International Law and Economics,* vol. 11, no. 2-3 (1976): pp. 319-36; "The International Community and Multinational Corporations," in Sauvant, Karl P., and Farid G. Lavipour, (eds.), *Controlling Multinational Enterprises* (Boulder, CO: Westview Press, 1976), pp. 215-41. For further elaborations, see Wang, N.T., "The Design of International Standards of Accounting and Reporting," *Journal of International Law and Economics,* vol. 11, no. 3 (1977): pp. 447-64; "Analysis of Restrictive Business Practices by Transnational Corporations and Their Impact on Trade and Development," in Schachter, Oscar, and Robert Hellawell, (eds.), *Competition in International Business* (New York: Columbia University, 1981), pp. 3-37; and works cited in note 36 for this chapter. For reports on the current progress of negotiations, see United Nations, *Report of the Commission on Transnational Corporations* (various issues) and the *CTC Reporter.*

Chapter 6

1. For a general survey of issues, see Smith, David W., and Louis T. Wells, *Negotiating Third World Mineral Agreements: Promises and Prologue* (Cambridge, MA: Ballinger, 1976); Kapoor, Ashok, *Planning for International Business Negotiations* (Cambridge, MA: Ballinger, 1975); de la Torre, José, "Foreign Investment and Economic Development: Conflict and Nego-tiations," *Journal of International Business Studies* (fall, 1981): pp. 9-32.

2. See also the relevant parts in a series of industry studies by the United States Centre on Transnational Corporations: *Transnational Corporations in Food and Beverage Processing* (New York: United Nations, 1981); *Transnational Banks: Operations, Strategies and Their Effects in Developing Countries* (New York: United Nations, 1981); *Transnational Corporations in the Fertilizer Industry* (New York: United Nations, 1982); *Transnational Corporations in the Power Equipment Industry* (New York: United Nations, 1982); *Transnational Corporations in International Tourism* (New York: United Nations, 1982); *Transnational Corporations in the Bauxite/Aluminum Industry* (New York: United Nations, 1981); *Transnational Corporations in the Copper Industry* (New York: United Nations, 1981); *Transnational Corporations in the Agricultural Machinery and Equipment Industry* (New York: United Nations, 1983); *Transnational Corporations in the International Auto Industry* (New York: United Nations, 1983).

3. The model contract combines joint venture and product-sharing features. For a brief description of the terms, see Brown, Chris, "Tough Terms for Offshore Oil," *The China Business Review* (July-Aug., 1982):

pp. 34-37. See also *Alternative Arrangements for Petroleum Development* (New York: United Nations, 1982); *Main Features and Trends in Petroleum and Mining Agreements* (New York: United Nations, 1983).

4. Vietnam has laid claims to offshore oil areas under bid by foreign oil companies. Other countries with territorial claims include Japan and the Philippines.

5. An example of an empirical study of cultural differences among nations is Griffeth, Rodger W., Peter W. Hom, Angelo DeNisi and Wayne Kirchner, "A Multivariate Multinational Comparison of Managerial Attitudes," Academy of Management, *Proceedings 1980,* pp. 63-67.

6. The Shanghai Communiqué and other documents associated with the normalization of United States' relations with the People's Republic are reproduced in Solomon, Richard H., (ed.), *The China Factor* (New Jersey: Prentice-Hall, 1981), pp. 296-314.

7. The French language is reputed to be capable of a greater degree of precision. It used to dominate international usage, but its dominance has been eclipsed in recent practice. In the United Nations, both English and French are working languages; Spanish, Russian, and Chinese are all official languages. In practice, English is predominant. In commercial transactions in China, contracts are usually in English or Chinese, and where both texts exist they are equally valid. A comparison of the texts, however, often reveals subtle differences.

8. For example, the answer to the question "You have not eaten yet?" when one has not is "Yes" in Chinese, meaning "Your statement is correct, that is, "I have not eaten yet." In English, the answer should be, "No."

9. During the visit of one senior Chinese official to the United States, the last question was asked in full view of the televison camera.

10. See articles by Edwards, Robert Randle, and Li, Victor H., in Wang, N.T., (ed.) *Business with China: An International Reassessment* (New York: Pergamon, 1980), pp. 24-29; 37-43.

11. For estimates of the distribution of gains between transnationals and host countries for exports of a number of primary commodities (notably pineapples, bananas, tobacco, copper, and tin) in some Asian countries as measured by retained value, see United Nations, Centre on Transnational Corporations/Economic and Social Commission for Asia and the Pacific (CTC/ESCAP) Unit on Transnational Corporations, *Transnational Corporations and Primary Commodity Exports from Asia and the Pacific* (Bangkok: 1981).

12. *Alternative Arrangements for Petroleum Development* (New York: United Nations, 1981); *Main Features and Trends in Petroleum and Mining Agreements* (New York: United Nations, 1983).

13. Pye, Lucian, *Chinese Commercial Negotiating Style* (Cambridge, MA: Oelgeschlager, Gunn & Hain, Publishers, 1982), pp. 1-23.

14. For a demonstration that the very process of talking between adversaries can exacerbate tensions, see Schelling, Thomas, *The Strategy of Conflict* (Cambridge, MA: Harvard University Press, 1960).

15. See the lists enumerated in Tung, Rosalie L., *U.S.-China Trade Negotiations* (New York: Pergamon Press, 1982), pp. 191-95; Searls, Melvin W., "Business Negotiations in China," The American Chamber of Commerce in Hong Kong, *Doing Business in China* (Hong Kong: *South China Morning Post,* 1980), pp. 138-46.

Chapter 7

1. Based on interviews and basic research by Chi Wei Yen and Jennie Chien.

2. This literature includes: *American Industrial Report, British Industry, European Industrial Report, French Industry and Technology, Japan Industry and Technology, Electronic Technology* and *Petroleum Production and Processing.* See Gorman, Tom, and Jeffrey S. Muir, *Advertising in the People's Republic of China* (Hong Kong: China Consultants International, 1979), pp. 46-79.

3. Early translations of foreign names frequently used archaic words or characters denoting animal or barbarian origin.

4. The Chinese name of Chemical Bank is an example, since "chemical" in colloquial Chinese, especially in southern China, means poor quality or fake. The importance attached by the Chinese to having good and avoiding bad connotations is illustrated by the high premium paid by the Chinese in Hong Kong for desirable car license-plate numbers. Apart from low numbers, which give the impression of a well-established family background rather than a newcomer to wealth who could not afford to buy a car in the early days, numbers with several 8s command a price of thousands of dollars because they sound like prosperity. In contrast, the number 4 sounds like "death."

5. An example is Coca Cola. The Chinese phonetic equivalent means "good taste and happiness." Another example is Pepsi Cola which is translated as "all happiness."

6. See, for example, "The 1980 Exhibition of the People's Republic of China, based on interviews with the Editor," *China-International Business,* vol. 1, no. 4 (1981): pp. 339-42; Gay, Verne, "The Marketing of China: Some Observations from the American Executive Suite" (New York: 1983) (mimeographed).

7. Based on the author's field visits and basic research by Carol J. Ryan.

8. Han, Kehua, *The New Development in Tourism in China* (Beijing: National Tourism Administration, 1983); Goldsmith, Carol S., "Tourism in China," *China Business Review* (July-Aug., 1981): pp. 11-17.

9. Tung, Rosalie, *U.S.-China Trade Negotiations* (New York: Pergamon Press, 1981), pp. 92-118.

10. "Joint Venture Hotels Increase with Growth in Foreign Contact," *China Trade News* (Mar., 1983): p. 4.

11. Hoving, Thomas, "More than a Hotel," *Connoisseur* (Feb., 1983): p. 78.

12. Based on interviews and a research paper by Debbi E. Soled.

13. "Cracking the China Market." *Asiaweek,* Sept. 11, 1981, p. 52; Hoopes, Townshend, "Showing the Flag in China," *Publishers Weekly,* July 31, 1981, pp. 27-29.

14. Based on interviews with several publishers.

15. *American Bookseller,* Feb., 1980; interview with E. Falken, Litton Educational Press, March, 1982.

16. Conversation with E. Falken, May, 1983.

17. *Publishers Weekly,* July 18, 1980, p. 12.

18. *FBIS,* Mar. 12, 1981, p. B6; *Publishers Weekly,* Sept. 5, 1980, p. 18; interview with S. Gelardi, Academic Press, March 1982; interview with F. Kaplan, Eurasia Press, March, 1982.

19. Benjamin Company press release, March 30, 1981; conversation with Roy Benjamin, March, 1982, and May, 1983.

20. *Advertising Age,* Dec. 14, 1981.

21. *Ibid.*

22. Goldsmith, Carole S., "Chinamags," *China Business Review* (Sept.-Oct., 1981): p. 32.

23. *Industrial Marketing* (Nov., 1980): p. 77; interview with J. Dingee, Chilton Publishers, March, 1982.

24. Conversation with Harvey Winter, March, 1982.

25. Based on a presentation by Chester Moss at Columbia University and interviews and research by Betty Wang and Cynthia Wang.

26. Based on Mun, K.C., "The Experience of Joint Venture in China," a paper presented to the Academy of International Business; interviews by the author and research by Leung Kin Chiu.

27. Based on a presentation by G.J. Figueredo at Columbia University.

28. Based on a presentation by K.W. Liu at Columbia University, and interviews by the author.

29. Based on field work and research by Peter Wu Kwok Lai, and S.K. Kwan.

30. Based on interviews by the author and basic research by Kevin M. Kelly.

31. He is currently Commissioner of Human Rights, New York City.

32. Based on interviews and research by S.L. Lum.

Index

About the Author

N.T. Wang received the A.B. from Columbia College and the M.A. and Ph.D. from Harvard University. He is the director of the China-International Business Project, senior research associate of the East Asian Institute, and adjunct professor at the Graduate School of Business, Columbia University. He was formerly director, Information Analysis Division of the United Nations Centre on Transnational Corporations and has headed a number of United Nations missions to developing countries. He has been a Distinguished Exchange Scholar to China and a visiting professor at the Chinese University of Hong Kong, University of Pittsburgh and City University of New York.

Dr. Wang has written or contributed to many books and articles on development and transnational corporations. These range from *Business with China: An International Reassessment,* and *Taxation and Development,* to *New Proposals for the International Finance of Development.* He has also directed and authored numerous publications for the United Nations.